YeeHaw! Hang on for the Ride!

a celebration of life and love.

BilliJo Doll

PublishAmerica
Baltimore

First printing

Hardcover 978-1-4560-0139-1
Softcover 978-1-4560-0138-4
PUBLISHED BY PUBLISHAMERICA, LLLP
www.publishamerica.com
Baltimore

Printed in the United States of America

In The Beginning

As I sit here in my temporary office, I pause in my writing and thought process to look out the window. Bougainvilleas are amassed with flowers yet they barely block the million dollar view of the Pacific Ocean and beach down the hill from me. There are no houses or anything else to mar the view between this house and the sea.

And I ponder how it is that my life has brought me to live near this quaint ocean-side Mexican village.

I am a fourth generation Montana rancher. Now entering my 'golden' years, I no longer own cattle, live on a ranch, or am actively involved with what defined my life for decades and defined my family for centuries.

I was conceived on my parents' honeymoon — a trip to Square Butte in November to go Mountain Goat hunting. For years my mother joked that she got a billy goat and a BilliJo during the same weekend.

Actually I am not named after a goat; I am named after a little girl whose dad was a trainer on the tracks. He was a retired jockey turned race horse trainer. My mom was a jockey. And, although she did not like little children, she thought Joe and Billie's daughter, Billie Jo, was cute. Mom simply changed the spelling of the name when she gave it to me.

Jenny Schimnick was the nurse when I was born in Havre, Montana. When Mom put my name on the birth certificate papers, Jenny walked out of the room with a backward comment. "I hope she forgives you some day." I have never felt as though there was anything to forgive as far as my name is concerned. My name is as unique and as individual as I am.

Jack and Jenny Schimnick became my first memory of loving people. For a few months they were next door neighbors to my parents. They were beloved friends for years. I remember going to their house and playing with the toys they had … maybe for their grandchildren.

Then we moved out to the hog farm. I am told I should not remember those years, but I do have very clear memories. I remember playing alone in my sand box, I remember running through the house playing with Bruce Martin — my first playmate and boyfriend, and I remember the awe inspiring view of the river, the trees, and the railroad tracks below the house.

As far as I know, Bruce's mother, Sharon Henderson Martin, still carries a picture of Bruce and I in her wallet that was taken when I was about two years old. Sharon has loved me since the day I was born. Sharon and her husband, Clint, invited me to her parent's 50th Wedding Anniversary twenty-five plus years since her parents had seen me as a toddler. Sharon took me by the hand and led me to the front table.

"Do you know who this is?" she asked her parents.

Her mother looked at me, as if about to say my name and Sharon said, "It's our BilliJo."

When I was in my thirties, I met a woman who was Clint's sister. She had a scrapbook of me — of every time I was in the county newspaper — following my growth through school, marriage, divorce, and college.

Sharon's little sister married a party buddy of mine from Turner. She babysat Bruce and I when she was in her early teens and we were toddlers. I never saw her again until her parent's 50th Wedding Anniversary.

At the Anniversary party, I took a walk around the park at which it was held. I came across some little girls playing; one little girl fell off of the teeter-totter. With her knee bleeding, I picked her up and carried her to the party. She pointed out her parents. I carried the crying child to them. Her mother asked me who I was; I told her.

In shock, she said, “Do you know who you hold in your arms?”

“No,” I answered.

“She is my daughter, Billie Jo. She is named after you.”

For years Clint and Sharon lived outside of Chinook; we always stopped to visit when we went to Havre. Sometimes Mom would drop me off at the Martin’s so I could play with Bruce and Brenda while she shopped in Havre. When the Martin’s moved to Grassrange, I lost that close contact. Yet, over the years, we would see each other at the county fairs, Brenda visited me while I was in college in Bozeman, I stopped to visit Clint and Sharon or they would drive to Lewistown to see me, and we exchanged Christmas cards for years.

Friendships that last over a half a century are precious. Clint, Sharon, Bruce, and Brenda Martin are much cherished friends.

I do not remember my brother Levi’s birth. I do remember my mother pregnant with him. I remember the day we moved from the hog farm. I felt afraid. I did not know what was going on but I knew it was big. I was in the back seat of the car with my brother; Levi was screaming at the top of his lungs. My Auntie Diane Jones was in the passenger seat and Mom drove. Mom told me to get Levi to quit crying. I was helpless to do so. I started to cry as well. My mother told me to quit my crying or she would give me something to cry about. She ‘gave’ me something to cry about because I could not stop crying. The second time she threatened to give me something to cry about, I swallowed my tears before she hit me again.

At the age of two years and seven months old, my life changed dramatically for the first time.

The Ranch

The ranch we moved to was south of Malta and was almost totally different from the pig farm. There were cows instead of pigs, bigger pastures, drier landscape, and the house was very old instead of new and on the prairie instead on a hilltop overlooking the winding river. On the hog farm, my dad, was a partner and worked with his oldest brother. On the ranch he worked for my maternal grandfather, Irvin (I. H.) Halverson, who lived about 150 miles away. The pig farm was less than five miles from town and right on the highway. The ranch was nearly 20 miles from town and a good three miles away from the highway.

Yet with all the stark contrasts from the life I had known before, I thrived in my new life.

I loved the cows and the horses. My mom, Louise, being a rancher's daughter, had me break my first horse at the tender age of four. That was my age, not the age of the pony. My first sentence, as recorded in my baby book from back at the hog farm, was "Me a cuff cowboy." And tough, I was.

I knew I was tough from a young age. Mom told me I had to be tough if I was going to be a female rancher.

First-born children, regardless of gender, in a ranching family are needed to work outside as soon as possible. It is logical; there is more work needed to be done outside than in the house. Mom was the first-born in her family too. She totally understood this need. Dad was the tenth child in a family of eleven kids but he embraced the concept readily. It was not odd for me to drive tractor, harrowing the spring pasture, dragging a 'harrow' to break up cow turds, by age of four or five. It was normal to 'drive' the pickup while dad fed at age three. Dad would put the manual transmission in first gear (compound), jump out of the moving vehicle to climb into the back of the truck to throw bales of hay off of the pick-up to feed the cows. While he fed the cattle, I stood on the seat of the truck and steered. Instead of going to pre-school, I helped pick rock. I helped to move cattle to another pasture for them to eat fresh grass as soon as I was old enough to straddle a saddle. Before I was old enough to ride by myself, I rode behind mom on her horse. This is normal on a ranch.

Dad decided to start artificial inseminating (AIing) the cows to improve the herd when I was about six. I got to help Mom with the detecting (detection or locating and finding cows cycling and ready to be bred); all three of us kids helped her. By age ten detecting several hundred head of cattle was mostly my responsibility. I had hay fever allergies so I did not 'get' to help with haying often. At age thirteen I was sent to AI school to learn how to breed cows. My parents wanted me to go far in life … as far inside a cow as necessary to breed one, all the way up to my armpit.

So my summer days, from 4ish AM to 10ish PM, were spent riding horses, finding the cycling cows, and penning them. First shift, which I often got out of, was from 4-8 AM and included morning breeding of the cows penned the previous morning. Afterward, we went back to the house for breakfast three miles away. Second shift was from 9:30-10:00 to noon, then home for dinner. After dinner I cooled off in the reservoir or took a nap. Third shift was from 2:00 to 5:00 PM and home for supper. Last shift was from 7:00 until 10:00 PM with the breeding of the cows that had been penned the previous afternoon. Then home to bed to start it all over again the next day. This lasted for 42-45 days, fully two breeding cycles for cows, then bulls were turned out with the cows to breed any that were missed or did not 'catch' when AIed.

How many ten year old kids work 12-15 hour days seven days a week?

The answer is: all of them on a western ranch.

Papa bought the ranch from brothers Brewer and Carl Anderson. The bothers continued to come out and help dad, especially Carl. Not until recently have I realized Carl was probably schizophrenic. I did not find him odd as a child; I found him to be kind albeit very quiet. He let me ride on the top of the tractor when he drove it. I was never afraid of him. I took care of him in a nursing home some twenty-plus years later; it was there I learned he had a mental illness.

Carl was not the only person in my life with a mental illness. My mom's mom, Ann Halverson, was diagnosed as having rapid cycling bi-polar disorder. Although, now I think maybe she had schizo-affective disorder. When she was 'good' she was generous and kind. She bought clothes, furniture, and toys for herself, her children, and her grandchildren. It was not until I was an adult did I realize most people did not get a houseful of all new furniture every couple of years (or months). I have had the set of living room furniture she gave me for the past twenty-nine years and the set I bought new for the past sixteen years; Grandma would roll over in her grave if she knew that. During Grandma's bad times, she was unpredictable. I felt afraid when she was grumpy and in her odd tormented world of abnormal fixated thinking. She was never loving physically (hugging) but she was always generous in her giving. She believed that if a person held a child after the child was of age two, the child would become spoiled. My parents embraced this idea. There were no hugs or touching (unless a spanking from Mom) in our family.

I think my mom was about half afraid of her mother. Mom always gave in to Grandma's demands. One of her demands was to allow the grandchildren to come stay for weeks at a time.

These visits to my grandparent's ranch were a dichotomy of joy and fear.

I loved my Grandfather and he loved me. Papa was not a perfect man; he could be quite dishonest in business affairs, totally unforgiving, and in his later years he had an affair. But he loved me and I knew it. Through him I learned the reality of "love covers a multitude of sins" (fragment of a Bible verse). When he had to "run to town" (or Zerbe Brothers Tractor and Implement dealership) to buy parts for broke down farm equipment, he would always stop by the house and pick me up to go with him. I learned to read from him by the writing on the dashboard of a pickup. I had no idea what "alt" meant in English. I knew it meant "old" in German, my grandmothers' native language. I figured, it was an old pick-up truck.

Papa also taught me about financial management. He said in order to have material resources when I was older, I needed to learn to spend less than I made. It was such wise and simple advice. I have avoided debt and paying high interest rates most of my life. I learned to save money and to pay cash for many of the things I have wanted to buy. This financial management is why I could vacation in Mexico during the winter some years later.

Grandma would mostly ignore me while I was at the ranch. She did not have me help her cook, clean, pick eggs, or feed the chickens. I played with her Breyer horses for hours. Grandma would always take me to town to get a haircut. Mom would tell Grandma to not get my hair cut. Grandma would take me to the barber (not the beauty shop where she had her hair done) and damn near get my head shaved, my hair was cut so short in a "pixie" cut. I hated my "boy cut" short hair.

I hated it when kids would ask me if I were a boy or a girl. They would say I looked and played like a boy but I dressed like a girl.

My grandparents also had a hired man, Hank Grittner. Hank was from Minnesota. He came to Montana to find a job after World War II. My Papa saw Hank working — unloading grain at an elevator, I think. Papa knew he wanted that strong man to work for him and began to woo Hank away from the other farmer. Hank went to work for my Grandfather in 1957 and was still on the ranch when my mother sold it in 1999. He now lives in a nursing home — fully in his right mind but unsteady on his feet — waiting to die (Hank has since died prior to the publishing of this manuscript. He is buried next to my Grandmother in the family plot.).

Hank never married. He had a sister in Minnesota. His only close family was my family. Hank did not give kids the time of day much. But I still have the rocking horse he gave me for Christmas when I was two. I remember when he went to town for his weekly drunk, he would always bring home a Nut Goody candy for me. He is a gruff guy with a loud, opinionated voice. He KNOWS the local news and weather, what is right and wrong, all about everyone in the county, and how to do everything. And he, like Grandma, is of German nationality or heritage.

Papa was a Norwegian.

The three of them would have terrific screaming fights and yelling matches. So bad and so loud was their fighting that the neighbors, the Brandts who lived a half mile away, could hear their bellowing.

Hollering at one another was thought to be a normal way of life. My parents yelled a lot, too. Yelling, fighting, and hollering were all a predictable part of every day. What was not predictable was Grandma's moods and behavior.

I remember once, at school when I was in high school, one of my classmates worked as a waitress. She told the story of how this crazy woman had come into the restaurant, ordered and ate a meal, and then did not have any money to pay for the meal. My classmate said the deranged woman ranted on and on about how could the owners and staff at the cafe not believe who she was, how important she was, and the fact that she really did have a lot of money. She just happened not have any money on her at that time. Then the classmate turned to me and said, "She's your Grandmother, right?"

Yes. Right. She is. Embarrassingly so, yes, Grandma was my grandmother.

Grandma's father, William Schilke, had a mental illness, too. I do not know what. Neither does any living person. I remember him as a sullen, uncommunicative man, sitting in the corner of the living room. There are stories of him banging his head against a brick or concrete wall. Maybe he was trying to quiet the "voices" in his head? His wife, Pauline, was also quiet but, I think, more due to being trodden down by the heavy burdens of life. When they immigrated to America, Pauline was very sick on the ocean voyage. Did she have sea sickness? No, she had morning sickness. She was pregnant with daughter number three, my Grandmother. Ann is not my Grandmother's real name but she would never let anyone know her name given at birth; she kept her "real name" a secret even unto death.

My great-grandparent's homestead in north eastern Montana was a barren, rocky area of the county on which it is impossible to grow a productive farm. My Grandmother stayed in a dormitory in Peerless for her freshman year of high school; she had to quit school after that year and go to work. She secured a job herding sheep for a big rancher further north in the county. The first thing Grandma was able to buy with her own income was a rawhide bridle and a horse. No one remembers the name of the horse, but when the shaggy pony died, Grandma tanned its hide. I have the rawhide reins and quirt, and the horse hide.

Grandma prided herself on being a "good girl" and staying away from going into the irrigation ditches or into the barn with the hired men on the ranch where she worked. Yet, she got "caught" at a dance when she was eighteen. My mother was born five months after my Grandparents were married. Grandma never forgave Papa. She tried many, many times over the years to forgive herself, I doubt if she was ever successful. Grandma finally came to grips with my mother's existence on her death bed fifty-some years later.

The second life-altering event happened, not solely because of my Grandmother but due to a combination of a couple of things.

Staying at Grandma's I was my normal, happy, chatty self when Grandma undressed me for bed one night. Raising my shirt up over my head, she said, "If you don't stop all your yapping, they're going to cut your tongue out and you'll never be able to talk again."

Weeks later I had a tonsillectomy.

I was four years old.

I had no understanding of what was going on.

After waking up alone in the dark, in the hospital bed, my throat felt as though it were on fire. It hurt so bad I wanted to cry. I put my hand to my mouth and felt … I still had my tongue. The doctor missed. I could not cry. I could not make a sound. The next time, he would not miss and he would cut out my tongue.

My life as a wallflower had begun. I was basically silent, or at least very quiet, for almost thirty years and muteness still dogs my trail. Writing is the way I express myself.

Only Sharon Emond seemed to notice my sudden turn towards non-talking. My family went to the Emond family's ranch to visit a month or so after the tonsillectomy. Sharon made a comment about me, looking at me, about my silence — she said something to the effect of my throat should not still be so painful that I could not talk. I could only stare back at her. She has had a special place in my heart ever since for noticing, for expressing her concern.

Mitchells

Sharon Emond's maiden name is Mitchell. The Mitchells - all of them - are my third memory of loving people, after Jack and Jenny Schimnick and Clint and Sharon Martin.

Three Mitchell brothers owned three ranches side-by-side next to our ranch, on the way to town. Lawrence and Roselyn Mitchell were Sharon's parents and I knew them the least. They had the middle place but they had already sold it and had moved to a ranch in the Bears Paw Mountains. Next to our ranch lived Orville and Phyllis Mitchell. Jim and Dorothea Mitchell lived at the third ranch, the ranch closest to town. These people are hardworking, tough people. And some of the most kind and loving people I have ever known.

One time, when I was six, we were at Jim and Dorothea's ranch for a visit. Their three daughters were several years older than me and were not playmates. I lurked in the doorway between the upstairs where the girls were and the living room where the adults visited. I stood somewhat behind Dorothea's chair. She turned to me and asked what I was doing. I was bored. I stole a glance at my mom; we were not allowed to be bored — if I could not find something to do Mom would find something for me to do, usually a job of some unpleasant sort. So I said nothing to Dorothea.

She said, "Come here."

I went to her. She picked me up on to her lap, cuddled me, and rocked me as she continued to visit with Mom. I froze in panic and terror. I finally garnered enough courage to ask, "What are you doing to me?" Touching, holding, hugging a child of my advanced age was NOT allowed in my family!

She stopped rocking and looked at me. "I'm rocking you. Don't you like it?" Her voice held surprise and concern.

I shook my head mutely.

She let me climb off her lap.

Before we left their home, I went into the kitchen and stole a pencil. This was my first act of theft. To prove, at least to myself, I was not worthy of a kind and loving embrace.

Orville and Phyllis lived only six miles from us. Orville mentored my father in a lot of aspects of ranching. Although Willie's modern techniques such as cross-fencing the pastures were foreign to Orville. My dad had been a farm boy in Minnesota. There are similarities between farming and ranching, so much so that most people think of them as one in the same. But the two occupations are VASTLY different!

When I was in college in my thirty's, the Range Specialist made the comment to me that my father was one of the best ranchers in Montana. A compliment from the Specialist was a rare commodity indeed. With pride, I told the Assistant Dean of the College of Agriculture what the Range Specialist had said.

"No," Dr. Clayton Marlow said.

I immediately felt like a fool for bragging and for repeating the comment.

Clayton continued, "Your father is one of the best ranchers west of the Mississippi."

And he is.

From a western point-of-view, nothing much exists east of the Mississippi worth talking about.

Back to the Mitchells … Orville wore jeans, cowboy boots, denim-blue wrangler shirts, and rolled his own smokes. I never saw Phyllis wear anything but a cotton house dress. When Dad would go over to their place, he would dump me off with Phyllis.

Orville and Phyllis had two sons and no daughters. By this memory, the boys were probably already in college.

I do not think Phyllis really knew what to do with me, a little girl. So she treated me like any other visiting lady. She would brew tea. We would sit at the table, drink tea, and visit. She would look at the clock and say, "It's time to start dinner for the men."

She taught me how to peel potatoes.

I loved them like surrogate grandparents. Years later I would take my own children to visit them as if they were my son's grandparents. Orville and Phyllis never had any grandchildren that I know of; one son and his wife left Montana and the other son never married.

Years later I was in the divorce process and stopped to visit Orville and Phyllis. They had moved to Stanford Montana. Phyllis lay on the couch, dying of cancer. She had finished sewing her dress to wear for her burial. But she did not want to talk about any of her pain, her treatments, or her dying. She wanted to talk about my divorce. She hurt for me; she could not imagine going through life without Orville's love. She hurt that I did not know the love of a good man. And that is what she wanted to talk about — the importance of the love of a good man - to encourage me.

To her dying day, she thought of others and what she could do for them.

Phyllis was "older" when she and Orville married. She was 25 and he was 30. Their love and devotion for each other is unparalleled in my experience. Her funeral was one of the hardest things I ever saw — that tough old cowboy Orville awash in grief at the death of his "little buddy" after more than 50 years of marriage.

For three years after Phyllis' death Orville often mentioned in letters and conversations that he sure missed his little buddy. In the end, on oxygen from emphysema, living in an apartment in town instead of in the country on a ranch, and especially feeling the loneliness for his little buddy, one morning Orville put a .22 to his sternum and pulled the trigger. Late that evening, his nephew found him but Orville had lost too much blood to survive.

No one bothered to get a hold of me and tell me until after the funeral. That is one thing I have accepted but not forgiven. No resentment attached, simply unforgiven.

School

I had to start first grade at age five so we could keep the school bus route open. That ploy only worked for two years. By the time the school board closed the route, my life had changed again. By then closing the route was no big deal. But I am getting ahead of myself.

Unforgettable in the first grade was my first creative writing assignment. Mrs. Stickly gave us the assignment to write about something memorable in our lives. At age six how many memorable memories does a child have? What I wrote about caused her to immediately call my parents in for a private parent-teacher conference. That set precedence in my educational years for creative writing — none of my teachers have ever liked neither my perspective on history nor my imagination. None of them have ever written a science-fiction novel series that is still on the shelves of major bookstores either. Haha!

Beth

A family moved to town after school started. Their oldest child, a girl, had started first grade in the other town and did not want to move. Her dad knew of my father and family, so he told his daughter something.

One day a blond chubby little girl, whom I had never seen before, walked up to me and said. "My dad says you're going to be my friend."

And so it was and is and always will be.

I do not make it to Seattle to visit Beth very often. She travels to Montana more frequently. The last time she was at my home in the summer, we sat in my shaded back patio and visited. She made the comment about how my life and garden-yard was so peaceful and tranquil. Yes, I am at peace. Beth knows as few people do how troublesome my early years were for me. She is a soul-sister. She has a calm center much like her mother had. Beth is and was a great comforting person in my life.

Marla

I do not remember meeting Marla. I do not know how our parents knew each other. There was some race track connection. Her mom, Sandy, sewed for Marla and me matching pink western pants suits. We were so cute.

For two years we were nearly inseparable. We both loved horses. Then they moved away and I never saw her again.

A half a century later, Marla found me on Facebook. She told me she never forgot her best friend from first and second grade. As we shared our histories, I soon realized our lives took dramatically different courses. Yet, we have two strong connections: our early friendship and our faith. I rejoice she is back in my life again.

Jeanette

Years into my adulthood I worked for the Federal Government, they did a background check on me for Federal Security reasons. I had to give them the dates of when I met the people I listed as references, people who had known me for many, many years. I phoned Jen.

"We met on July 12th — our brothers' mutual birthday," I said. "Do you remember what year?"

She told me immediately.

"How do you remember that?" I asked.

"I remember because I was so lonely in the first grade. But that summer I met a friend and I have never felt lonely again."

When we were 18 years old she eloped with her best friend; they have been married ever since.

Although for years we did not live far apart, I do not see her often. But I always remember with joy the years we had racing our horses across the prairie in pursuit of or being pursued by imaginary Indians, posses, or other types of notorious villains. We stole canned food, usually cans of tuna fish and mandarin oranges, out of the pantry and had our canteens of water so we could be gone all day with our horses.

Our mothers became best of friends as well. They belonged to a bowling league. There were three kids in each family. The other four kids were easy for babysitters. But, babysitters would get so frustrated trying to get Jen and I to do what we were told, they would quit after the first night or two. We were not bad children; we simply do (note, not a past tense verb) not like being told what to do. If we wanted to pretend her bed was a campsite on a cliff where we could sit around an imaginary campfire and sing old cowboy songs all night long. We did so. If we wanted our bacon-lettuce-and-tomato (BTL) sandwiches different from the other kids, we told the babysitter just how to fix our sandwiches — then the other kids would want theirs done special, too. Including my two Jones boy cousins, all eight kids were a babysitter's nightmare.

Jen and I are just free spirited girls who love horses and all that goes with that life. I think her daughter is much like us.

Ludell and Lynne

I met Ludell when we were in the second grade and Lynne was in the first grade. Her family has a ranch 36 miles south of town. They had bought a house on the north side and for the entirety of their school years, the four kids attended town school. Her mom, Marlyn, was a teacher and taught at the country school where Ludell went to first grade. Marlyn got a job teaching in town after Ludell's first year in school.

Jen invited Ludell to her birthday party. Lynne is eleven months and two weeks younger than Ludell. Where Ludell went, Lynne went.

I met them both at the same time.

This family continues to play a strong role in my life.

I think Jen and Ludell are the closest. Yet the four of us are nearly as close as sisters. We try, not always successfully, to have our own reunion for the four of us every August.

Lola

I do not remember when Lola and I became friends, maybe after Marla's family left town. Lola was the last child in a large family who lived on a farm across the river on the edge of town. Her older brothers taught her how to walk across the railroad bridge over the river to get home — saving a long trek around on the highway. I was always very afraid to cross that bridge with her. What if a train came and hit us? What if I fell into the water and drowned? I did not learn how to swim until I was in my thirties. But I loved going to her house, I never said "no" when I was invited in spite of the terror of crossing that bridge.

When I contacted Lola about this story and asked her permission to tell it, she asked me if I remembered one of the last times we played together at her house.

Yes I do.

We had gone exploring in the fields and came across a dead bloated cow in an irrigation ditch. For some unknown reason that would only make sense to country kids, we decided to jump on the cow's over extended belly as though jumping on a trampoline. It was a great amount of fun until the cow's intestines ruptured!

Playing with Lola was always wonderful country kid fun. Our friendship, along with Jen, was very close throughout grade school.

But my behavior began to bother Lola once we got into the fifth grade.

We celebrated my birthday one year with a night at the annual wagon train.

Every year there is a wagon train that lasts four to five days. In those early years, it always started out in the Little Rocky Mountains and slowly wound its way to town where there would be a parade and a big Labor Day weekend celebration.

The night us girls went to the wagon train, we had a few beers to share.

The following week, Lola wrote a letter to Jen and I stating due to our choices, she could no longer be our friend. That really hurt our feelings and we did not talk to her for years.

I think maybe Lola avoided us as well.

After we were grown, I tried feebly to talk to Lola a few times. She always seemed to side-step away. At our twenty- year class reunion, I cornered her and told her straight out that I had something to say to her.

She fidgeted.

I would not let her slide away from me.

I told Lola how much I admired her for having the strength of character at such a young age to not give into peer pressure. I told her I was sorry for choosing booze and partying over our friendship. I told her I was sorry.

What she told me broke my heart.

Lola said that it was the hardest thing she ever did — to write that letter and to stick by her decision. She was alone for probably close to four years before another group of girls accepted her into their clique. She said those four years of incredible loneliness, of no close friends, was so discouragingly difficult. Yet, she was firm in her conviction for the direction of her life-style and she stood by her decision. She has such a strong inner spirit.

It is no wonder she is still married to and in love with the boy she fell in love with in high school.

I still hurt for the pain I caused her.

Lola has no resentments toward me, yet we have never been able to renew our friendship. I think, deep down, my actions caused scars in her spirit where she cannot allow me access. She is a great wife, mother, and grand-mother. She is one of the most wonderful women in the world.

May I never hurt another person the way I hurt Lola so many years ago.

Vinee

I say Vinee and I have been friends since her birth; she's a week more than two months younger than I am. We are third generation friends.

When my father's family moved from Perham, Minnesota to Havre, Montana, they lived across the street from Vinee's grandparents, Thomas & Alice Velk. Grandma Doll, a single Catholic woman with a busload of children, and Alice Velk, a married Lutheran woman with a houseful of children, became good friends. My dad, Vinee's uncle her mother's eventual husband, and one more friend of those boys all had birthdays within weeks or months of each other. Those four young men terrorized the Hill County countryside together.

Vinee's parents and my parents often took the drive to go visit when we were young; it was maybe 60 miles across country but would have been over 130 miles by the highway.

Although friends as children, we did not become the closest of friends until we were in our twenties. I love her. We have been through incredible tragedies together — always supporting each other. She was there for me when my third baby died. I was there for her when her son, Levi (yes, he was named after my brother) was killed in an automobile accident.

When the tears and sobbing came at the catharsis of writing this tome, I called Vinee. Whenever there is something going on in my life, I call Vinee.

Peggy is the other person who bears me up though all life's events.

Peggy

On my eighteenth birthday, at Bible College in North Dakota, a gal from my home town had a little hot cocoa party for me in my dorm room. She invited another Montanan whom I had not met, Peggy.

Peggy and I have been best of friends ever since.

For well over twenty years now Peggy and I have phoned each other every weekend, ever since about the time her father died and my divorce. Sometimes we talk more often. Like Vinee, she has been by my side, supporting me, throughout the majority of my adult life.

I could not have gotten through some of the hardships had it not been for these two women, Peggy and Vinee.

Yes, this book is more about the people who have shown me and taught me how to love than it is about the events in my life that shaped me. The thing is, many do not even know how they have touched my life and how important they are to me and to my development into the woman I am today. I share the life-changing events as well, because, along with the people, events shaped my life. Yes, by listing Peggy I am getting ahead of the story, again, because I did not meet her when I was a child. But there is a reason I procrastinate to move forward.

The next life changing event is, even yet today, so difficult that it is hard to write about it.

My sister, Lesli Ann was born three and a half years after me. She was everything I was and am not - blond, beautiful, and with an engaging personality. Everyone loved Lesli Ann; even people who did not like kids liked her. She emanated joy. A special child destined to become an angel.

One day when I was in the second grade; Levi was upstairs in his room playing 'army man' which he spent nearly his entire life doing; Dad was out farming; Mom, at first, was sewing. Lesli Ann asked to go outside to see Dad. Mom bundled her up, kissed her on the forehead, and told her she loved her.

"I know, Mom," she said as she happily went out the door.

Mom's sewing machine broke or quit working. She went to the barn to work on training Red Wing - a beautiful sorrel horse. Mom rode the horse to the house; this was the first time she had ridden the gelding outside of the corral. On the way to the house, she knew something was wrong.

We kids had the run of the ranch; we could and did play anything and go anywhere on the ranch we wanted to do or to go. We were taught young how to kill rattlesnakes and how to open tough gates. We were always safe.

What is thought to have happened is that Lesli Ann went to the chicken coop instead of going to where Dad farmed and saw that the chickens were out of water. She had watched Dad chop holes in the ice for the cows to drink all winter. Her little bucket was on shore, dad's axe was in the icy cold reservoir with her body when she was found.

She was not quite a month past her fourth birthday. She died on the first day of spring.

Jen remembers when my parents picked me up from school early that day. She wondered why. When she learned Lesli Ann had died, Jen wondered why my parents did not pick her up from school as well. She knew that I needed her.

Everything in life changed.

I refer to times in my childhood as "before Lesli Ann died" and "after Lesli Ann died" so stark is the line between the two. Most changes in life are gradual. The changes after this event were not slow, although the depths of some of the changes were more gradual. My parents friends changed, the atmosphere in the home changed, and their behavior changed.

Other things happened in second grade that affected me strongly as well. My eye sight had gotten bad, I am nearsighted, and I had to get ugly cat-eye frame glasses (because they were the cheapest frames). Many families have nicknames. My mother called us: Honey Bee, Kewpie Doll, and Tinkertoy. My father called me "Ugly," Levi was "Homely," and Lesli Ann was "Cutie." The ugly glasses reinforced the esteem pain.

Levi quit calling me "Ugly" when I was 28 years old. My father did not always refer to me as "Ugly" — just often enough for my heart to scar. Occasionally, even to this day, he continues to make negative references to my looks.

When I was in my thirties, I was at Dad's ranch for branding calves. I am not a morning person. It is not wise to try to engage in interaction with me prior to a cup of coffee. I am quite neanderthal before my first sip of that caffeinated hot drink. As I stumbled my way to the coffee pot, my father made an "ugly" comment. I gave him the finger. Instant silence filled the room. Only when I made my way to the table with my coffee cup did I realize they had company.

A prairie dog hunter from New York was visiting and sat at the breakfast table as well.

Oh well.

Before I left the house, my step-mom told me I had hurt my father's feelings.

Later, at the branding site, both my father and I were at the tail-gate of a pick-up truck filling vaccine syringes. In our usual way of no eye-contact communication, I said, "(his wife) said I hurt your feelings this morning when I flipped you off."

He answered with silence.

I continued, "I am sorry I hurt your feelings. But I am not sorry I flipped you off. "

He made no comment.

"You said a smart-ass thing and I responded. The next time you make a comment about me being ugly, I'll probably flip you off again. Flipping you off is an appropriate response to your inappropriate words. But, I did not mean to hurt your feelings and for that, I apologize."

We were almost done filling syringes.

The one sided conversation continued. I looked at him. "If I ever say a smart-ass thing to you, I suspect you will flip me off. That's okay. Just know, I will continue to flip you off when you say such shit to me."

We were done with the syringes. He glanced at me briefly and turned to go back to work.

He has continued to make the comments rarely. I ignore him and his ugly smart-ass comments. And I have never given my father the finger again.

Other Changes after Lesli Ann's Death

My father has always been a dependable, stoic, hard-working (stubborn) German. Recently I was told by a man, "I don't know your father, but I think you have his character." Hmmm ... it could be that stubbornness is a character trait that runs in the family. I prefer to think of myself as having tenacity.

Dad is a good man — he does not drink, smoke, chew, chase women, or have any other obvious vices. He does not talk much. I think, maybe, because he spoke German when he was a child and when he married Mom he still had a brogue. He has not had any noticeable accent or mispronunciations for decades now. After Lesli Ann's death, he retreated further into himself and into his silence. There was a gulf in the family from the emotional separation from my father. Dad did not have the coping skills needed to deal with Lesli Ann's death; however, his lack of skills did not cause him to make glaringly evident poor choices at that time.

Louise, on the other hand, has always been and will always be a very gregarious, life of the party, knows no strangers, and needs people type of person. She enjoys excitement and chatter around her most of the time. After Lesli Ann died, Mom fell off of the deep end in drinking and chasing around. It did not happen all at once, but over the next few years Mom made more and more wild choices.

No one can judge her for her lack of coping skills. My father blamed her for Lesli Ann's death. She was the mother, she should have been with her children and not training a horse.

Wrong.

No one, no mother, no father, no guardian, can be with their children at all times in order to keep them from harm. The people who try to always keep their children from injury retard the emotional maturity of those children. Living, celebrating, and exploring life is the healthy way to grow up. Accidents happen. Sometimes terrible and tragic accidents occur. Accidents are never anyone's fault.

How any one of us gets through the tragedies of life is directly proportional to the support we have after the calamity occurs.

The greater support, the better chance of emerging on the other side less damaged. The lesser the support, the greater the damage to the soul of the person and the worse the chances are to emerge on the other side without disfiguring soul-scars.

None of us had the needed support necessary to have gone through the catastrophe. Mom reacted to that lack in a more obvious way than any of the rest of us. It is as simple as that.

There was a huge outpouring of cards, letters, and expressions of sympathy from the community, family and friends. Many people remember vividly when my sister died. Yet, Mom did not get the counseling or whatever depth of support she needed to heal.

Mom has apologized to me at least a half a thousand times for not being more present in us kids' lives when we were young. I tell her every time that she is forgiven and that I hold no resentments. My life would have been different, and I think worse, had she exercised her strong will and her strong personality more in an attempt to curtail my strong will and my strong personality. Her preoccupation with Lesli Ann's death and her own inner pain actually gave me a reprieve to live my own life and to travel my own road toward my own destiny.

After Lesli Ann's death, Mom got a job as the secretary at the grade school, a position she would hold for nearly ten years. Hence, no more need for a school bus. She also gave up jockeying and took up bowling. To this day, I hate bowling. It was a night to drink, to get drunk, and to drive home in an inebriated state.

Mom also began to occasionally party with high school kids. Both Levi and I remember nights of being made to lie down on the floorboards of the back seat of the car so that the teens with whom

Mom bought booze for, drank with, and drove around with would not know neither that she had children nor the fact that they were with her.

The speed limit in Montana at that time was "safe and prudent." Mom could make it to town in about ten minutes at an average speed of 100 miles per hour. Using seat belts were not allowed in our family vehicles. Also not allowed was any sign of fear such as a sharp intake of breath.

My youngest son thought, when he was in high school, that trees grew faster than I drove. I have a reason for driving carefully when other people were in the vehicle with me.

One time, the Ophus kids were in the car with us. Mom was driving her usual speed of about 90 mph while reading a letter. We had a tire blow out on the car. Mom maneuvered the car safely to the side of the highway. The Ophus kids never rode to town with us again.

I do, occasionally, read a book while driving. Although not as often as I once did. I can also engage in a variety of activities among which are: completely changing clothes, applying make-up, and writing notes to myself. I seldom, however, talk or use the cell phone while driving. That is a dangerous activity in which to engage. I have read signs that state: Honk if you love Jesus, Text if you want to see Him soon.

Okay, that was not true. I fall asleep when I drive. Music does not keep me alert. I talk on the phone when I drive whenever there is cell phone coverage in order to remain awake while driving. I do try to drive in a safe and prudent manner however, and I seldom speed.

Grade School

For the most part, my grade school years were the idyllic years of youth. I loved the ranch. I loved riding horses. I loved the cows. I loved everything about my life except the way my parents fought. Mom does not remember them fighting much. Oh my. This is a point on which we differ completely. I have not asked my father what he remembers.

I did not love school. Mom made me wear a dress every day. When I was in the fifth grade, she let me wear a nice pants suit to school on Friday's. Into high school, I regularly wore dresses. I think I was the only girl in my class who had to wear a dress for so many years. I know none of my friends had to wear dresses. Today, I wear a dress or a skirt nearly every day; at my age (or my hip size) skirts are more comfortable than jeans.

I tolerated classroom necessities. I am a horrific speller. Without spell-check, I would not be an author. If a speller-checker could get wore out, mine is close to crashing because I use it in every sentence I write. Editing my own writing is an arduous process — for both me and for spell-check. Once I have done my best on a manuscript, checking my spelling and grammar are major tasks for proofreaders. I have more than one proofreader.

Math is a four-letter word. I was taught not to use four-letter words. When I started college at age 30, I tested out at a junior high level math. My youngest son thinks I am still at that level. I still avoid math. When I need computations done, I call my brother. Levi is a Professional Engineer. Using mathematical computations is his livelihood. Besides, Levi is the smartest person I have ever met.

I liked science. I totally loved reading. I liked recess. Everything else was just tolerable. Luckily I have a high IQ that helped me get through school.

I liked boys, too. The first boy I kissed was Jerry Allen Hanson. Once, when his family was out at the ranch visiting, I hid him in my closet while I played dolls with his sisters in my room. Every so often, I would slip into my closet and give him a kiss. He just stood in there, grinning; he never complained. Our childhood friendship ended when our parents no longer visited back and forth after Lesli Ann died. He has been married to his high school sweetheart, Tammy, since she graduated from high school, the year after we did. They are an awesome couple. They have stuck together. I admire them greatly.

One day, while digging to China with Jerry Allen in their back yard, Rick Starkey gave me a ring. I remembered we were younger — maybe age five, Rick set me straight, we were seven. I thought he got the ring from a Cracker Jack box. No, he has informed me the ring came from a Captain Crunch cereal box. I gave the ring back to him a week or so later; he thought my dog had chewed it up. No. It was me who nervously chomped on the little plastic ring. I do not know what causes a seven year old boy to like a seven year old tomboy/girl. Country Western Singer Lynn Anderson had a song out about that time "I Wish I Were A Little Boy Again." Only, I did not change from being a tomboy to being a girl. And I did not know how to react to Rick's offer of a ring; I did not know what it meant or what he wanted from me. From then on I was about half afraid of that guy and avoided him for the next thirty years. Only after he was engaged to his wife did I learn what a great person he is. He, like so many mentioned in this book, is of solid, moral character. He is a very admirable man.

My first boyfriend in school was Joe Miller. I was nine. By this time, Jen's folks had gotten a divorce and she lived in town. The three of us would ride bikes around town. Both Jen and I liked Joe. We all three got to go to a movie one night. Joe sat between Jen and me. He held my hand. Wow, what a thrill! That relationship ended when Jen and I moved on to the fifth grade and Joe did not. Joe, a handsome blond man, has a beautiful blond wife, Dianna, three gorgeous blond daughters, and two darling blond granddaughters. He is a lucky man. Dianna thinks she is lucky they found each other. I agree.

Most of my guy friends were just that, friends. I loved it when my folks would go visit the Watson ranch. Johnny Watson was one tough kid and a great playmate for riding horses and climbing trees. He had to be tough; his father was tough on him. We remained friends throughout Johnny's lifetime. He wanted to date me in high school, but I knew better than to do that! No girl who wanted to keep her virginity dated a guy who won a State Wrestling Championship his sophomore year! Johnny was a tormented soul type of guy; may he rest in peace.

When Mom attended college she met my dad, who worked as a maintenance man at the college. Mom's roommate, Kay Ulrich, married a man named Rummel and got pregnant not many months before Mom and Dad married. Kay was from Phillips County where the ranch I grew up on is located. Her oldest son is five months older than me and one of my good longtime friends. He liked to climb trees, too. They had a great old pine in their yard in town; we spent many an hour up in that tree. Our parents never complained about all the pine sap we got on our clothes. At least, I do not remember his mom or my mom complaining about it.

No one else, outside of my sons, has caused me to laugh so often and so much as Kay's oldest son. He has a wonderful wife and three great sons. And I love his mother, Kay Hould, whom I still call "KK" too. In many quiet, subtle ways she has given me tremendous emotional support throughout my life. Kay's youngest son, Beaner, was too young for me to have as close a friendship with. I like and admire him, as well; he is a fine man.

KK was one of the first single mothers in town. Back in those days, divorced women were suspected of low character. KK held her head up, proud with self-respect. She did not cower, ashamed of her divorced status. Quietly she raised her sons to be responsible men. KK was one of the women I had as a role model when I became a single Mom. She is still one of the women I admire for her bearing of grace and dignity.

Mom and Dad liked to play cards with other couples. They belonged to a monthly card club that got together with other couples frequently, more frequently than only once a month. Jen's parents, my Auntie Diane and Uncle Jess and two other couples are the families I remember the most.

There were the three kids in Jen's family; two boy cousins, Wyatt and Jess Jr. (girl cousin Sheila was born later); and the three more kids. With my brother and me, the ten of us would play tag, hide-and-seek, or cowboys and indians for hours. Jen's sister did not seem to like to run and play with us much and one of the other kids was somewhat too young to keep up.

One of the other boys was in my class; he was a rather quiet guy. I always liked him. I still like him because of my memories of him. But he does not hang out with the classmates any more. I wish he would. I think he would find most of us would like to renew our friendship with him. The past is past; come be a part of this loving, accepting, supportive group. Quit being apart.

I have nearly 80 great classmates and many more great schoolmates. There is hardly an asshole among the assemblage. It has been awesome to watch and to be a part of this group of people — the huge family of the citizens of Malta.

Cousin Wyatt is a year and three months younger than me. When we were really young, we thought we would get married someday - to each other. It did not happen. He was one of my best buddies and "tease-mates" for many years. I love him. I admire and respect him, too. He bought his family farm and has done well. Papa would be proud of him. Wyatt raised sheep for a long time … an endless topic for teasing. He would just chuckle and not take offense.

Cousin Jess Jr is five years younger than Wyatt. He tried his hardest to keep up with the older kids when we were children and he usually succeeded. I love Cousin JJ, as well. He is the most straight-forward, no-shit type of man I know. He takes the teasing well, too. When

Sheila, their much younger sister, got married, I asked him when he was going to get married.

He answered, "It'll be a cold day in hell before I get married!"

"Oh good," I said, "a winter wedding. Will it be this December?"

I think that was the only time I rendered him speechless for a moment.

Both of my boy-cousins are bachelors.

All three cousin siblings are very close. I think that is cool.

Cousin Sheila is too much younger for us to have been raised together. I know her the least. She has one of the most beautiful smiles in the world and she is one of the most self-assured women I know. Sheila is also the Mayor of our home town. I so admire her self-confidence and personality.

Until Sheila was born, I was Auntie Diane's only girl. A lot of people thought she was my mother. Partially, maybe, because I spent so much time with their family but mostly, I think, because I resembled her more than I looked like my own mother. To this day, people will comment, "Oh, you must be Diane's daughter."

No, I am Louise's daughter. But I am a loved-like-a-daughter daughter of Auntie Diane's. Throughout school, 4-H, and my career — Auntie Diane was on the mat fighting for me. No one herald me more. No one.

The resemblance is not only physical between Auntie Diane and me. We both adore the color purple. When she died of leukemia, I think hers was the only totally purple funeral in history. I miss her.

But I look like my mother too, especially now that she quit frosting her hair blond and I am getting … older. We sound alike on the phone, we walk alike, we look alike … both when we walk toward someone and when we walk away from someone.

In the last five years I have been slapped on the ass, only to turn around and hear the other person, in shock, say "Oh, you're not Louise, I thought you were Louise!" more times than I would like to admit. Recently, a friend of Mom's took a picture of us walking away. Mom and I walked hand-in-hand along the beach. Oh my, talk about looking like twins from the rear! Mom hated the picture, but I kind of liked it. We are quite a bit alike.

Mom asked me once if it bothered me when people would comment about how much we were alike. "No," I answered, "because I always tell them I have all of your good qualities and none of your bad."

I have made my own mistakes. Or, let's call them "errors in decisions." And I have made a lot of them.

Once, when driving my youngest son to his doctor's appointment, he stated, "Mom, I know you do not like it when people tell you that you are like your parents. But, Mom, you are."

I replied, "I know that, young Mr. (his dad's name)-BilliJo."

He did not talk to me for miles.

Nurture and nature are the strongest of teachers.

I have heard that a child's personality and character are developed within the first five years of their lives. That may be so. I also know that a child's personality and character are already established when they are born. No child comes with instructions on how to raise that child. I had difficulty wrapping my head around how my two sons could be so different from one another when they had the same birth parents and I raised them the same! I quit complaining about it though when I told Jen of my frustrations; she had the same situation and she had twins.

When I was in the fifth grade my family did something outrageous. We adopted a baby girl. My folks named her gave her the middle name of Louise. For the next five years, that child rarely left my side. I often had to take her on dates with me. I took her to keggars as well and told her to stay in the car. Both she and Levi sat in the car while I drank beer at the keggar. When Levi got cold or bored, he would send her out of the car to go find me around the bonfire so we could go home.

Yes. I had a normal childhood. So did my brother and sister.

The day we picked her up in Helena from Catholic Charities, her little three-week old brown eyes looked at us, locked on me, and never left my face. She stared at my face as I hung over the back seat and looked at her lying in the front seat of the car for the entire trip back to Malta. Her birth mother was only seventeen. Maybe that is why we bonded so quickly.

She was a difficult baby. I think I have hearing problems in my left ear due to her incessant crying and my having to hold, carry, and walk her while Mom fixed supper. Gawd that kid cried. And cried, and cried, and cried. She hated water and totally freaked out at bath time. Mom had a terrible time finding a babysitter who would and could watch her.

Levi and I hated babysitting her, too. I do not think there has ever been or ever will be a child who cried as much as she cried. But Levi and I had a solution. We would get a tablespoon, yes a tablespoon not a teaspoon, and heap it as high as we could with peanut butter. Then we would shove it down her throat. We had to force her mouth open, which sometimes took both of us. She sure could clamp her teeth closed when she wanted to. Once we shoved the peanut butter down her throat THAT shut her up. She could not open her mouth to scream when it was so full of peanut butter. She could not talk yet so she could not tell on us. How or why she did not suffocate, I will never know.

Almost as amazing is the fact she still likes peanut butter.

The only time she ever got a spanking was when she wanted to come live with me in Tennessee and threw a fit about it. Although we have no shared DNA, she is as strong willed as I am. She does not use internet so we are not in frequent communication. Luckily for me, her daughter, and I chat regularly and she relays messages to her mom for me. Ally studies to become a doctor. As accident prone as she was as a child, and as accident prone her older brother Zach still is, it is good she has chosen the medical field. Zach enjoys his military career and I do not get to see him very often. He is engaged to a beautiful woman who loves him. He is a lucky man. I visit with my family members as often as I can via skype.

Hired men

My Grandparents were not the only people who had hired men. We did too. The problem in the first five years we lived on the ranch is that Dad worked for Papa and Papa was tight with a dollar. Papa gave Dad $300.00 a month. This was to go for all ranch expenses: his wages, food, clothing, repairs, feed, wages for others, everything. Needless-to-say, it was not enough money for a portion of the expenses let alone enough to hire someone to live in the bunkhouse and work with and for Dad.

Dad had a solution.

Fort Belknap Indian Reservation is south west of the ranch. Dad's brother, Herb, managed the St. Paul's Mission's ranch (the mission no longer owns that ranch). The nuns at St. Paul's mission school made the candy mints for my parent's wedding. Dad knew folks out there.

On about the tenth of each month that help was needed (calving, irrigating, and haying) Dad, and often I went along, would drive out to Lodgepole to Kirkaldie's store. There would be a few guys loafing around outside of the store. Dad would go in, buy an orange pop for me and shoot the breeze with the owner of the store.

At that time, Native Americans would get their 'treaty money' the first of the month. For some, by the tenth of the month, the money would be all gone, often due to alcohol consumption.

Dad would bring one of the loafers home with us to work for a month.

The deal was always the same. **If** they stayed the month, Dad would pay them $300.00. They also got room and board.

There was a terrific fight at home every month about this arrangement. Mom was so afraid of Dad losing his entire paycheck on his gamble. It was a hellova risk, but, what else was he to do?

So some guy would come home with us and Dad would work him. It was nothing for these guys to work 18 hour days irrigating and/ or haying with the addition of farming and working cattle. The fact they worked seven days a week goes without question. Dad sweated the booze right out of them. For the first few days, they were usually pretty sick. If the man complained about how hard Dad worked them, he would tell him he was easy compared to his first boss on a ranch south of Havre.

I think maybe Dad worked them harder toward the end of the month.

Long about the first of the month, George Powell would come to visit. I may not remember his name correctly. I remember him to be a tall lanky Indian man with a big black cowboy hat. I liked him and looked forward to his visits but I do not know why. I do not remember him ever giving me the time of day.

The hired man would think about his government check waiting for him back home and he would be "thirsty." He would ask George for a ride back to the reservation. George would say yes. The hired man would go to Dad to draw his time.

Dad would say, "Nope. Our agreement was for a month. You've only been here three weeks. You stay another ten days and I'll give you your wage. You leave now and you won't get a dime because you will have broken your word. Now what will it be?"

They would leave with George.

Never, not once, did Dad ever have to pay a hired man he hired this way. Never did my mom's fear of losing his entire paycheck come true. Not one time.

And I think there was an arrangement for George to show up like he did. I know my parents gave him butchered chickens, eggs, and garden produce. I do not remember them giving other people food when they came to visit.

And, at least one hired man we got that way, Leonard Whiteford I remember his name to be, came back several times. Someone explained it to me years later, after I saw Leonard stumbling pants-pissing drunk in Malta on the sidewalk outside of The Stockman Bar. Leonard liked irrigating for my father - it gave him some time to heal up between drunks, it gave him some honest work to do, and he got to eat my mom's good cooking which helped in his recuperation from chronic alcohol poisoning of his system. Through Leonard, I got to see the effects of years of heavy drinking.

Dad bought the ranch from Papa somewhere around the time Lesli Ann died. That fact and the murder of a Native friend of his on the reservation gave way to actually hired hired-men.

I was taught how to jump rope by a young hired man. I wish I remembered his name. I remember his surprise though, when at the supper table, I mentioned that all the girls in school jumped rope during recess and I did not know how. After dark, he took me outside, got a rope, tied one end to the yard gate post, twirled it, and told me when to jump until I got the hang of jumping rope. He got in trouble for his kindness to me. It seems, if you have time to do foolish things for little girls, you are not working hard enough. If a person worked hard enough, they would be too exhausted to do dumb things like teach a little girl how to jump rope after supper. He left the employment of my father soon afterward.

I have neither forgotten Mikel J. Barstad's name nor his impact on my life. Mikel worked for us twice. The first summer, he was a nineteen year old kid fresh out of 'Nam. At some point, one of his brothers came to visit. Paul was huskier than Mikel, had a deeply tanned chest, wore black shorts, and had very white legs. I called him "Brown-Black-and-White." They went on a runner and Mikel did not come back.

For some reason Dad rehired him again the next year. By then we had adopted my sister.

It is hard to explain my love for Mikel. He treated me like I existed. That may sound odd, but I do not know of another way to say it.

Here I am, a little girl, in a family where the old adage of children should be seen and not heard was prevalent; in a family with a very silent father and a mother who was so into her own pain she did not see others; in a family who lived miles from other people. Levi and I did not get along as children. He wanted to play 'army men' and dink around in the shop taking things apart and rarely getting them put back together. I wanted to chase the wind on a fast horse.

I was starved for … acknowledgment? Acceptance? Attention?

Mikel talked to me. He had the balls to change the radio station in the pick-up truck from KOJM 610 Country and Western station to the Rock and Roll station out of Moose Jaw, Saskatchewan, Canada. Shit hit the fan when we forgot to turn it back to the only approved radio station.

I loved him. I loved working with him. I loved riding with him. I loved hanging out with him. He took this mouse-in-the-corner and caused her to feel as if she had value as a human being. I have not seen him in decades; I have talked to him twice in over forty years. We are in contact again now and plan to stay that way.

Beth's dad, Byron Ophus, came to work for my dad when we were in junior high. I think he saved my life.

Dad had bought Orville and Phyllis Michell's ranch from them. At the time, he took me aside and said, "I will probably never be able to afford to send you to college because of this purchase, but you will always have a place to live. It will be your place when you grow up."

Hmmmm … that did not bode true. But for many years, I viewed that place as mine.

The Ophus family moved onto the Mitchell place.

From the time Beth and I became friends, I was at her house as often as possible. For the five or six years they lived in town, before Byron went to work for Dad, I was at their house at least a few times a week. Her brothers became my brothers. To this day I call them Brother Brian and Brother Bret. They do not belong to any religious sect. Her mother, Bev, became a stable second-mother. But it was Byron who made the biggest difference in my life.

From Byron, I learned I was an acceptable human being. I do not know how he did it.

We kids were sent from the room when Byron started to tell jokes. He was ribald. Maybe it is from him I get my sense of humor.

Byron was not the gregarious person my mom is, but, he brought life and laughter into our home. He could do amazing things like take out his front teeth and stick his tongue up his nose like a cow does.

He would sing, "Everybody's doing it, doing it, doing it. Picking their nose and chewing it, chewing it, chewing it. They think its candy but it'snot."

He would tease.

Byron use to say, "Real men don't wear underwear" so often that, at age five, my sister quit wearing panties. She absolutely refused to wear any. Byron got a great kick out of this. Mom was furious with him. She finally convinced my sister to wear old boy shorts of Levi's.

Byron got great amusement from anything a kid did.

He taught me how to play cribbage. A game of cribbage determined many things in our family: who had to wash dishes; who had to go to the highway to get the mail; who got the midnight heifer check during calving.

One time, when I was in junior high, Dad gave Levi and me the option of going to school or picking rock with Byron. Levi went to school. I did not.

There were a hellova a lot of big rocks on the hay fields that Dad wanted to break up and reseed into alfalfa. And I worked alongside Byron as best as any wanna-be-a-man girl could.

At noon we went to his house for dinner.

That morning, Bev and Byron had gotten into a fight. Bev had gone to town and had locked the house. There was no way to get in to get anything to eat.

Byron told me to go to the east (shady) side of the house and have a seat on the grass. He went to the garage, to the refrigerator there, and got two beers. We sat in the shade and drank our beer for lunch.

Never before had I felt such total acceptance from an adult in my life. I loved him, at that moment, more than I loved my own father.

We picked rock for only a couple of hours in the afternoon. My energy waned and when he saw that I was tired he took me home. When Dad asked why we were done so soon, Byron told him we had no lunch. My father just looked at me. I felt as though he were disappointed I was unable to work alongside of Byron all day without food or drink. I might have been thirteen at the time.

For my decision to work on the ranch rather than to go to school, though, I was awarded with a new saddle and a brand of my own. Dad tooled my name in the leather across the Cheyenne roll and my brand on the Horn. My saddle was my most prized possession.

That is to say my most prized possession in addition to my horse, Silver Tip.

I had many horses by this time; I do not remember all of their names. Tarbaby was my first horse and the first horse I broke. I broke a stud horse once named Smokey Joe; I never did like him much. Vinee has a list of the thirty or so horses she has owned over her lifetime; I do not know how she remembers all of those horse's names. Prior to Silver Tip, I had a bay mare named Chiquila. Years later an x-ray showed I had suffered two broken vertebra in my early life. I immediately knew when. T-6 broke when Mom hit a black cow late at night, driving home after bowling, drunk. And one of the many times Chiquila bucked me off L-5 broke. I know which time; it was after a branding.

I never went to the doctor for these injuries. Crying was not permitted, complaining was not permitted, and whining was certainly not permitted. "Cowgirl-up" and take the pain like a man. So I did. Physical pain and emotional pain were stuffed.

When Chiquila was sold, Mom sold her for $100.00 more than she had bought the mare. That $100.00 was mine to use to buy another horse. Byron knew a man with an injured gray mare. The man had never sold a horse for only $100.00 and he was not about to do so. Byron loaned Mom $5.00 to give me to add to the payment for the horse. I bought my favorite horse for $105.00.

Silver Tip was five years old, totally wild, and barely green broke. She had severely cut her right front leg, just above the hoof, in an attempt to jump out of the previous owner's corral.

But Byron knew I was man enough to break this wild Arabian mare.

Silver Tip did not buck. She was high-strung and danced around constantly with her hot blooded heritage. When she was really irritated at the concept of standing around waiting to go, she would rear up. This scared me. I feared she would go over backwards. I would fling myself forward in an attempt to get her front feet back on the ground.

One day, while 'standing' on the gravel driveway, she pranced around, began her antics, and reared up. Byron was on the ground and commanded me to do as he said. I trusted him implicitly so I obeyed.

"Lean back," he demanded as he watched her back legs. When they began to tremble, he said, "Lean forward." When she would come down, he barked, "Lean back!" Up she would go again. We did this over and over again until Silver Tip trembled from head to tail. Byron had me quit forcing her to rear. She never tried to rear again.

I never doubted I could trust Byron with my life.

Growing Up Afraid

When people would ask me what I wanted to be when I grew up, if I were honest, I would say, a hermit or I would say a rancher. If they said, "Don't you mean a rancher's wife?"

No, I meant a rancher.

If I feared their laughter at such a goal, I would give an acceptable answer = a nurse, a teacher, a … a … some career it was okay for a girl to aspire to.

But the only life-style I could think of, where I would be safe, was that of a hermit.

Between the knowledge that I was ugly, that I talked too much, and that I was not safe from some hired men and some babysitters had totally convinced me I needed to stay away from people as much as possible. I did not know how else to protect myself but to simply avoid human interaction.

My father did not abuse me. He did not touch me in any way, shape, or form. He did not hug, hit, or have any physical contact whatsoever. When I started to hug him, in my thirties, it was like hugging a pillar outside of a fancy building. Slowly, over the years, his arms came up. Then there was a bit of a gentle pressure. Then he returned the soft pressure of a genuine hug. Now I get full-blown bear hugs. Smile. Who says you cannot teach an old dog a new trick?

My dad's father, Ed, went to prison for incest when my dad, the tenth child, was two years old and my Grandma Mary Theresa Doll was pregnant with her eleventh child. I do not know how many of the living nine children Ed abused, but I know it was more than the one he went to prison for sexually assaulting. I have a vague recollection of him when he came to Montana to visit once when I was somewhere around three years old. I never knew him. Ed died when I was a teenager.

The kids in that family, my dad, uncles, and aunts, learned to turn a blind eye to problems in the family. My aunts and uncles had no protection from Ed's abuse. They did not learn how to protect their own children either. Grandma Doll was at a loss as to what to do; she talked to the priests about it — their only solution was for her to "put out" more. That did not slow or stop the abuse. Nothing in her life prepared her for Ed. She was 25 when they married, an old maid. She lived with Ed for over 20 years. And she had nothing to do with men for the remaining 50 plus years of her life. They never divorced.

When I was nearly a half a century old, a friend asked me if I knew when I started to hide from people. Yes. I started to run and hide when I was about three and a half years old. I knew every nook and cranny of the buildings on the ranch, in and around the barn, and calving shed. I knew where to hide. And hide a lot I did. I seldom felt safe. The only times I felt safe were with trusted playmates, with trusted hired men such as Mikkel and Byron, or with groups of children such as when our parents played cards.

This running and hiding also started the antecedence of being afraid of people, of being afraid of vulnerability, of being afraid of being known. Fears I have dealt with all of my adult life.

I am very slow to out-grow fear.

I believe our character defects are our character assets twisted. Solitude is an asset necessary in order to write. However, when it is twisted into isolation, it becomes, for me, dangerous. I could not be a hermit. I would go crazy in the silence of my own existence or due to the stinking thinking carried on in my brain. I need people.

When I first began to realize this, I was in my late twenties. I fought the concept for another nearly twenty years. I was afraid to let go of my fear. I was afraid to be vulnerable. I was afraid to let people into my life. Now I fully accept the fact that, for me, to be alone for any length of time is ludicrous. Today my life is full of people, full of love, full of experiences, and full of joy.

4-H

I loved 4-H. I loved being around the other kids and families at the meetings, I loved learning about animals, I tolerated the necessity of learning how to sew, and I loved the annual county fair.

My favorite meetings were held at Dr. Hitch's place. He was the county veterinarian. His kids and I were in the same 4-H club.

Another vet moved into the county. One day he held a veterinarian class for kids in 4-H vet. I was still too young, at nine years old, to take "Vet" but we had an older boy working for us at the time, and he was in Vet Science. I got to go along.

Jim Curtis, Kikker, the Veterinarian, went through several aspects about animal husbandry. At one point, he took a sheep's temperature. It was high. He asked the class if the sheep had a fever. Was the ewe sick? No one answered. I raised my hand. Kikker acknowledged me. The sheep's temperature was high because it was a hot day and her wool coat was very warm. Bingo. The little kid knew the answer.

I could not wait to get old enough to take vet science. For a while, I wanted to become a vet when I grew up. I held Kikker in high admiration for years. Kikker and I became friends when I became an adult. It has been a pleasure to be able to call him a friend and to be able to call upon him as a friend during the intervening oh so interesting years. I had the opportunity to go to work for Kikker on a part-time, on-call basis when I was in my late 40s. He was a great boss; he talked to me about moving back to Malta so I could work for him full-time. No way. The work and life of a veterinarian has got to be one of the most miserable jobs in the world. I really like Kikker and I love animals but I do not want to work in all kinds of weather day after day for ungrateful stressed-out ranchers.

In 4-H, I took market steer for a couple of years. I sobbed when I had to sell my beloved steers. My uncontrollable sobbing was totally uncharacteristic of me and irritating to my father. One year, I got a white ribbon on Icfano, my steer. Yet after the steer was butchered, his meat ranked second in "carcass." Dad figured if the damn judges could not tell when a live animal was a high carcass value, there was no use of me taking market steers to the fair.

I took breeding cows instead. I won blue, reserved grand, or grand champion every year on my breeding heifers.

The reason I enjoyed taking animals to the fair had nothing to do with ribbons and trophies. I loved staying at the fair!

I loved being around the other 4-H kids, the boys, and the freedom of no parents. I had to stay with Auntie Diane. She kept a closer eye on me than my parents would have!

There is a "rite of passage" around the age of puberty for country kids during the county fair.

This rite-of-passage was the opportunity to stroll around the fairgrounds with a kid of the opposite sex. If a girl was really lucky, the boy might win a stuffed animal for her.

I walked with some boys who were just good friends; I walked with some boys I liked. I don't ever remember holding hands with any of them so innocent was my affection. I may have held hands with Geno. I cannot ask him though. He was killed in a double car automobile accident along with several other teens before we graduated from high school.

I do remember wearing a black hat that belonged to a boy named Greg. Wow, did Auntie Diane give me hell for that one! I do not think I had the guts to talk to Greg ever again. Surely not at the fair that year, I did not want Auntie Diane to know to whom the hat belonged! That woman had a tongue with volume on her!

The other great thing about 4-H was camp. Phillips County, where I lived, and neighboring Blaine County, went together for 4-H camp out south of Havre, in Hill County, at Kwanis Camp. It was held after AI season so I went every year.

I felt very self-conscious in my swimming suit with my very darkly tanned arms and my starkly white legs. I felt self-conscious wearing my ugly black cat-eye framed glasses. But I loved camp.

Older girls taught us how to apply make-up and did our mascara for us.

There was dancing every night.

There were boys.

I never had a "boyfriend" at 4-H camp. There were two older boys who made a huge difference in my life though. And they were brothers.

Hugh Ross was a junior leader at 4-H camp one year. I do not remember the topic of the class or workshop he presented. It had something to do with feelings and emotions. I reacted and was taken aback by what he said. He noticed. Afterward, he asked me why I tensed and retreated.

I told Hugh that showing emotion, such as crying, was not allowed in my family. I told him that I had not cried in years.

I was maybe 12 or 13 years old.

He looked at me with eyes of concern and expressed his vexation. Basically, telling me that I needed to be in touch with my feelings. Hugh was about 16 at the time; he was a wise man beyond his years.

I left him, went away by myself, and cried. I did not shed the bitter tears of sobbing and soul-healing. I think that would have been too much for me. But the hard wall that surrounded my heart now had a little crack in it with these tears and the revelation of the need to feel and maybe express the feelings I felt.

A year or so later, I won a trip to 4-H Congress held in Bozeman. Hugh's older brother, John Ross, was there. He had broken his leg and was on crutches. He needed someone to carry his books and papers and to open doors for him because he could not maneuver both crutches and "things" at the same time. I did so for him. He expressed his gratitude.

These were simple acts of kindness.

I did not see my actions as kind. I saw John's appreciation of my actions as kind.

That is it.

No big deal.

It was because of John and Hugh that I made the decision to dedicate my life to helping others; to help kids not to feel the way I felt as a youngster.

These two teenage boys deeply touched my heart with their basic core personalities of loving kindness. In fact, they touched my life so profoundly that I wanted to name my first-born son Matthew John and call him Hue. Hew, as the name is spelled, means to cut or to chop. Hue means color. Believe me, my oldest son Matthew has added color to my life. But my husband did not want "John" as his middle name. Matthew Dan is called Matthew, not Hue.

Twenty-plus years after 4-H I met and got to know John and Hugh's parents, Warren and Betty Don Ross. They were a ranching couple out in the Bears Paw Mountains. I can see where the four kids in that family get their composure. I met the older two children as well. They are all such likeable, wonderful people.

The thing that struck me the strongest about Warren and Betty Don was that they would read the Bible out loud to each other at the table. Whether they did this at breakfast or supper or who did the reading and who listened, I do not know. Seeing the big old bible open on their kitchen table was an awe-inspiring sight.

The other fact that struck me was Betty Don could trace her Montana family back to the days of the first settlers in the state. Her grandfather was a "hundred dollar man." For the cost of one hundred dollars a person could walk along side of a wagon train going west. The man walked all the way to Montana from Saint Louis, Missouri beside a wagon train and created a new life for himself and for generations of his kin on the wild frontier.

King Alcohol

When I went to Germany, I obtained a better understanding of the relationship between Germans and beer. It is somewhat similar to Americans and coffee.

During my early years, Dad would often have a beer. Only once in my entire life have I seen him a little tipsy. One other time I remember him with a hangover. That is it. In over a half of a century, only two times that I am aware of, has my father ever over-indulged. When I was a kid, for him to come in the house, especially on a hot summer day, and have a beer with salt was very, very common. To have a beer when someone like when George Powell stopped to visit was normal. It was never an issue. He had a beer or two a day, and maybe a mixed drink or two when there was a party. Today, he drinks maybe a mixed drink or two a year and it is the same with beer — he drinks maybe a couple of beers a year.

Mom was known as a party girl even before she met and married Dad. But to label her as an alcoholic would be a misnomer. Alcoholism is a progressive disease. Mom has drunk, at times and for durations heavily, for 40-50 years without the continual progression of the disease.

There was and is always alcohol in their homes.

My first memory of me and alcohol was way back at about age three. I had a little blue plastic cup that I would raise above my eye level to the level of the kitchen table, and beg, perhaps silently, for some beer in my cup. I always wanted more

I was about six weeks after my sixth birthday when I finally got enough beer to get drunk for the first time. I loved it.

Mom got angry with my goofy behavior and put me to bed. I jumped on the bed. Jumping on a bed was a HUGE no-no in our house! We were not allowed to sit on our made beds, let alone jump on a bed. But I did not care. I was invincible. The feeling that being drunk gave me has to be similar to the elation of an explorer when they discover their treasure. Unvanquishable. Unstoppable. Unconquerable. The feeling must be akin to truly being on top of the world.

It is impossible to adequately describe the feeling to someone who does not have the disease of addiction. That euphoria is better than any orgasm. Unfortunately, it is also much more elusive than a great orgasm. In the early years of drinking the feeling is attainable but in the later years of drinking it is not. Chasing the feeling is akin to chasing a shadow — impossible to catch or to hold. The pursuit of the feeling alcohol gives an alcoholic drives many people to the gates of insanity and death. So great is the compulsion; so hideous is the obsession.

Mom made homemade wine. Dandelion, chokecherry, and rhubarb are the wines I remember. I loved them all. Rhubarb wine may have been my favorite; it has been too long ago to remember accurately. Mom would bottle and store this wine in the cellar to let it age. I would sneak down every now and then for a quick snort. When I would empty a bottle, I would hide the bottle to the back of the shelf.

Mom eventually quit making wine. She could not figure out how or why the bottles in the back would break their seal and evaporate all of the time.

I will never forget the look of confusion on her face as she stood holding an empty bottle of wine, wondering how-in-the-hell did another bottle of wine evaporate.

I never ever was suspect. Who would be suspicious of a six-seven-eight-nine year old little girl of "closet drinking?"

That is how and when living a double life-style started. On one hand, I was an average to good student with above average capabilities, I was very active in 4-H, I was a church goer, and I was a relatively squared away kid. On the other hand, I constantly looked for ways to obtain and to consume alcohol. I started smoking cigarettes at age thirteen. Drugs were just a way to augment effects of the booze.

Shoplifting increased exponentially with the increase in drinking. All money I obtained went to securing alcohol. Gifts, do-dads, and sometimes food were stolen. I stole booze, too.

I started to try to quit it all after I went to Germany. It took until the night of graduation to quit the drugs. Yes, that was a bad night. Thank God for Jen and another classmate.

Shortly after I turned nineteen I had quit drugs, drinking, and smoking — at least for a few years.

Junior High and High School

Thanks to the heavy use of alcohol and drugs, I do not have that many memories worth sharing of my high school years. A few times with great friends, a few memorable people, and a story my sons want me to share and a story my niece, Lesley (yes, Levi named her after our sister), wants me to share because of the value they put in mirth and a good laugh.

David Skiff

"Stork" moved to Malta when we were in junior high. We gave David Skiff the name "Stork" because of his height not because of any frequent activity to aid in the bringing of babies. I should know, I partied with him enough. And party a lot together we did.

All the girls liked Stork. I think the girls in the class were disappointed when he chose a pretty, shy girl to "date" in junior high. I gave up my "crush" on him somewhere about that time and simply became a friend.

I did not feel safe with a lot of the other guys in the school. "Bad" things happen to girls who get drunk and pass out. David was a safe guy to party with because his motivation was the same as mine = to drink, to get drunk, and to have fun. I was always safe drinking with Stork. I drank and partied with anyone and everyone but as far as guys go, I felt safe when Stork was around.

I have woken up in bed with Stork though. I had been lying on the kitchen floor in a house in Wolf Point. The tiles were cool. I had gone to the refrigerator to get a cold slice of pizza to eat and lay down on the floor to eat it. I enjoyed the cool tiles too much to get back up again, or maybe I could not get back up, I do not know. I do not remember anything after lying down on the floor to eat the pizza. Wolf Point is not a place for sixteen year old white girls to party. Beth told me the next morning that she is the one who undressed me, put my pajamas on me, and put me to bed. When I woke up, I startled to find Stork sleeping on the other side of the bed! He had recently had an appendectomy and wanted a comfortable place to sleep. He was in pain and he knew nothing would happen if he slept next to me. He was right. Ours was and is simply a good friendship.

Stork fell in love in high school and married the woman of his heart soon afterward. He and Terry have three confident young women as daughters. The love they all five share is a beauty to see. David has my greatest admiration.

I admire him not only because he was such a great friend so many years ago and because of his family today. I admire him because of his character. Yes, I did get to see the development of that character when we were growing up. And he **is** quite the character! I admire him today because of what I get to see in him as a man.

The mettle of a person is in their relationships. His love for his wife and three daughters is evident by the relationships they have. I hope David and Terry know that he ranks, with a few others, at the top of my list of admirable people.

Slivers

I have very open relationships with my sons, Matthew and Andrew. We can and have talked about every topic imaginable. I always tried to be honest with them and answer any questions they had.

Yes, my sons know my stories.

When I had my career, I would have the opportunity to go speak in other states. Mom would come and stay with the boys while I was away. Matthew came home for lunch because the junior high school was only a couple of blocks away from our home. It was too far for Andrew to walk home for lunch from the grade school. I told Mom how much I enjoyed the ten-fifteen minutes I had with Matthew every day.

Talking on the phone with Mom one night, she said, "Oh, I see what you mean about enjoying those few minutes with Matthew! And the stories he tells! Why, he told me this one story … I told him it had to be his Uncle Levi, it could not have been you!"

"What story, Mom?"

She told me.

"Yes, Mom, that was me."

"OH Honey Bee, it couldn't be!!"

Oh yes, it could.

A family of my favorite people to party with was the Zents. Janet and Marlene were out of the home by the time I met Wilbur and Ruth's family. Buddy (Wilbur Jr … no wonder people call him Buddy) is a year older than me, Rene is my age, and Cathy is a year younger than me. They all were quite the partiers.

Wilbur worked as a government trapper and was a very strict parent in many aspects. It was a rare time when he would let Buddy drive his truck around town. This was a very cool old truck. It was circa 1950's, baby or sky blue, and with a wooden floor in the box or bed of the truck.

The night before this particular night guys from the class ahead of mine had been driving around in a SUV-type rig. Some of the guys mooned us.

The night with Buddy, there was at least five or six of us in the cab of the pick-up. More kids wanted in the truck and to "cruise the drag" with us. I and another gal, who wishes to remain anonymous, opted to get in the back of the truck. The guys from the night before started to follow us around the cruising strip of the main street.

So the other chick and I mooned them.

Buddy happened to glance in his rear-view (no pun intended) mirror and caught us with our pants down. He slammed on the brakes.

Yeah, I had festering slivers for weeks.

Buddy was angry at us. He feared Wilbur would hear about the mooning and "ground" him from the truck.

The other chick let someone remove some of her slivers.

Not me. I was too embarrassed.

I have never ridden in the back of a wooden floor-bed truck again.

I never mooned anyone again, either.

Wagon Train

Some years the wagon trail to wind near our ranch. I was allowed to ride out and meet it a few times. I loved the wagon train. I loved riding over the prairie. I loved walking around the campsite in the evening and visiting with the folks from the other wagons. Those who tried to have a "buffalo chip" (using cow dung) fire I avoided their campsites. Cow patty fires smolder and stink. The food cooked over these fires taste like shit also. I suspect the tails of the 1800's wagon trains and buffalo chip cooking fires is not very accurate; my guess is the pioneers used sagebrush as their main source of cooking fuel while crossing the prairie. Sage smoke favored food is much more palatable than dung smoke flavored food. And the prairies were covered with sagebrush species.

At least once I was allowed to stay with Auntie Diane for the duration of the wagon train. One year I got heat stroke and people thought I was hung over. That was a bad year. I think I am lucky I did not die of heat stroke. Kikker left the wagon train and took me home; I do not remember if he hauled my horse back to the ranch or just me. I may owe him my life.

One year Byron rode with Beth, Brian, Levi and I along on the wagon train.

Levi teased and maybe bullied some of the little boys who rode on the school bus. I tried to defend them. Some of these little boys also rode on the wagon train. To be nice, I asked one cute little eight year old boy if he wanted to ride behind my saddle on Silver Tip with me.

Yes he did.

He rode with me all day. I could not get the kid off of my horse! I figured he liked riding with me because it was better than riding in the wagon over the rough bumpy prairie sod. Years later I learned he had a childhood crush on me.

Years later I became friends with his older brother's wife. The wife asked if her husband remembered me. Oh yeah, I was the one who protected the little boys on the school bus from my brother.

More years passed and the cute little brother asked to be my friend on Facebook. Sure. I said I did not think he would remember me.

He not only remembered me, he remembered the name of my horse over thirty years later! Gotta love any man who remembers a girl's horse's name after that many years had passed.

Speech and Drama

I was not allowed to be in sports. Sports would take too much time away from the ranch and work. Not that I was athletic or anything. That was in the days before girls' volleyball. I love volleyball and did play co-ed intramural volleyball in high school and, as an adult, played co-ed volleyball in a city league for nearly ten years. When I was in high school I wanted to be in track, but of course, that was impossible during the spring calving season.

I got to be in Speech and Drama.

At first, I thought it was the worst thing in the world. But I would take any excuse to leave the work at the ranch. So, okay, Speech and Drama it is.

I think I remember the look on head Coach F's face to have read something like this: "Omg, WHAT am I going to do with THIS one!"

Coach F taught me oh so much more than government and current world affairs.

He had me try every Speech and Drama event in the book. I failed miserably at every single one of them. It is physically and mentally impossible for a reservedly shy kid to get up in front of others and speak! I would cry on the bus prior to the meet. I got ulcers. I got the lowest score in every round of every event. But, hey, someone has to come in last!

I would not quit.

Part of the "not quitting" was the fact I was too engrained in the art of stubbornness — oh, wait, I mean tenacity. The other aspect was the fact I would do anything to go to town to party. I did not smoke while "in training" that would break training rules. I was accused of it once, but I never did that. I did, of course, drink. But that was a way of life, not any act of rebellious "breaking the rules."

Toward the end of that miserable first year in Speech and Drama, my classmate, Shirlee Miller's debate partner quit or was unable to go to District. Debate is one of the hardest events in Speech and Drama. NOT the event for me! But, I went to Coach F and volunteered to be Shirlee's partner for District. This was about two weeks prior to District. There was no way a GOOD contestant could have totally gotten ready to debate the topic for the year, let alone ME.

At District the top six contestants went on to State. There were only five debate teams in our District. By volunteering, I had a sure trip to State.

I think it was the second time I read something in Coach F's face, this time, I think I read: "Holy Shit, this kid is serious." Or, maybe it was some other words of shock going through his head such as "Oh god, no, ANYONE but THIS kid."

In spite of his incredulousness, he did not say no. He, Shirlee, and the other coaches worked with me for hours every night to that I would not totally embarrass Shirlee and the team.

I totally embarrassed Shirlee and the team.

I do not like controversy; I do not like argument; I do not like dispute.

Shirlee has a gentle spirit. Yet, in her gentleness there is a solid core of strong character. She carried us through the rounds of debate with grace and dignity.

I was the fool.

That simple act of volunteering changed Coach F's perception of me. Somehow, he saw, buried deep within me … potential. The difficult task was to quarry out what was so submerged and buried so deeply.

The next year, it was more of the same … trying different events, speech events as well as drama events.

I failed.

My failures were not as dismal as during the first year. There were a few times I was not dead last in a round. There may have been a shy, scared freshman from another town who would get last place once in a while.

State was held in Malta that year; I got to go to State again.

We did not give up. The coaches did not give up on me and I did not give up trying.

I was no longer crying before every meet. I no longer had a problem getting up in front of peers and judges. I did, however, have a problem with essential things like eye-contact and voice projection. I feared looking at people. I did not like it when they looked at me. My voice would get quieter and quieter until no one could hear me. They would lean forward to catch my words. This attention would scare me further, so I would speak even quieter. And so went the downhill spiral.

The third year, we found the key to my initial success.

Coach F had me portraying Anne Boleyn, one of King Henry the VIII's to-be-murdered wives. It was a simple sketch … she was locked in a tower awaiting her future death … the only acting I had to do was to pace and seem to be afraid, yet accepting, of my upcoming demise.

The thing is, in the year 1536 no one wore glasses. I had to take mine off.

Bingo.

I cannot see you; therefore, you cannot see me.

Well, maybe I did not have that much of an ostrich point-of-view. But it is what "worked" for me.

I went from dead last to winning rounds to placing in the meets. I do not think I ever came in first that year, but I scored points for the team. And I learned that a little soap on the fingers near the eyes "helped" me to cry in the sketch and judges thought I was "in touch" with my character. I went to State again; this time on my own accord and ability.

In high school, I always tried out for the annual play. Coach DQ was an assistant Speech and Drama coach and Director of the plays. My freshman year I was a stage hand for the play. During my sophomore year, I had a part in a whodunit drama. My junior year Coach DQ cast me as the lead role in an Orphan Anne themed production.

These roles also helped me eradicate any trepidation of being in front of people and grow in confidence — as long as I was not looking at an audience or crowd or engaging another person in real conversation. I still, occasionally have difficulty engaging in idle chitchat in a social setting. I am too serious a person to enjoy talking about the weather, although I have learned to do so. When speaking from a podium, one does not have to really listen to the other person. A speaker has to listen to the audience's body language, but not their words. Truly it is easier to be a speaker than a listener.

My senior year I won first place at many Speech and Drama meets; I won first at District; I also won first at State in Serious Solo. I played the part of Doodle's brother in James Hurst's short story, *The Scarlet Ibis*. I still have my gold medallion I won at State.

Thanks to coaches like Coach F and Coach DQ. These men, in their kindness and perseverance with me, taught me how to begin my trek toward the confident woman I am today. For years now, thanks to them, I have had no problem speaking in front of an audience. I learned the only way to get over a fear is to walk through the fear.

This is not to say I do not have butterflies in my stomach before a speaking opportunity, I do. I do not allow the "butterflies" to stop me from sharing. I know the "butterflies" are more about the hope that what I share will touch the heart of someone in the audience than any fear of standing or speaking in front of people. These days, when I speak, it is often to tell my story.

I owe a lot to Coach F and Coach DQ. I would not be who I am without their influence. I love them both.

I have not seen Coach DQ since I was in High School. I see Coach F every few years. I had a short stint as a Speech and Drama Coach; I saw him at a Speech Meet when he was a judge. He got a kick out of the fact of me being a Speech and Drama coach. He made the comment that the most successful high school students are the ones who take Speech and Drama. Judging by the people I know, I would agree with him.

Coach F also attends my High School Reunions. At the twentieth, he said something to the effect of "So, you're still single?"

Yes, except for the seven year marriage to my son's father.

No boyfriend?

No.

Then he made some comment alluding to me owning a lot of sex toys due to being single. I was shocked speechless that my esteemed coach would say such a thing to me.

The next day I had a come-back.

"Hey, Coach F, do you remember what you said to me last night?"

Nod.

"Just so you know, I don't own any toys."

Pause; he made no comment.

"When I feel the need, I go to the grocery store."

He gave me a blank look.

"I shop in the produce department."

The look on his face was still blank.

Patiently, I explained: "I buy bananas, cucumbers, zucchini, and other such shaped fruits and vegetables. I go home, I perform orally, and then I swallow."

His shocked silence only lasted a moment before he burst into laughter.

I love my sense of humor.

Hazing, Teasing, and other forms of Bullying

I have not always been able to joke about oral sex.

When I was in the second grade, someone started to call me BJ. The nickname stuck. For the next twenty years, I was only known as BJ. After I went to work at my career in Chinook, when someone phoned and asked for "BJ" the Conservation District Administrator would say to me, "BilliJo, someone who used to know you is on the phone."

During the summer between seventh and eighth grade while at 4-H camp, an asshole from Chinook started to call me a different bj name; he referred to me as "blow job." He was also on that school's junior high football team and he went on to be on the Sugar Beeter's high school wrestling team as well. Every time he saw me, he would call me blow job. Soon other assholes did the same.

Once I entered the café where the Chinook wrestling team had just finished eating a meal. The asshole, which started it all, stood at the cash register to pay for his meal. He greeted me very loudly, "Hey Blow Job!" Everyone in the entire restaurant turned to stare at me.

I had no idea what a blow job was. I knew the jerks who called me that were making fun of me; others around them would snicker. I knew I did not like it. But I did not know what it was that they called me.

After a couple of years of this, I finally asked a classmate what a blow job was.

The only reason I can think of that caused me to ask a classmate of mine this all important question was that in junior high he made up a "cuss word" we students could use in class that our teachers would not know we were cussing. "GDSOBFCS" we would mutter or say when we were not happy about something. "God-damn-son-of-a-bitch-fucking-cock-sucker" became our string of cuss words. We thought we were so suave and cool.

When I asked this class mate what a "blow job" was, he looked at me quizzically. "You know," he said, "a cock sucker."

Oh. Okay. Right. Of course. Thanks.

I had no idea what a cock sucker was.

On the ranch, the bulls had penises; I assumed my father and brother did also. Cows had vaginas; so did my mother and me. We did not use "cutesy" or slang words for genitalia.

It was not until I was 27 years old and divorced that I learned what the assholes referred to me as.

At that time, I lived in Malta and had become reacquainted with some old high school friends. A friend was upset one day because someone she knew had been making fun of me and my name. I decided to ask her what the hated nickname meant.

She looked at me with the same quizzical look my classmate had given me over ten years prior. She started her explanation in the same manner "You know," she said, and then she continued, "oral sex … ."

No wonder with that appellation no decent boy from my home town wanted to go out with me in high school. No wonder I had the reputation I had.

I lived for twelve years in the same town as the asshole that started it all. He has the reputation of being a total jerk, asshole, and creep. As far as I know I never saw him when I lived in his hometown.

During my twentieth class reunion, I learned there were still assholes in my class who referred to me as blow job behind my back.

I do not have any time for assholes. I will behave in a polite manner to them. But that is about the extent of my interaction with such people.

When my friend explained the term to me, I began to tell people my name is BilliJo, not BJ, or Billie, or anything else. BilliJo is one word, even though the "J" is capitalized in the middle of the name. "Jo" is not my middle name. My middle name is Marie.

I think it was one of my first acts of self-confidence and self-esteem as I stuck to correcting anyone who referred to me as BJ.

My Auntie Diane said she could not stop calling me BJ.

Byron had given her the nickname of "Fluffy" due to her weight. Byron liked big women. He would say for men to marry a fat woman; fat women gave shade in the summer and warmth in the winter.

Diane hated her nickname. I called her Auntie Fluffy. When Auntie Diane told me she could not quit calling me BJ, I told her I could not quit calling her Auntie Fluffy.

She quit. So did I. We had mutual respect for each other.

Some people still call me BJ. Some people, whom I know hold no malice and I let it slide. There are damn few people in this group. Most other people I correct when they incorrectly state my name as BJ. To me using my proper name when talking to me or introducing me to other peoples, is an act of respect. I do not accept disrespecting behavior toward myself any longer.

My name is BilliJo.

Getting Locked In

There was a boy who moved to town our senior year in high school. Everyone liked Danny Thomas. Danny was friendly to everyone: the popular kids and the kids other students made fun of. Looking back, I realize Danny was a very sensitive guy.

He befriended me, the girl people made fun of and called blow job.

The week we graduated from high school was a week of partying. There was school sponsored all-night party. This party was supposedly designed to keep us from drinking. That ploy did not work. We were allowed to come and go at the party. We would come in the building and dance awhile and then we would go outside, cruise around for a while and drink.

A popular cheerleader, a basketball and football jock, and another basketball jock invited me to go cruise the drag with them in her robin-egg blue Mustang. Never had these two jocks invited me to drink with them.

Feeling honored at the invitation and being totally shit-faced drunk, I walked out of the door with the three of them. The basketball jock and I walked across the street to her car and got into the back seat.

I was so drunk that I did not notice the other two stayed on the side of the street of the building in which the party was held.

The jock started an attempted rape.

The two across the street laughed when they saw the car bounce up and down. They thought sexual action was taking place.

No it was not. I kicked the shit out of the jock and the cheerleader's car. He tried to get me to quit kicking by saying I would kick out the back window.

I wish I had.

He finally opened the door and crawled out of the car after I handed a hard knee into his crotch a time or two.

Completely pissed off, I also crawled out of the car. I stocked past the two grinning fools of classmates and stumbled into the party.

I remember two people looking at me strangely, chaperone Coach F and classmate Danny Thomas.

Danny took me by the arm and led me back outside. The two assholes were across the street tending to their injured jerk of a friend or laughing at him rolling around on the sidewalk holding his injured parts - I do not know which.

Danny led me to his car and opened the driver's door.

"Get in," he ordered me.

I did.

"Lock the door," he commanded.

I pushed down the old-fashioned door lock on the passenger side door.

"Lock the back door," he demanded.

Obediently, I reached back and pushed down the back passenger door lock.

He reached in and locked the back door on the driver's side. Then he pushed down the lock on the driver's door.

He said, "You are now locked inside of my car. You cannot get out until I let you out." Then he shut the door.

I fumed. How dare he lock me in his car! There was a party going on and here I was — locked in a car!

I was too drunk to realize all I had to do to get out of his car was to pull up the lock on the door, to pull on the door handle to open the door, and get out of the car.

Danny returned to enjoy the party. I stayed locked inside of his car, safe from assholes who try to take advantage of dumb drunk girls.

Six weeks later Danny and I were driving around town while drinking. We got quite drunk. Our topic of conversation was suicide. We had a classmate in the hospital getting his stomach pumped from a suicide attempt overdose. The other guy, despondent over a break up and his inability to woo her back had swallowed a bottle of pills.

Danny and I, in our drunken state, decided that an overdose was not the way to commit suicide. We decided a high-powered gun to the head was a more sure fired way to complete the task.

A week later it was the Fourth of July celebration. I remember vividly walking naked across my studio apartment; I was headed to the bathroom to take a shower after spending the day at Nelson Reservoir.

Through my right ear, I heard the beginning of the firework display in Trafton Park. Through my left ear, I heard Danny's gun go off.

Later some of us learned of Danny's tragic family and past. On the outside he was a charming, happy, loving, lovable young man. Inside he was tormented.

The torment became more than he could cope with.

I still mourn him and the loss of his life.

Yes, my oldest son's middle name is in honor of Danny Thomas, my classmate.

Grandma Doll

During the few years, from age thirteen to sixteen, of extremely rebellious activity, my parents tried several ideas and methods to 'help me grow-up' as my behavior was seen as immaturity. I was, as the label is now, "ungovernable."

My parents helped Grandma Doll move to Malta so I would have a consistent place to stay when I had to be in town, rather than with friends. I guess they thought my friends were bad influence on me. Rather, I was a bad influence on them.

I can understand, in the years before welfare or public assistance, Grandma Doll raised ten children without a husband to provide for them. I understand she was one tough lady. But to think a 77 year old woman could help raise a 13 year old brat is beyond me. I guess my folks were at the end of their rope in trying to find solutions to curtail my behavior and attitude.

Not that my behavior was glaringly, obviously, or loudly rebellious. I never talked back to my parents. I certainly never yelled at them. I simply, quietly did whatever I wanted to do. I had a total "fuck you" attitude. What I wanted to do was to drink as much as possible as often as possible. And, this is what I did. I drank.

Having me work like the loafers from the reservation did not curtail my drinking, hiding the alcohol in the house did not curtail my drinking, and forbidding me to stay in town did not curtail my drinking. Nothing any one could do would have stopped my drinking.

Of course, Grandma could not keep me from drinking either.

Grandma would fix supper for me. I would not be "home" to eat. She would keep the plate of food warm for me in the oven. Sometimes I was too drunk to eat. Sometimes I had the munchies and would devour the supper.

When I got home, she would meet me at the door of her apartment and ask, "Have you been smoking; have you been drinking?"

"No, Grandma," I would lie.

"I can smell tobacco on you."

"My friends smoke, Grandma, but I don't."

"I smell alcohol."

"How could you? I haven't been drinking. Maybe the breath mints (or gum) I have kind of smell like booze."

She would step aside, defeated. I would push past her and go downstairs to my room.

My room was in the basement; her bedroom was upstairs. There were two bedrooms in the basement. She moved me from the one I slept in originally to the one below her bedroom. She would also turn on the electric mattress cover so I would have a nice warm bed with nice warm flannel sheets when I went to sleep. I never thanked her for her kindness.

I think she made me change bedrooms so she could monitor my activities better. There was a back door. I would unlock it and sneak out the back in order to go party more.

Grandma was unreasonably afraid of having the doors unlocked. She was absolutely convinced that if her back door was unlocked, a drunk would leave the bars, stumble down the street and go behind the apartment building, open her back door (subconsciously or intuitively knowing that the door would be unlocked), come into her house, and rape her. Maybe everyone has unreasonable fears, I do not know. I do know I still find this irrational fear of hers ludicrous. I know there are twisted sick people out there who would rape a damn near 80 year old woman; I like to think these sick men are rare and none in Malta, Montana.

She caught on to my sneaking out at night. She hung a bell on the doorknob. Sometimes I would remove the bell on my way downstairs. She caught on to that act, as well.

It could take me up to 45 minutes to get that door open without ringing the damn bell, but I would do it.

What I do not understand is that sometimes, the bell would not ring, but Grandma would suddenly sling open the kitchen door and catch me in the act of opening the back door. I would lie and tell her I was just on my way upstairs to go to the bathroom. She never confronted me on my obvious lie — how could I be on my way upstairs when I had the doorknob to go outside in my hand or the door half way open?

The only bathroom in her apartment was between the kitchen and her bedroom. I smoked pot in her bathroom.

When Grandma would ask me about the smell in the bathroom, I would tell her my bowel movements stunk so badly that I burned a little incense in the bathroom to cover the odor. I do not know if she bought that lie. Marijuana was a new concept for her generation.

Sometimes I would be too sick with a hangover to stay in school all day. I would go back to the apartment after the mandatory class of English. I always told her I had trouble with my menstrual cycle and that I had cramps and needed to lie down. She had to know no one got their period or ovulated every week. But, she would always let me in the house and she would go to the grocery store across the street and buy a 7-Up for me. To this day, 7-Up tastes like a thoughtful medicine to me.

Some nights I would stumble into her apartment to catch her sitting in the living room praying the rosary for me.

Of all the kind things she did, praying the rosary for me was the one that actually touched my heart at the time. As I have looked back several times since her death, everything she did for me were acts of loving kindness. I just never noticed or just did not care when I was a teen.

I never let her know. I pretended that act of love, praying for me, did not affect me. I was so selfish and self-centered that I did not even care or notice the warm bed, the warm food, the many little acts of kindness and love. I did, however, notice her praying the rosary.

I felt badly that she worried for me. I did not understand why she worried about me. I was invincible when I drank. I was on top of the world, unstoppable, and unconquerable. Plus, I did not think I would live to see the old age of thirty.

"Eat, Drink, and be Merry for tomorrow may never come" - I took that saying to heart. Ever since Lesli Ann died, I wanted to die, too.

I was told that God loved Lesli Ann and wanted her to be with Him. In my child-heart, I thought: Did God not love me, too? Did He not want me to be with Him, too? I took risks with my life when I drank— maybe to subconsciously "help" God get me to die and to be with Him.

Grandma Doll also believed idle hands were the devils workshop. I was not allowed to be idle. Even when watching TV, I had to be "doing" something. She taught me how to crochet, how to embroider, how to needlepoint, and how to cross-stitch. None of these things do I remember how to do. When I was pregnant with Matthew and sick, Beth taught me how to knit. I still knit, although not as well as Beth.

My youngest son, Andrew, feels ignored if a person is doing something while visiting. One of the hardest things I ever have had to learn is to just sit and listen when chatting with him. To honor and respect him, to express my love for him, I had to learn to sit and visit. He was in college before I fully was capable of doing so for any length of time.

Grandma also quilted. For some unknown reason, I loved her big old quilting frame. Equally unknown, she never taught me how to quilt. I wanted her antique quilting frame when she moved; I did not know how to quilt, she gave it to someone else. Today I quilt. I do not like to sew the tops; I only like to hand-sew the quilting. Many years ago I bought myself, in an antique store, a laptop quilting frame. It is handier than Grandma's big old one and an antique, but I still wish I had hers.

I do have many things Grandma gave me. She gave me the last quilt she ever quilted, the last afghan she ever crocheted, the last pillows she worked needlepoint on, the last quilted pillows she sewed the tops for. She made me my first down pillows when we moved to the ranch when I was three, I still have them. She sewed for me a new set of down pillows when my folks built the new house when I was thirteen, I still use them. I have her ironing board and still use it; although, I do not iron everything I wash like she did. I have her hand-written recipes cards and I use her recipes. I have never been able to master her home-made egg noodles. I have never tried to learn how to make head cheese, blood sausage, or pickled pigs feet from a butchered hog.

When I was much younger, every autumn Dad would butcher a hog or two. Grandma would come and help him process the meat. Mom was glad she had the job as secretary in town and did not have to be around the mess they made in the kitchen with their processing. Some of the sausages tasted great, others I did not enjoy so much. We always had fresh lard with which to cook and with which to make the best pie crusts in the world. I still love side-pork and any dish made with pork except when added with sauerkraut.

I embrace my German heritage quite well except when it comes to sauerkraut and cooked cabbage. Two dishes I could live without.

Remembering their butchering helped stimulate my imagination when I wrote my first war-survival science fiction novel, *The Seekers*.

Remembering my Grandmother helps motivate me to try to be a better person.

I will live the rest of my life in a manner of amends for the thoughtlessness of my behavior for the years of living with my Grandmother during high school.

After I graduated she moved into an independent living complex. Whenever I would go visit her, she would meet me at the door.

"Are you still drinking?"

She would not wait for an answer, yet she would peer up at me in a hopeful manner.

"Are you still smoking?"

Again, she did not wait for me to respond. Her eyes would slide away from mine.

"I'm still praying for ya."

She would turn and hobble slowly into her apartment, expecting me to follow.

When she was 93 years old, still living in her own apartment, she had her first and only heart attack while sitting under the hair dryer getting a perm at the beauty shop. They rushed her to the hospital.

The young doctor (maybe 60 years old) talked to her about a pacemaker after they revived her.

"Sonny," I am told she said to him, "it's okay. I am an old woman. I am ready to die. Just call my family for them to come and say good-bye."

That was on a Friday night. They called me at the bar. I lived 90 miles away. I did not go say good-bye. They called me again on Sunday, at the same bar, and told me she had passed away.

I went to her funeral. I stayed sober throughout that ordeal.

The rest of this story will be told later in the book.

Germany

Another thing my parents did to assist me in growing up was to sign me up as a foreign exchange student to go to Germany, the land of my ancestors.

My family hosted many foreign exchange students and young adults over the years. The first foreign exchange student was Braulio from Brazil. The second was Fritz from West Germany. Through the program Braulio was affiliated with, I went to live with Fritz's family for three months. I was sixteen when I went to West Germany. I never lived on the ranch again full-time until engaged to be married four years later.

I fully enjoyed my three months in West Germany. I have always wanted to return, yet, never have.

For "foreign language" in school, we had German. I had five years of German in school plus a few words and phrases from Grandma Ann when I departed for the country of West Germany. Yet, the first question asked of me when I arrived, "*Bist du mude?*" (Are you tired?), was incomprehensible to me. Because of the accent I could not understand the words of this simple, basic question.

I believe immersion is the best way to learn a new language. By the time I left West Germany, some of my dreams were in German. To this day, I use German words when I take notes. Often it is easier for me to say something in German than in Spanish. When I speak in German, it is confusing to my Mexican friends. My sons grew up knowing German commands (Clean your room, come here, I love you). But when first in the country, I was lost.

I do not sleep well on an airplane. After twenty-six hours of flying, driving from Frankfurt to Struth, a meal, and little visiting I was totally exhausted. But when Anne, Fritz's girlfriend, and Anita, the house-maid, asked me if I wanted to meet a gal who spoke English I could not say no.

Unbeknownst to me, my first night in Germany I went to a Bible Study in the living quarters of a nurse at the nearby hospital.

Arriving in her small apartment, there were a few other young ladies and candles burning in a quiet setting. After being introduced to Elfrieda and our short conversation, I sat on a couch and promptly went to sleep. When the study was over, they woke me up. Anne, Anita, and I walked back to the house in the comfortable silence of people who cannot communicate in each other's languages but are at ease with one another.

Elfrieda had asked me if I would like to meet American men.

Duh.

I am sixteen. I really like boys. Of course I would like to meet American servicemen.

Anita Hefner, the housemaid, was a strong Christian young woman who was also my age. She became a bosom buddy of mine. I think of her often. I wish we had never lost contact. She was a fantastic person and friend. She and Anne had patience with my inability to speak fluent German that Fritz and his parents did not have. I pray Anita and I will meet again. She is one of the finest people I have ever met.

A few weeks after my arrival, Elfrieda asked my German house-parents, Fritz and Helga, if she and her boyfriend, Erik, could take me out for a night on the town. Young Fritz, the son, was not home that day. The parents said yes.

When Erik and Elfrieda came to pick me up, young Fritz was not happy about me going to town with this other young couple. His parents allowed me to go anyway.

I was ready. There is no drinking age in Germany. I fully expected a night of drinking and singing as is common among the Germans. And to which I had become accustom quite rapidly.

So, with my cigarettes and a little money in my pocket I climbed into the backseat of Erik's car. Only to read a sticker on the dashboard that said something to the effect of: smoking is stupid. Hmm, I thought, I guess I will keep my smokes in my pocket.

Erik drove to Ansbach, the major city only a couple of miles away from the farming village in which we lived. Struth is on a hill; Ansbach is in a valley. Down through town and up the other side of the valley we went, making a right hand turn into the gate of a United States military installation. Elfrieda made a comment I did not understand about the guard being a brother. He just waved us through the gate without asking to see any papers or identification. I had no idea security was so lax.

Erik and Elfrieda had been quiet throughout the drive. I had no idea what to expect. Erik stopped the car in front of a church.

WHAT!?

Oh, I could see a movie theater next door. Maybe that is where we were going to go.

Elfrieda and I got out of the car. Totally confused and still having no idea what to expect or what was in store, I did not fully grasp Erik stayed in the car.

We went inside what would be called the fellowship hall attached to the church.

There were young men, soldiers, all around the room.

I stayed close to Elfrieda as I glanced around at all these potential kissing partners.

She walked up to an older young man. I learned later Scott, the missionary, was of the ripe old age of 26. Scott was a good five to eight years older than most of the other guys. He was the only one of the guys who was married. His wife and three children were not present that night.

Elfrieda introduced Scott and I. "Scott, this is BilliJo, who I told you about."

We shook hands.

As we shook hands, she continued. "Erik and I have another invite out. Make sure she gets home."

With that, Elfrieda turned, walked out, and left me standing there, shaking the hand of a total stranger in a church fellowship hall filled with total strangers.

At least they spoke English.

That night was my first introduction to a Pentecostal church. I had never heard of the Pentecostal movement. I was raised strict Catholic. My father is one of the most devout Catholics I know. I was raised celebrating every religious holiday, saying the rosary, observing holy days of obligation, adhering to strict Lenten self-denials, memorizing specific prayers, and attending Mass at least weekly. I even remember Mass in Latin and covering my head with a doily.

As the reader may know or imagine, a Catholic Mass and a Pentecostal "come alive" service share nothing in common except for maybe the word "God."

Raised in Montana in the era in which I was raised, I had seen one Afro-American person in my entire life prior to the airplane trip to Germany. A Black man worked at the race tracks at the county fair one year. The next Afro-American people I would see were a family who got on the plane in Detroit. There were several Black men in the room in Germany. To my mild surprise, they did not sit together in a segregated area of the hall.

The amazement of unsegregated Blacks was the least of my astonishments.

I had never seen, heard of, nor witnessed such a loud outpouring of music and praying. Catholics do not pray out loud, loudly, and in a different language.

After the service, Scott asked me if it was okay for me to join them at the Christian Servicemen's Center before taking me home.

I was not about to say no. Part of me was too afraid to say no; the other part of me was too curious to say no. I had no idea what I was getting myself into. But, they seemed like a nice, friendly bunch of young men. And, I thought, I had gone to church all of my life. The drinking often followed the fellowship or church service, especially when we attended Saturday evening Mass. There is the common saying: When four Catholics get together, there is always a fifth.

We all climbed into a van that another older man drove. Later I learned the driver was the oldest man of the group. He was 28 years old; he was really, really old. He drove to the heart of Ansbach, into the "old town" section behind the city wall.

Most, if not all, of Germany's cities once were protected by a large wall that surrounded the cities. As the fear of invading hordes of barbarians or armies during the Dark Ages waned so did the need for protection behind the walls. The cities grew around these fortress-like abutments. The old parts of town still had cobblestone streets and such an antique, historic atmosphere. I loved to wander the winding twisting streets of old town Ansbach.

The Christian Servicemen's Center was on the second or third floor of a building that housed a dentist office on the first floor.

There was no drinking for this group of guys. When we arrived, there were other young men already there. One sat at a piano, one had a guitar, and they all sang hymn-like songs. I sat on the floor with other guys and listened to them sing these unfamiliar yet happy songs.

Much later, 2AM if memory serves me correctly, the older GI loaded up the van with the people he had to drive home. I think he took me home first.

This first astonishing introduction to a different way of life did not frighten me off. Two days later, Scott came to pick me up for another service. This night was a Bible Study held inside the church sanctuary.

Soon I was skipping school, an act definitely not new to me, and spending my days at the Center. Some of the guys actually lived at the Center. Whenever they were not on duty or on call, all of them would hang out at the Center. I spent as many evenings as I could at the Center, as well.

Me hanging out with a dozen or two young men from the age of 18 to about 21 was great in my book.

I loved the way they shook hands whenever they met each other or when someone entered the Center. I loved the way they took the time to talk and to listen to one another. I thoroughly enjoyed the collection of German comic books they had — Astrix and Oblix. I loved everything about their friendliness and genuine care for one another.

The way they talked of God and of a personal relationship with his Son, Jesus was new too. This concept was familiar to me.

My mom's brother managed a Christian summer camp for years. Along with 4-H Camp, I went to Bible Camp every summer. Yet, the message did not get through to me those summer days spent at Pines Youth Camp on the Fort Peck Dam. I went for the swimming, horseback riding, over-night hiking trips, and, of course, boys.

The summer before I went to Germany I dated a guy who worked at the Christian Youth Ranch in the northern part of the county. Mike attended Bible College in Nebraska; I do not remember where he was originally from. Mike was nine years older than me. My dad about could not handle the fact that I, at age 15, dated a man of 24. But I think the only reason Mike dated me was to goad my dad. When Mike first asked me out and I told him I could not go out with him until he came to our house and talked to my father, he seemed to find that funny. When he drove the 50-some miles to have that visit with my father, Dad hardly said a word. Mike finally slapped the arms of the chair in which he sat, stood up, and said, "Well, then, I guess I can date your daughter."

Our first date was to go to a popular movie. Standing in a line that snaked around the corner of the Villa Theater, we waited patiently for the line to move forward. Soon, my father and brother were in line behind us. They did not talk to us. I was morbidly embarrassed; Mike found it funny that they had come to town as well. He laughed out loud at the idea that my father brought my brother with him for them to spy on us at the theater. My father and brother sat across the aisle and about two rows back from us in the movie house. Mike got great mirth from all of this. After the movie, he told Dad that he wanted a few minutes alone with me. Dad did not say a word as Mike and I walked off together and got into his little car. About fifteen minutes to a half hour later, we met my father and brother at Joe's In & Out and I rode home with them. Not a word was said. I do not think Dad ever fully trusted Mike and I. But Mike was a "gentleman" in the old-fashioned meaning of the word; Dad had nothing to worry about.

Mike talked to me about God and Jesus, too. But there was something about the guys in Germany … I got to see them live their faith on a day by day and night by night basis. And I wanted what they had.

August 4th was on a Thursday. I had gone to the bank that day and had taken out enough money for cigarettes for a week. I attended the Bible Study that night. When the offering plate was passed, I put my entire week's allowance of cigarette money into the plate without thinking. When I realized what I had done, the plate was in the pew behind where I sat and I tried to get my money back. Tom, a young man sitting next to me, asked me what I was doing. I told him. Scott told us to shush. I turned back around to face the front and pondered what I had just done. I did not hear a word Scott said that night.

Afterward, before we left the church, Tom said he wanted to talk to me. He led me across the aisle to a different pew. Elfrieda joined us, although she said not a word. I realized later, she was there to pray for me.

Tom told me the things I had heard all my life, about Jesus being the Son of God. This was nothing new. I had heard about Christ all my life. Then Tom said something that struck a chord in my heart. He said something to the effect of: a Christian is not sinless, they just sin less when they follow God and His Will. Learning to follow God's Will has been a life-long process ever since.

Ever since God chose to take Lesli Ann instead of me, I had felt as though I was not "good-enough" for God or anyone else. The fear of not being "good-enough" is one of my greatest liabilities to this day. I felt as though I was not good-enough for God to love me, not a good-enough daughter, friend, or student. The list could go on *ad infinitum*. In fact, I was not good-enough at anything. I was not good-enough and therefore, I was not loveable.

For some reason, the concept of not having to be "good-enough," of not having to try to be good-enough, of just trusting God to help me through life … I grasped at it like a drowning man reaches for a life-preserver.

Tom asked if I was ready to pray.

Yes.

He said to repeat after him.

Being Catholic, I thought I had to say the exact same words he said. I listened carefully but when I tried to repeat his words, my memory failed me and I just talked to God from my heart.

My life changed again.

Mom sent me money for my seventeenth birthday; I bought a Bible. I devoured everything I could learn from it and the guys from the Center.

Helga held a birthday party for me. It was held in the flower garden. She served cocoa with whipped crème and chocolate slivers on top and fruit desserts. The Gerhart family (my host family) gave me a *drindle*, a traditional German dress. Teens from Struth gave me a teddy bear and perfume. I still have the dress and teddy bear. My seventeenth birthday was one of the most memorable birthdays of my life.

Barely a month later, it was time for me to return to the United States. I arrived in time for the end of football season and Beth's birthday.

I tried living at home but I could not. I would say good-night to my parents and go to my room to read my Bible. My dad would come into my room, rip the Bible out of my hands, and throw it across the room while he yelled at me.

The trip to Germany was to help me grow up; it was not intended to make a "religious fanatic" out of me. Dad had been taught that only Priests were educated enough to read the Bible and understand the context and content. Other people who read the Bible would get an incorrect interpretation. That is how all the crazy denominations got started. His reaction was only in fear for his daughter due to what he had been taught and raised to believe.

Dad and I were unable to work through our differences. I moved to town. At first I lived with Grandma Doll, but that was about like living at home. Byron quit working for Dad and I stayed with them in a motel trailer park; the six of us were in a tiny little two bedroom camp-trailer. Two weeks later, Bev suggested I find somewhere else to live.

I still attended keggars, only I did not drink, I brought a pitcher of ice tea with me. Or I did not drink as much. I was still "me" — strong willed and defiant. I only had my drinking friends. I did not know to whom or where to turn for help and knowledge for this new way of life.

The first time I lived in Tennessee, I drove down to Atlanta Georgia to visit a high school classmate, Ron Stuff.

As we sat at the Pancake House waiting for our breakfast order, he turned to me and said, "When did you become a Christian?"

"Between our junior and senior year in high school," I informed him. "Did you not notice a difference in me?"

"I noticed you didn't party as much."

"I still went to parties because I didn't know what else to do."

"Why didn't you come to me?"

"I didn't know you were a Christian."

"Why not? You knew I went to (such and such) church."

"So, I went to church, too."

Going to church does not make a person a Christian any more than baking or eating muffins makes a person a biscuit.

He went on to tell me that when I was in North Dakota, the school sent a press release to our hometown newspaper announcing that I played my saxophone in an evangelistic ministry. It was then that he and his family learned of my conversion.

"When my mom read that in the newspaper," he said, "her jaw didn't only drop open in shock and surprise, her whole face fell on the floor."

Yes, going from drinking and partying to proclaiming the gospel was quite a change for me. I do not think I ever was a "religious fanatic." I did want to learn all I could about a different life-style of trusting God in my daily life.

Church and Bible College did not teach me how to trust God. The organization dedicated to helping drunks stay sober taught me how to trust God in all aspects and situations in my life.

The Orahood Family

For this uncertain period of my life, this family deserves a chapter unto themselves so strong is their effect on me. I could write chapter about stories about the cows I owned, the horses I rode, or the fun times I had with friends. But this book is about the people and events that shaped me as a person. This family continues to influence my life.

For almost five months I lived with the Orahoods in town my senior year in high school. I was so afraid Marlyn would send me home to my father that I tried very hard to not be a problem in their household. The only boy in the family, Tim, remembers me spending most of the time sitting quietly in the corner chair in the living room reading.

I visited the family during a Christmas vacation when I was in college nearly fifteen years later. I met Tim's future wife, Sally. Tim laughingly told her that college had been good to me — I had learned how to talk.

The three Orahood girls, Ludell, Lynne, and Lori, shared a bedroom in the basement. I shared a twin bed with Ludell.

I only needed an English class and the Government class to graduate from high school. I had those classes in the morning and would skip school in the afternoon. There probably has not been another student in the history of that high school who skipped school more than I did and who did not get caught nor expelled.

There is a big south-facing picture window in the Orahood's living room. I would curl up in my favorite chair in the sun and read.

One day, Ludell and Jen skipped school with me. Actually, they did this more often than once but not all of the time. I do not remember if Lynne was there or not this day; she was the better behaved of the four of us and seldom, if ever, skipped school with us. To our embarrassment, Wesley was home. He was hung over from the night before and had not made it back out to their ranch. To further our embarrassment, Marlyn came home at noon. As a teacher, she always stayed at the grade school during lunch. For her to catch us was unthinkable.

I do not remember them saying a word of chastisement to us.

Instead, I remember Marlyn fetching a glass of wine for Wesley and sitting on the arm of his chair with her arm around him while he sipped the "hair of the dog that bit him the night before." This picture of a simple act of loving kindness between a married couple is forever etched in my mind. I had never witnessed anything like it in my life. No wonder all four of their children are still married to their original spouses.

When I lived in Glasgow I grew to know Lori as an adult. I watched her and her husband, Wayne Shipp, interact. By this time they had been married or together for over a quarter of a century. I wish everyone could know such a loving expression of vows in their marriages. I have told them how much I admire them. I could go back to my behavior as a teen in the Orahood home at the Shipp's home and quietly sit in the corner and watch Wayne and Lori — I am in such awe of their love and commitment to one another. How they treat one another and how they talk to one another is with such respect. After so many years together, they still kiss upon seeing one another or leaving one another.

Once when Wayne and I worked together, he was upset. He told me Lori had gone to bed the night before without kissing him. It was the first time in their marriage she had done so. He did not know what was wrong. He was preoccupied with worry. Lori came into the office. She walked around the counter to get to her husband's desk. She leaned down kissed him where he sat in his chair and they put their arms around each other. He asked her about the night before. She said she had been very tired and he had been busy doing something. She simply had gone to bed. He said to her even when or if he was busy doing something, please interrupt him and give him a kiss good-night. She said okay. Then she kissed him again.

I had to turn away for fear they would notice the tears in my eyes at witnessing such a loving interaction. Not that I think they would have noticed. They were too busy looking into each other's eyes with that goofy teen-age love-stuck expression on their faces.

Wesley and I share birth dates. I forget Ludell's and Lynne's birthdays. I have never known Marlyn, Tim, or Lori's birthdays. But I never forget Wesley's.

A couple of weeks before I went to Germany, Ludell, Lynne, Jen, and I took five horses, one horse for each of us to ride and one green broke horse for us to use as a pack horse, from the Orahood ranch and rode off into the Larb Hills for a week. Jen and Ludell have the blackmailing photos that document our trip. We did not know how to pack a horse; Jen's husband packed professionally into the Bob Marshall Wilderness — I hope that is the only reason why he laughs at the photographs. I suspect he laughs at the pictures for other reasons.

Ten years later I was going through a divorce. Ludell and Jen (who had learned how to pack a horse) took me again on a horse trip into the Larb Hills. They knew I needed them, the horses, and the country-side in order to deal with what was going on in my life.

How can I explain what this family has given me throughout the years?

They were just being themselves. They did not do anything special for me. I did not know that when I was younger. Their open door policy was one of the greatest acts of love any family has ever done for me. When I stayed with them those months, I felt secure. I felt safe.

The girls' doors are still open to me at any time. Lynne has told me, "You know where the coffee pot is, you know what bed you can use. Even if we're not home, you're always welcome here and you always have a place to stay."

Coffee is of vital importance in the Orahood, Heaton, Brewer, and Shipp families.

I wish to include here a tribute I wrote for Casey Brewer's family after his death from leukemia.

Ludell said at the event of Casey's wake that everyone has a purpose in life and when that purpose is fulfilled, God takes the person home.

Casey was a spark, whose purpose was to start a fire.

A song from the early 70's (late 60's?) lines were something like: It only takes a spark to get a fire going and soon all those around warm up to its glowing. That's how it is with God's love, once you've experienced it. You spread His love to everyone … .

The Orahood clan are coals of glowing love. And Casey was a spark that flew out of the coals to start a fire.

One of my favorite scriptures is found in a little book towards the end of the Bible. John wrote: Beloved, let us love one another. For love is of God and everyone that loves is born of God and knows God. He that doesn't love doesn't know God, because God is Love.

Many times during the last two years of Casey's life, I heard someone from the Orahood clan say, "For a non-religious family, we sure do pray a lot."

Thank God they are not religious. There were a lot of religious people in Jesus's day. Once a few of them came to Him and asked Him what was the greatest commandment. Jesus simply said, there are two great commandments, and the second is like the first. One, love God; two, love others. All laws, guidelines, and commandments can be summarized in those two. We are called to love.

When Ludell phoned me and said the doctors cannot do any more for Casey — his life was in God's hands. She asked me to pray for a miracle. I did. I prayed God would spare Casey's life so Casey could live his life as an example of God's love. God answered my prayer, but not in the way I thought. I thought 40-50 more years. God gave 4-5 more days. Yet, in those days, God made Himself real to many people in the ICU and waiting rooms. People got to see the power of prayer and the power of God's love.

Love is not a novel idea to Casey's family though. I remember the kindness and consideration with which Marilyn and Wesley treated each other when I stayed with their family back in high school. They have given their children and grandchildren a role model of love.

Today when I visit Bobby and Ludell, I receive a big hug from both of them. I get to watch them kiss each other, be considerate to each other, and generally treat each other as though they were newlyweds and not an 'old' married couple. Hugs from their children; there is love all around.

Visiting Donny and Lynne, I get introduced to young people with hyphenated last names. As soon as a young person enters their home, their name is immediately hyphenated to include the Brewer name. Not only are their children's friends treated like family, so is everyone who visits. When I stop to visit again, there are hugs and a warm welcome … coffee, a bed, a shower, whatever … make yourself at home. It is like I never moved out of the Orahood household. I know I am not the only person treated with that love and welcome. It is Brewer's lifestyle. It is a lifestyle of loving.

I do not get to see Tim and Sally much. When I do see Tim, I ask him about his family. Tim's voice warms and his eyes sparkle as he tells me about the women of his household. His love for them, his wife and four daughters, shines forth through his stories, his laughter, and his warmth of voice.

I got to see Lori and Wayne quite a bit when I lived in Glasgow. When Lori came to the office to talk to Wayne, she did not stand behind the counter. She walked around it over to where her husband sat, leaned down to kiss him, and then stood with her arm around his shoulders. Wayne put his arm around her; in that loving position, they visit with one another for a few minutes.

Toward the end of Jesus's life, He gave His followers some last minute instructions about sharing the good news of access to God through Himself, Christ. One of His followers asked a question. It seems Jesus and His followers also hung out in the temple church just like the religious folks, also prayed, and also gave to the poor. How were people to tell followers of God from the religious people? Jesus answered, people will know you are my disciples by your love for one another.

In Casey's brief spark of life, he fanned the coals of love that he found in his family to set a fire of love racing through the lives of hundreds of people.

Thank you Orahoods, Heatons, Brewers, and Shipps for being an example of God's love to me and to so many other people. Keep fueling the flames.

The day in high school that Marlyn told me it was time for me to move on; I felt an incredible sadness and fear. I knew Dad had been calling her on the phone telling her to send me home. I knew Ludell was five months pregnant and planning her wedding. I knew there was not much room in that twin bed for the two of us and her growing womb.

But I did not know where else to go. I did not want to go home to the ranch.

I do not remember much of the next six-weeks. I know of some of the places, houses, and homes where I stayed for a night or two. Finally another classmate who was pregnant invited me to live with her while her soon-to-be-husband was gone to National Guard boot camp.

When I graduated from high school, a man I had known all my life came to talk to me. He owned the Villa Theater at that time. He planned to be away for the summer; he needed someone he could trust to manage the show house and to make the nightly deposit. He knew he could trust me with his business and with his money. He asked me to manage the theater. So I did. I kept perfect account of the books and not once was that man shorted as much as a penny. The owner said I could have a coke and a bag of popcorn a night. This became my daily meal as most of my money still went to booze. When I had saved up enough money, I rented my own apartment.

I do not recommend for sixteen or seventeen year old girls to leave home. But for me, it was what I needed to do in my life's journey.

Early Adulthood

Mid-way through my senior year, I had quit trying to not drink. When I rented my own place, my apartment became a party place that summer for many of my friends and classmates. It was in a big old building kitty-corner across the street from the show house. That grand old building has since burned down. I had "Jesus" posters on the walls and booze in the refrigerator.

I was miserable inside. I felt especially lousy after Danny committed suicide as I felt as though I were responsible for his death due to our conversation not many nights before.

One night in August, I lay on my sofa-bed in my studio apartment praying. I told God how unhappy I was — that it was too hard to try to live for Him. I did not have a clue how. Unmistakably, I heard in my mind, "Go to TBI with Sharon and Curt."

"What?" I thought.

Again came the words, "Go to TBI with Sharon and Curt."

I graduated with Curt Thims, I knew his older sister, Sharon Thims. But I did not know them well enough to call them "Sharon and Curt." To me, they were Sharon Thims and Curt Thims. Having attended their church a few times, I had heard of Trinity Bible Institute (TBI), so was familiar with TBI. Instantly I knew what I was to do and with whom. I fell asleep in peace.

The next morning I phoned Mrs. Thims to tell her the news. Within days, I had moved to Ellendale North Dakota with the older Thims children and had started to attend Trinity Bible Institute.

It was there I met Peggy.

I did not receive financial assistance from my parents to attend college. And because TBI was not accredited at that time, I did not receive student financial aid either. The first semester almost wiped out my savings. I moved into an apartment and went to work at the local nursing home as a nurse's aide.

I did not enjoy North Dakota. It was a terrible winter; often my car would not start. Walking to work or to school was to risk hypothermia and death. Yet I always showed up. Classes were difficult for me; I did not have the background of being raised in that denomination with all of the scripture verse memorization and familiarization with the Bible.

Late in the spring, I talked on the phone with Harold and Luanne Melder, an interracially married couple I had met in Germany.

Come to Tennessee, they invited.

So I did.

Eighteen years old and with no obligations, I visited my family over the summer. Mom and Dad had split in January; I spent the first month of the summer with my father and the second month with my mother. Then I hit the road.

Arriving in Cleveland, Tennessee, I learned Harold and Luanne were out of town on vacation. I enrolled in the local Bible College and got a room in the dorm.

I did not fit-in in the Bible Belt. Because Mom made me wear dresses to school, the social control of the school in which all females were to wear dresses at all times was not that big of a difficulty for me. I cannot exactly put my finger on why I was uncomfortable at that school. Part of it, I am sure was the oddities of the South. May it never rise again. I know the other half of my children's relatives are all Southerners. But, bless their hearts, Southerners are an inbred breed of strange cats. At the time, Tennessee ranked 49th in education in the nation. Montana ranked in the top 10. I joked, but not often nor to too many people, that Tennessee ranked 49th in education and that it showed.

The other part of my not fitting in at Bible College was, I think, my association with Harold and Luanne. There was a subsequent and automatic ostracization that went with hanging out with an interracially married couple.

In Montana, one's family may not like it much if their child dates or marries a Native American, but it is not grounds for possible murder.

In those years, the KKK (Klu Klux Klan) was still very active. While I attended college that year in Tennessee, a Black man was murdered in North Carolina for dating a White woman.

As had become my pattern, I rented an apartment after the first semester and got a job. The differences were that I had a roommate named Thea, and I worked in a Mexican restaurant, El Burrito, owned by a Black woman.

Harold and Luanne had one vehicle. Frequently when Luanne had the car and Harold needed to go to the grocery store, he would call me and ask me if I needed anything from the store and could I take him with me when I went shopping.

One time, after I picked him up, we drove down the main thorough street of the city. The KKK demonstrated on the corner of the denomination headquarters of the church of which we attended Bible College. I witnessed a Black man turn pale with fear. Harold slunk down in the seat. He said for us to talk German in the store so that people would think we were foreigners.

So we did. People would look at us and Harold would start to talk loudly about things of no significance such as today is Tuesday and I wish it were Thursday. The people staring at us had no idea what he said. I would answer just as loudly about such nonsensical things such as I was tired and needed to eat *wiener schnitchel*. Our sentences and our conversation was gobbledygook but no one understood the words. So we would chatter back and forth without really saying anything.

Thea and I never met our landlord. He owned the local Ford dealership and one of the managers from the dealership also managed our apartment. I was afraid of the man. He once put his arms around me and asked me for "some sugar" — the southern term for a kiss.

The manager had an equally scary plumber work for him. One day they both were in the apartment with me. I do not remember where Thea was. I phoned Harold and told him I was afraid of these men.

They talked in low voices in the bathroom and I had no idea what they planned.

Harold came over in his karate uniform. He had a black belt. He hung out with me until the white men left. They quit talking quietly among themselves and left as soon as the work was finished. They never bothered me again.

I did not realize until later that Harold was probably as afraid, if not more so, of them as I was. And, later, he commented that he never in his life thought he would be asked to protect a white girl from white men.

Harold was from Birmingham, Alabama; Luanne was from Green Bay, Wisconsin. They met in the army. They had the most beautiful children in the world, both in looks and disposition.

Tyrel was the name of their oldest son. He was such a gentle, kind soul of a delightfully wonderful little boy. I watched him play in the sandbox with the other children of their neighborhood — all of whom were white. And all of the children with whom he played, their parents who lived in that apartment complex attended the same Bible College. One of the moms of one of the other children brought all of the children peanut butter and jelly sandwiches and Kool-aid. She brought treats for all of the children except Tyrel, that is.

I do not understand prejudicism. I understand the definition; I understand the concept. But I cannot wrap my head around it. As I will never know what it feels like to walk on the moon, I will never know what it feels like to hate someone due to their race or color. All races have their assholes; all races have their wonderful, kind, loving people. To judge someone because of their nationality, race or looks is stupid.

I tried to not drink while attending Bible school. I only drank and got drunk once in Tennessee and ended up somewhere in Georgia. THAT scared me straight. On December 4, I quit drinking. I had already quit drugging the night I graduated from high school a year and a half before. I had quit smoking, I think, when I was in North Dakota.

In January of the next year, I enrolled in the local community college for additional classes. In a history class, I met a boy. Unbeknownst to me, he followed me around for a couple of weeks before he spoke to me. Soon he asked me out on a date. Our first date was for lunch at the local Cracker Barrel restaurant on a Wednesday early in February. Before long, he bought a meal for me nearly every day. We would take the left-overs home for Thea.

Thea and I had a budget of $5.00 a week for groceries for the two of us. One person could not live on $5.00 a week, let alone two people. Her family brought some frozen meat and other things; we traded some of it with Harold and Luanne for WIC commodities; and this boy's frequent taking me out to eat was how we survived those few months of mostly ramen noodles.

Marriage

This young man asked me to marry him about six weeks after we started dating. I freaked and went home to Montana for Spring Break.

I had not gone back to Montana for Christmas; I felt I did not have the funds with which to do so; my parents never did help me with college. But when this young man popped the question, I suddenly found the funds with which to go home.

The ten days on the ranch in the springtime, during calving, convinced me I loved Montana more than I loved the young man. Decision made, I flew back to Tennessee to let him know my answer.

He would not take "no" for my answer. He was persistent. He said for me to allow him to accompany me to Montana. He said he loved me enough to go and live anywhere I wanted to live. Dad's hired man was killed in an automobile accident. My father called and asked me to go to work for him. I told Dad what the young man had said about going with me to Montana. My father reluctantly hired both of us.

On the drive to Montana I quickly educated the young man about aspects of ranching. He readily adapted to ranch living, or so it seemed. I do think he is naturally gifted to do well at whatever he does. He learned to ride horses and to run haying equipment readily. I agreed to marry him. We set a date for the following February. Having not had sex yet and being of the horny age of twenty, we pushed the date up to October.

In those early years, I often said that the man I knew disappeared at 2:05PM the day we married and a complete stranger took his place. As soon as the marriage vows were said, he seemed to change.

As his wife, I now was his property. I was expected to do as he said (commanded). Six weeks into the marriage, I was pregnant. As soon as Matthew was one month old, we moved back to Tennessee because unbeknownst to me prior to marriage, my husband had decided he hated Montana. One of the reasons he had for pushing up the wedding date was that he felt he could not continue the muse of pretending to enjoy my lifestyle, my world, my love of ranching.

I tried, I truly did. But I cannot be the concept of what some Southern men think of as a "submissive wife." And I strongly disagree with the idea of a man having the right to discipline his wife in order to get her to behave in a manner of his liking.

My folks, for all of their disagreements, worked together. Neither of them had specific jobs in the house or around the ranch. In fact, I think Dad was a better cook than Mom. I have heard stories about their first year or so of marriage to my mother when he had to teach her how to clean house. Remember, Mom is the oldest child of a ranching family. She was outside working with her father as soon as possible; she knew how to ranch. Dad was the tenth child in a farming family; he knew what needed to be done and how to work or help in the house as well as outside.

The idea that I was the only one to cook, to clean house, to take out the garbage, and to pick up his dirty underwear off of the floor was an idea I could not grasp, accept, or concur with. The statement I was to obey him was not in our wedding vows. The idea that it was only the man's job to bring in income was foreign as well. Although, I did want to stay home and raise my children myself — not hire someone else to raise them. So that aspect was understandable. Except for the fact, he went to college and did not have a job. I was the only one with a job — six days a week I delivered the local newspaper in the neighboring county. I would come home exhausted from that one hundred mile a day drive around two counties in the hot sun to find him sitting on the cool living room floor watching TV. He would then expect and insist that I not take five minutes to rest, but immediately fix something for him to eat. In "Southern talk" correct grammar would be "to fix him something to eat." I wanted to "fix him" alright.

I also learned to hate TV. My husband would watch TV from "F-Troop" reruns at 4:00 until Johnny Carson was over. The children and I were to be absolutely silent when he watched his TV.

That meant no noise whatsoever. No cooking or cleaning in the kitchen. Supper had to be done prior to F-Troop. No playing. No talking. No music. No nothing.

Training a baby to cry only prior to 4PM is impossible.

I became pregnant again. I missed riding horseback, I missed cows, I missed my ranching life. And although we lived in what Southerners think of as the "country" - there was still a house or business every tenth of a mile, I missed the country. And, I thought, I hated Tennessee. I was going back to Montana with or without him.

My husband came along. He had just graduated from four years of college at the two year community college with a computer programing degree. He thought he was ready to accept a great computer programming job.

The nation slumped into an economic regression. Jobs were not to be found. No jobs. Not for people with or without a degree, let alone only a two-year degree. We traveled throughout Montana that summer looking for work. Nothing was to be found.

The doctor told me I had to quit riding in a vehicle. That the position of my legs bent day after day and the pregnancy caused a reduction in the blood flow to my legs. We had to settle down somewhere.

Billings is the largest "city" in Montana. We thought if my husband could find a job anywhere, it would be in Billings.

We were wrong.

My husband substitute taught junior high school in the Heights. Then he got a very part-time security truck guard job. Between the two part-time or occasional positions and my Grandfather's generosity, we survived until Andrew was born.

A week after Andrew was born, Dad loaded us and all our things up and brought us back to the ranch. Not to work, but to have a place to live for the winter.

Of course, my husband wanted to move back to Tennessee. An idea I was 100% against. There was no way in hell I was going to leave what little support I had through my family to live in the isolation of his family again.

With the name of "Billy Joe" people in Tennessee thought I was Southern — until I opened my mouth and the Yankee sounding words came out. I fought allowing my speech to slide down into Southern slang, ya'll. I had two Southern women friends, my old roommate Thea (who was originally from Ohio, but who adapted to the South easily) and a gal named Janice. Although we were close, I never could grasp the Southern culture and life-style. I was and always will be an outsider there.

Back in Montana and my husband's unsuccessful job search, he had spent seven months looking for work. One day I went to town and got a job, immediately. Andrew was less than three weeks old. My new job was at the Good Samaritan Nursing Home where I worked part-time as a nurse's aide.

Within a month, he got a job at the newspaper as a typesetter and printer's assistant.

We moved north of town about five miles and rented a ranch house. Life was good. I would go for walks along the banks of the Milk River with my two baby boys. I loved living in the country. The landlord's daughter babysat when I had to go to work. She would even do a load of laundry for me. Her helping me out by doing laundry is a fact to this day that I appreciate.

Then the newspaper was sold. The new owners, partners, also bought the Chinook Opinion and the Harlem News in the next county. They decided that the Phillips County News did not need two Printers and that the Printer for the Chinook Opinion would soon retire. They gave my husband an ultimatum: move your family to Chinook or find a new job.

We moved.

This was the twelfth move in six years. Twice we lived in one house for two years in a row. Moving was a way to stay isolated from other people knowing what goes on behind closed doors.

We found a little farm house to rent about seven miles from town. I became reacquainted with Vinee. This was Peggy's hometown; she lived twenty miles away in Havre. Life was good again, except for that damned TV.

There were other problems in our marriage as well. But for the purpose of this telling of the story, I will limit the disclosure to simply non-stop television and silence. Truly, constant television watching is not a divorce issue. Other things were. I cried for the first six months of my marriage. Then my father said, "You made your bed, now lie in it." This means, I made the decision to marry the man, now deal with it. I quit crying and began dying - inside.

My husband did not seem to mind much what the boys and I did during the day as long as I cooked breakfast for him and had supper waiting when he got home — whatever time of day that was. Often I would have no clue when to expect him home for supper. I drove out to where Vinee lived as often as I could. I became acquainted with other families with young children in the area. I became involved with a local church. I helped the landlord's son when he needed help on the farm.

This help on the farm was in the form of driving out to the field to get him when he wanted to leave the tractor out there or something as simple as that. The sporadic ride to the field or bring the 4-wheeler back from the field took all of ten minutes once a week or less often. Infrequently I would ride (horseback) for him as well when he needed to move his cattle to a different pasture or gather bulls. There were always others with us when we needed to ride and work cattle.

I became pregnant again. I did not tell my husband right away. I did not tell him because something felt different with this pregnancy. Something was different plus the fact I was not happy I was pregnant with our third child. Life with my husband was very difficult for me.

Vinee helped me get a job at the local stockyards. There was a weekly cattle sale every Friday. They also held horse, sheep, and pig sales along with the cattle sale occasionally.

My official title at the stockyards was that of a "back penner." This title meant I trotted along behind a sold animal to pen it in a designated corral for whoever bought it. Then I jogged back to the gate to get another animal to pen. It was great exercise. Some days, when we had bigger sales, Vinee would bring an extra horse to town for me to use. Those days were not as much exercise and much longer sales, but I did the job with much more pleasure astride a horse.

One Friday, there was something very seriously wrong. I was bleeding. I stayed at my job until the sale was finished. My parents taught me to never quit work or do a half-assed job at my employment.

I went home and called my doctor in Malta. He told me I needed to go to the emergency room in Havre. I called the emergency room. I told them what my doctor had said and asked, for some reason, who was the doctor on call. They told me the names of two doctors on call. I said I would go to a veterinarian or die before I would let the one see me. The hospital staff was not impressed with me and my attitude. Oh well. They also did not know my history with that esteemed pediatrician asshole of a medical professional; he took my virginity away from me. May he burn in hell.

I did not know the other doctor, but agreed to see him. The emergency room staff wanted me to come right away. But I could not. I had to make supper for my husband, so it would be ready for him to eat as soon as he got home — as I had been taught by him to do so. I had to make arrangements for my two sons for baby-sitting. Again, the staff was not impressed with me. But they did not understand why I said the things I said or why I had to do the things I had to do.

I started supper and called a friend so see if she could baby-sit the boys. This family lived in another farm house on the way to town.

The landlord's son stopped by, he was all excited about his hay. He wanted me to go with him to look at the bales he had stacked behind my house. I did. Yes, he had harvested his alfalfa perfectly and the hay was full of protein-rich leaves. Done examining the hay, he looked at me. He commented on how pale I was. I told him the doctors thought I was losing my baby.

He said, "Why in the hell did you walk out here to look at my hay then?"

I went because it was important to him to show me his great hay. He had been so kind to our family that it was important to me to return that kindness by looking at his hay. His wife was also pregnant and he was excited about the possibility of our babies being life-long friends.

Back at the house, I finished supper and packed a bag of clothes for my boys. As soon as the table was set, I heard my husband drive up. I met him at the door.

I said, "Supper is ready. Hurry up and eat it, you have to take me to the hospital. I have called the neighbors and asked them to watch the boys. The doctor thinks I am losing the baby."

He looked me in the eye and said, "What did you do to kill it."

I did not answer. I had no answer to that accusation. We held eye-contact for a moment longer, then I looked away and he walked past me to the table.

I did not realize when a woman loses a baby that she goes through labor. The labor pains had started. I was in so much pain from then until I came out of anesthesia that I barely remember dropping the boys off at the neighbors or the trip to the larger town. I remember nothing of the ER room. All I remember is my husband's non-stop talking accusing me of having an affair and of killing the baby so no one would know that the child would not look like him — because, he reasoned, a child of his could not die. It had to be someone else's child.

Apparently he kept his tirade up in the hospital as well because the doctor performed an autopsy on the fetus.

The verdict, the doctor told me, was that there was nothing I did and nothing I could have done to cause the baby's death. He said that either the egg was too old or the sperm was too old when they got together and they did not divide correctly to produce a child. He also said that I should have lost the fetus in the first trimester and not at five months. I have seen five month live birth fetuses and yes, my baby was deformed greatly.

Miscarriages are considered to be "biohazard waste material." Biohazard waste, at least in that hospital at that time, are thrown into an incinerator and burned. I did not consider my naturally aborted child "biohazard waste." I asked for the fetus.

I phoned a nurse I knew and asked for her advice. She said when she worked in a hospital in another town, when there was a miscarriaged fetus, she would phone the cemetery manager. Both the nurse and the grave digger were Catholics. They would bury the dead babies in the cemetery at night.

I and the gal who had babysat the boys that night drove to my home town and I buried the fetus near the headstone of my sister, Lesli Ann. I did this in broad daylight. No one was going to tell me I could not bury my child.

I named him Aaron James, wrote his name in the family bible, and did not tell people about naming him or burying him. Months later my sister named her son Zachary James. Years later my stepsister gave her son the middle name James. To my knowledge "James" is not a family name. None of my father's ump-teen relatives are named James; no one in my mother's family carries that name; I know of no one in my step-mother's family with that name. But for some unknown and uncommunicated reason, all three girls gave their sons the middle name of "James."

My husband kept up the daily barrage of trying to get me to tell him with whom I had an affair; who was the baby's father and what did I do to kill the baby. He would even follow me into the bathroom with this non-stop onslaught of verbal bullshit. Gone was the television watching; in its place was this insane mindset.

Five days after Aaron died I started drinking again. A month before he died I bummed a smoke and somewhere in that time, I started smoking and have never been able to quit again for any length of time. Fourteen days after Aaron died I started smoking dope again. I just could not deal with my child's death accompanied by my husband's accusations associated with our child's death.

By this time, my husband had decided that I had an affair with the landlord's son; to my husband, it was the landlord's son whose baby I supposedly killed.

Life got worse.

One day, Peggy came to visit.

It is important to know a little bit about Peggy's character. Peggy is the nicest person in the world. She is very shy and embarrasses easily; her face turns brilliant red often at my teasing. She would not hurt a soul. I think she has never hurt anyone's feelings. Her words are always kind, loving, and thoughtful. She is the most gentle-soul I have ever met.

Peggy and I sat across from each other at the table. She said, "What happened to you?"

I asked what she meant.

"When we were in college, when we first met, I admired you so because you were so independent and had such a strong character. What happened to you? You are not the person I met ten years ago. Why have you let your husband beat you down like this?"

We may have engaged in further conversation on this topic, I do not remember. I remember the shock I felt at her words. Not because of their truth or because of any hurt associated with the words. I felt shock that PEGGY, of all people, would say such things. I hung my head in shame at her words because for I knew she was right.

Years later when I reminded her of the conversation, she could not believe she said those words. The words were not from her but from God. Peggy would never say anything like what she said to me that day. She would not perceive the words as loving. But God would. God gave her the words to shock me into action.

Ten months before Aaron's death, I reached out to the local County Health Nurse for help. I had taken the boys to her office for their inoculations and knew she had a huge rack of pamphlets on various topics. One Monday, I phoned and asked if she had a pamphlet on "stress." She asked if there had been a lot of drinking over the weekend. No, I proudly had told her, we do not drink. She asked about the behavior in the family members. I told her. She recommended I attend a group. I did. There I learned about such things as "detach with love." I started to learn about co-dependency and how it differed from healthy interdependent relationships. I started to change. My husband noticed the change, and because he was looking around to have an affair, he assumed I was already having an affair.

I know he was looking around for another woman for two reasons. One is he started to go fishing several times a week without me. He never brought any fish home. I started to check the odometer on the pick-up. The fishing hole was about two miles away, a round trip would be approximately four miles, yet, on the nights he would go "fishing" there would be around fifty miles added to the odometer. That was a bit over the distance to Havre and back. The second reason is, one night he was angry with me because his best white western shirt was not clean. He planned to wear it to go fishing that night. Vinee was with us that evening and I served supper. When I got to him, I said as I dished up his plate, "Well, if you catch something, don't bring it home to me." Vinee was shocked I would say such a thing. I did not think she would catch the double meaning to my words. But he did bring it home; I contracted chlamydia.

The summer Aaron died was a summer from hell. My husband's mental state deteriorated and the bombardment of verbal accusations now sometimes lasted nearly all night long. Often his tirade was accompanied with midnight phone calls of accusation to the landlord's son. Of course, this caused problems in the landlord's son's marriage as well.

One night my husband got out my gun and threatened to shoot me if I did not confess to the affair he *knew* I had. I would not confess to something I had not done. He went outside and shot it off over and over again into the landlord's son's excellent stack of hay behind our house. I often wondered if all of the lead bullets ever caused any stomach problems with any cattle that were fed the hay that winter.

I obtained the phone number for the local crisis line and wrote it on the bottom of a Kleenex box I kept on the dresser by the bed.

Vinee had moved north of town 55 miles. They planned a vacation and asked that I feed their cows and do chores for them. I welcomed this escape from my husband. But he showed up at her place. He feared the landlord's son was with me.

Out came the gun again. Again I would not confess. He threatened to shoot himself and went outside. Soon there was a shot. Then silence.

I waited. My nerves were strung as tight as they could go. I would not go outside to see if he shot himself. I waited some more.

He stalked into the house. He was angry. He asked why I did not care enough to come running outside to see if he had shot himself.

I feared if I had run out the door, I would be met with a bullet in my chest. But I did not tell him this. I also knew he was too self-absorbed at the time to kill himself.

The next day, when he was outside for a moment, I called the County Sheriff's office. The idiot deputy sheriff said he would come get me but not my husband. I had to do Vinee's chores. I could not be taken away in a squad car! I could not leave my children with their seemingly insane father. We argued; I hung up on him and called Peggy.

A friend of Peggy's and an acquaintance of mine were getting married that night in the nearby little town. I told Peggy where the emergency phone number was written on the Kleenex box; we met in the bar after the wedding ceremony. She discreetly handed me a little slip of paper with the crisis line phone number on it and begged me to be careful.

Back at Vinee's, I called the number. The woman advised for me and the boys to go to the domestic violence shelter due to the threats with the gun. I feared greater retaliation from my husband if I were to do so. I could not go into the shelter as she suggested.

My husband moved in with the landlord's oldest son (I was accused of the younger one). I got evicted due to the accusal and the problems caused by my husband's behavior. All I could find to rent was an old farmhouse with a wood burning "furnace" in the basement. It was nearing winter and I had no wood. The only job I had was at the stockyards through which I made about $50.00 a month.

Soon afterward, my husband moved into the old farmhouse with us.

There were two bedrooms on the second floor of this quaint old house. One night I was in bed nearly asleep and the boys were asleep in their room when my husband got the gun again. The boys woke up this time. They had been asleep the other two times. Due to their father yelling, they ran to their mother. They were five and two years old. The three of us cowered together as their father waved the gun around with his now-common speech of demanding I confess to what I did not do.

He fired the gun out the window. We three ran downstairs; I carried Andrew and half-carried Matthew. For some unknown insane reason, I stopped at the foot of the stairs. May I never forget the sight of him at the top of the stairs waving the gun and threatening us. I have no further memory of that night. At that point my mind disassociated and shut-down so great was the stressful situation.

The next day, after my husband went to work, I phoned the crisis line and made arrangements for the boys and I to enter the shelter. I quickly packed a couple of bags of clothes. I called a friend for a ride to the nearby town where the shelter was located.

Arriving at the designated place to meet the woman who would take us to the shelter, I learned the shelter was full and the domestic violence staff would have to put us up in a local motel. I tried to make light of the situation to the boys; I tried to have them think this was some sort of fun vacation. It was truly a dive of a motel. It was difficult to convince them, even at their young ages, that this place was a place for a fun vacation. Yes, I maintain the importance of being honest with one's children. However, I felt I needed to project a cheerful attitude so they would not suffer any further trauma.

That is enough of this stage of my life. Needless-to-say, life did not get better overnight. In fact, due to the drinking and befuddled thinking, more traumas occurred over the next two years. It is difficult to remember anything positive from that period. The love and support from Vinee and Peggy was about all I had left.

I had been kicked out of the church due to the elders believing the lies. My so-called friends associated with the church turned their backs to me, although to this day they are friendly when we meet on the street. There is a difference between being a friend and being friendly. I lost my home, my marriage, my baby, my family as I knew it, my church, most of my friends, and my reputation.

I started to get unwanted, unwarranted phone calls and visits from men at night, including the Pastor of the church I had attended. Vinee came to stay with me to help protect me from the visits; the calls and visits stopped once the men learned I was not available for what they wanted.

I was turned in to the Child Protection Agency and was investigated for child abuse. My husband had a couple of his friends call in the allegations. I felt as though I was in danger of losing my living children.

I felt all I had left was Jesus.

When I read the Bible I would read verses that said, "I love you," "I have called you," and "you are precious to Me." But in my feeling shame that people believed I had killed my baby, I, again, did not feel loveable to God.

My new landlady advised, due to no ability to heat the house and due to the fact I was a woman alone living in close proximity to a bar and a reservation, that I find somewhere else to live; I secured a job as a housekeeper/cook/hiredman on a ranch in the northeastern part of the county. Within a month there I suffered an open compound fracture of both fibia and tibia while breaking a horse.

Because of months in a cast and months learning to walk again, I lost both that job and the job at the stockyards. I moved in with Vinee and her family for a short period of time. My father had an empty house on the ranch; the boys and I moved back to the ranch. I traveled to check out the possibility of attending college and was violently raped. Over the twenty-five months of drinking other rapes occurred, although none as violent as the rape in the college town. Seemingly totally defeated and beaten down. I cowered at the ranch.

This is to be a positive discourse of the supportive, loving people and events. Obviously my marriage and the events over the next year or two do not fit into the description for the book. But, it was and is one of the most powerful life-changing events of my existence. With the never-to-forget traumas were equally never-to-forget moments, like pictures in a frame, of … joy.

Vinee had been raised as stoically as I. Uncharacteristically; she gave me a big bear hug of love and support during this time. We hug nearly every time we see each other today.

One day, she arrived at the house without a furnace, crying. I did not cry when Aaron died. I had quit crying six month into my marriage seven years prior. I did not cry in mourning over Aaron's death until I was in therapy a year later. I mourned his death alone in sadness and then the mourning was cut short with the accusations. Vinee cries. She is one tough ranching woman, she is physically stronger than many men yet, she has the tenderest of hearts. She cries easily.

Crying, she asked why I lied to her. She had just spent 45 minutes with my husband, listening to his "side of the story" and he had convinced her of my affair.

I said nothing.

She asked why I just sat there and did not defend myself.

I said that I did not have the gift of a silver tongue like my husband. I had no words of defense. I could not convince her or anyone else in the community or county of my innocence; I did not have the ability or the words. All I could state is the truth — I had not had an affair. The baby was his child and I had not killed our baby.

She said she still believed my husband, but she loved me and would stick beside me because I was her friend.

Other people have heard this part of the story and asked why, if my friend believed my ex-husband, why would I want her as a friend? Please understand. It takes a great love to go against one's convictions in order to support a friend. By saying what she said, by honoring our friendship ahead of what she truly believed was factual at that time, she cemented her love for me and my love for her.

When I was in the cast after breaking my leg, Vinee hoisted me up on one of her horses so I could ride. The view from on top of the Cherry Ridges of the Little Rocky Mountains, the Bears Paw Mountains, the Sweetgrass Hills, and the Cypress Hills (in Canada) is one of eye-watering beauty.

The orthopedic surgeon who screwed my leg and ankle back together again had said that I would never walk again without a severe limp. I would never walk without a cane. I would never run, hop, skip, jump, dance, or … insert my foot in a stirrup again.

Never tell a stubborn person that they will never do something they really want to do. To tell me I would never insert my foot into a stirrup was near unto fighting words. Fists clenched, I set out to prove that man wrong.

It took me three years before I could insert my foot into a stirrup. And another two or three years before I could put weight on that foot in a stirrup. My right leg is still weaker than my left — when I walk and when I ride. I own a beautiful diamond willow cane; I only need to use it in the spring and fall in Montana when the weather is changing rapidly.

I moved to Billings to stay with Mom while I attended hydrotherapy to learn how to walk again.

Once, while I was hobbling difficultly with my cane, a young girl opened a door for me. She looked up at my face with all the innocence of a Girl Scout doing a good deed. Her beatific face fell, "You're not old," she said accusingly.

I wanted to slap the child.

Instead, I determined I would not spend my life walking with a cane. I also decided I needed to learn how to walk more gracefully; I enrolled in dance class. Seldom does anyone notice a limp.

I felt miserable in Billings. Mom knows of my love for the country and ranching. She talked to a cousin of hers I barely knew. Rolly begrudgingly allowed me to come out to the ranch he leased near Columbus to help him ride. It was at the end of calving season and he needed some help. He did not think a crippled female would be of much assistance. The emphasis is on the "female" more than on the "crippled" part. Rolly did not help me on the horse. It was all I could do to climb awkwardly on. My right leg/foot dangled worthlessly. I was totally meritless help a foot. Yet, my ability to ride and work cows caused Rolly to quickly learn to respect me and we became fast friends.

The best time that spring of my stay in Billings was on Rolly's ranch on the Yellowstone River. I would drive to his ranch for two days and a night and then drive back to Billings for two nights and a day for hydrotherapy and a shower. The boys stayed in Billings with Mom full-time.

The Halverson family considered Rolly to be a bit of a coyote. He had a few peculiar habits. One was the fact he did not drink coffee or have any breakfast in the morning. No coffee was a fact I complained about every day I was there. Near the end of that time we started to have coffee in the mornings; a habit, I believe, he still embraces.

Rolly would work until the day's work was done and then eat. Sometimes we ate our one daily meal at 2PM, other days it was nearer to 10PM. Some days we would eat in town, other days we ate what was available in his rented house. Two days in a row he fed me dried-out baloney with moldy cheese sandwiches on old dried bread. I refused to eat my sandwich the second day. I had been taught, you eat what is in front of you. Seldom do I refuse to eat the meal set before me. I did not refuse the meal the first day, but the second day I did. He was shocked when I told him we were going to town to eat. No one talks to Rolly that way.

I had heard of him dragging hired men off of their horses and taking the boots to them in his anger. For those who do not recognize that term "taking the boots to them," it means literally throwing a person to the ground and kicking the shit out of them. I told him he was never going to do that to me. Again, I surprised him. I am serious when I say; no one talks to Rolly that way. He is well known for his behavior when angered. No one wants to anger Rolly. His rage is a very frightening thing to behold.

We worked together; we rode together; we drank together; we played pool together. I think he saved my sanity during a time of great difficulties.

Soon our friendship reached the ears of my Grandmother Ann. In her insanity, she determined that Rolly and I were sleeping together. Of course she shared her suspicion of incest with other family members. The family arranged for Cousin Allen to ferret out the truth.

Cousin Allen was a very large man who lacked in IQ but who was a professional gambler-type of guy. He could read people. Allen lived in Great Falls. Upon the family's request, he drove to Billings and took Rolly out on the town to get him drunk and talkative. Allen quizzed the drunken Rolly about our relationship. Rolly was truthful and honest in his confession of his admiration of me as a worker; he told of how well I knew how to work cows and how to ride a horse. There was no sexual relationship between us whatsoever.

Cousin Allen, was my mother's first cousin. He only knew me as his cousin's kid. Allen also learned to think highly of me through Rolly. Throughout the rest of Allen's life he always stopped to see me wherever I lived, whenever he drove through town. I learned to love this mountain of a man. In his simple mindedness, he was as gentle, kind, and loving as anyone could be. It was a huge loss of a loving, supportive person in my life when he was murdered.

Physical therapy over, I and the boys returned to the ranch. I started to look for a job. One day I stopped to see my Auntie Diane; she told me that the Soil Survey office was about to look for a "cartographic aide" and for me to race right over to their office and talk to the boss. I did. I caught him in the middle of writing the "want ad." The paper was covered with scratched out words.

Writing was not his strong point.

He hired me on the spot. I did have to fill out the Federal employment paperwork which is several pages long and an arduous process in itself.

My career with the Federal Government had started.

Early Years with the United States Department of Agriculture (USDA)

When Auntie Diane told me to apply for the job, I had no idea what was a "soil survey" or a "cartographic aide." I needed to support myself and my sons somehow. I did not pay rent to my father; I helped out when he needed help instead and I raised Chinese Pheasants for him. But there were utilities, gasoline, and food bills I needed to have money to pay.

As a cartographic aide, I was to finalize the soil mapping of up to seven Soil Scientists onto milar maps to send to the state office for the eventual publishing of a county-wide soils maps. My office was formerly the storage room. My desk was part of a sheet of plywood held up by crates. USDA does not go "all out" in rural offices to equip them with fancy, expensive furniture.

The job was okay. The Scientists were out in the field all day mapping the soils of the county. I could play my music and talk to myself all I wanted. But I longed to be outside. The window in my office was probably six feet from the floor. I could only look up at the blue, blue sky. The building was air conditioned and the weather that summer was very hot. I remember walking to therapy and seeing 113 degrees on the bank clock. Yet, I still wanted to be in the country and outside. My boss sensed this and occasionally had me spend a day in the field with a Soil Scientist.

The convenience of, the approximation to, and the understanding of my boss made it easy to attend group therapy and individual therapy sessions weekly. At the suggestion of a schoolmate, I phoned the local CDC Center. I did not know CDC stood for Chemical Dependency Center. I only knew my schoolmate had recommended that I see the therapist, Bill.

I was a mess. With the mental stress of Aaron's death, the divorce proceedings, my physical inability to walk well, the rapes, and probably confusion in general due to alcohol and drugs I did not know what direction was "up." The fact that I functioned at all was solely due to dumb tenacity. Like a mule, I simply plodded forward, putting one foot in front of the other, not knowing what was wrong in my life and not knowing where I was going or why.

Bill enrolled me in three consecutive out-patient co-dependency treatments over a six month period. Plus I had one or two weekly one-on-one sessions with him. Finally, he suggested I attend an organization known to help people with the drinking disease.

I was shocked at his suggestion. I did not think I had a drinking problem. Booze was the solution to all of my problems. When I did not want to deal with or face a situation, I went to Billings to drink. My mom managed a state owned liquor store. She had an impressive collection of wine in her basement. She was one of my best drinking partners. We could sit in her hot tub, drink bottles of champagne, and talk for hours.

Whenever I felt a feeling I did not want to feel, I drowned the feeling with alcohol. It was a simple solution to all life's situations and problems.

Bill told me later that he knew if I had what he called "an alcoholic mind" that I would take him up on a dare. He dared me to go to six meetings without drinking between meetings.

No problem. I had gone seven years without drinking; I sure in the hell could go six weeks without drinking.

There were more than six meetings a week. But only one meeting was "open." Meaning open for attendance to whoever had an interest in learning more about alcoholism and the organization that helps alcoholics. Closed meetings, I thought, were only for those who have the disease. I attended open meetings because I did not think I had the disease. I did not drink like our old hired man of many years before, Leonard Whiteford.

I could not stay sober. I could not stay sober for six damn meetings, six damn weeks.

The more I tried to control my drinking, the more out of control it became.

I had become dependent on narcotic drugs when I broke my leg. At one point, a pharmacist told me I needed to get off the prescription because people became addicted to the drug. I phoned the orthopedic surgeon that screwed my leg back together and asked him about it. He laughed and told me to not worry about it and to go to a different pharmacy. So I did. Later I learned it is suggested to only take the morphine prescription for pain for a maximum of six weeks; I took it for nine months. I learned that I really like morphine. It gave me the perfect high. I would be just stoned enough to still function without feeling. I hated to feel.

Off of the prescription, my behavior when drinking became more erratic. I could not determine my behavior when I drank. It seemed that sometimes I could drink a few drinks and be totally shit-faced drunk; other times I could drink like a horse all night long and barely catch a buzz. It was not so much the drinking I tried to control as it was my behavior when drinking that I wanted to control. My behavior was as erratic as one can imagine. Either I was very friendly or I was a total bitch. I tried to limit my drinking. That did not work. I tried to change the type of booze I drank. That did not work. I tried to only drink with friends and have them help curtail the amount or the behavior. That did not work. I tried to only drink in the safety of my home. That did not work. I determined to never drink in the mornings; I would set my watch ahead so that it read PM — I reasoned, it was afternoon somewhere in the world. I decided to never drive drunk. That did not work, I had to get home. I determined I would not drink around my sons. That was easy when they went to Tennessee to visit their father in the summers. That decision was very difficult when they were with me for ten months of the year.

Often people are confused about alcoholism. It is not so much the amount of alcohol consumed that determines whether or not a person is an alcoholic; it is the phenomenon of mental obsession and physical craving that are the determining factors. I simply could not not drink. The more I tried to control my drinking, the more it controlled me.

Another year went by in my confused, disorganized life.

By this time, the USDA offices had moved into a larger building on the south end of town. And I had changed jobs. Now I had the title of a "conservationist aide." This meant I worked in the same office as Auntie Diane and I assisted the Soil Conservationists with whatever they needed. Mostly I assembled conservation folders. This was a part-time job, as was the cartographic aide position. The Phillips Conservation District hired me to work on their irrigation water project.

Then the Conservation District hired a guy to also work on the project. They had me train him; then they promoted him to be my supervisor along with giving him a sizable raise, well above my wage. I admit, when this happened, I did not like him. He and I did not get along well at first.

I did get along with another single man in the office. One day my supervisor for the Conservation District and my friend planned to go out to the bars for the evening. My friend invited me to go with them.

My supervisor asked my friend, "Why in the hell did you invite her! She's a castrating bitch!"

My friend said, "No, she's not. You just have to get to know her. I admit, she is hard to get to know. But once you get to know her, she's a great gal."

So started my D & D dates.

Nearly every weekend D & D and I would go to the bars. My friend knew of my desire to not drink much, or at least of my desire to control my behavior when drinking. These nights on the town were good. My friend made sure I ordered water; I did not act the asshole. My supervisor liked to dance; so did I. Soon other single people who worked for the government from that county as well as the neighboring county would join us at the bar on the weekend. D

& D and I were consistent; the others came and went as often or as seldom as they wished. I seldom, if ever, got drunk on these "dates." And I became very close friends with my supervisor.

Other things happened though. Once I had a beer or two with my pizza for lunch across the street from the office. That afternoon I could not think. I could not remember how to turn the computer on or how to input data. I went home.

During my weekly attendance at the open meeting, I learned of the third tradition — the only requirement for membership was the desire to stop drinking. An attendee did not have to have the disease of addiction; an attendee did not have to be an alcoholic to attend closed meetings! I had a desire to quit drinking. I had the desire to stop drinking for six damn meetings so I could prove to the therapist, Bill, that I was not an alcoholic. I figured it out. Due to the number and days of the meetings, the least amount of days needed to make six meetings was ten days. HA! I would only have to not drink for ten measly days to prove I was not an alcoholic! Ta da! The answer, to get that sonofabitch off of my back, was only ten days of not drinking. Not a problem.

And I could not do it.

Frustrated I would bang my fist on the table. I had stayed sober for seven years; why in the hell could I not stay sober for ten damn days!

The others in the meeting would smile gently and say irritating things such as: "cunning baffling, powerful"; "keep coming back"; and "maybe you should get a sponsor." Because I thought my will power was so great, strong enough for me to stay sober, and would keep me from drinking one grumpy old fart would give me his suggestion. He would suggest that I buy a bag of prunes and a box of Exlax and eat all of it. I was to then use my will power to not shit. I was to call him in the morning when I was successful in using my great will power to not take a dump. I never was stupid enough to try his suggestion.

Then Grandma Doll died.

I stayed sober all through the days with the family and her funeral. Returning home, in the silence of the boys being in Tennessee, I was alone with my head and my thoughts. I was tormented by the fact I had the opportunity to say "good-bye" to Grandma and I did not do so.

I drove to Billings. Mom was not home. I went to a late night meeting that Thursday. That is the last I remember for three days.

I "came to" walking down the hall toward the bathroom in the trailer Rolly rented near Columbus. Returning to my bed, I was affright with wondering where I had been and what I had done. I did not talk to Rolly much the next morning. I was afraid to ask him when I had arrived at his place or what I had done. I simply headed home. It was Monday morning and I was expected at work that day.

Needless to say, I did not make it to work that morning.

Fueling up on the north end of Billings, I checked my watch and headed north. What is normally a four hour drive took me ten hours. I cried so hard, often I could not see to drive. I knew, without a shadow of a doubt, that liquor had me beat. I knew that my solution to all life's situations was no longer to be my solution. I knew that my "best friend" had turned on me and had become my worst enemy. I knew my life had to change, again. I knew I would have to learn how to live without the assistance and help of John Barleycorn. I accepted these facts wholeheartedly albeit with huge mourning loss.

At times, especially family gatherings, I still mourn the loss of alcohol in my life. Everyone in my family drinks. Drinking alcohol is the culture in which I and my family of origin were raised. Drinking alcohol is socially acceptable. To drink alcohol is expected. To have alcohol available at all family gatherings is expected. To not drink alcohol is considered odd and abnormal.

Yet, I know I have the disease of addiction, of alcoholism, and I cannot drink alcohol in a normal manner. When I accepted that fact, that miserable lonely day driving from Billings to Malta, my life began to change again.

To this day, I have not felt the need to drink alcohol or to change how I feel by ingesting drugs or alcohol.

Bob

I decided to try the suggestion from the people in the group to get a sponsor. I asked a woman; she had lost a leg to diabetes and her health did not permit her to assist me. I asked another two women; they were so into each other that neither one of them had any time for me nor do I think they knew the steps needed to be taken to show me the way out. I asked the last woman who was active in meetings; I soon learned her suggestion for when I was jonesing for a drink was to go to the bar and get a man for the night. Apparently the women she tried to help attempted to stay sober one man at a time. That method was not for me to try. Since then, I have known other people who have tried that method of sobriety. I have not known anyone for whom sex has worked in keeping them sober.

I asked Bill if it were okay for me to ask for a man's help.

Immediately he was suspicious of my motives. "Who?" he asked.

I gave him the names of three men I had learned to respect. Bill thought any of the three would be alright.

I went to the first man; he said he was too busy to help me. I went to the second man; he said that I did not have a snowball chance in hell to stay sober and he was not going to waste his time on a twinke like me. I went to the third man; he said yes.

The relationship did not last long. I did not like the way the man treated me; he insulted me, he put me down, and he ridiculed me. I was not in boot camp. There was no reason to treat me with such invalidation. I did not feel I needed to be treated that way. I went back to the first man; he said he was still too busy to help me. I went back to the second man; he reluctantly agreed to help me.

In our discussion, he asked what I wanted. I had been told to find someone willing to talk about money, power (control), and sex. I told him this. He said he was willing to talk about the first two but not the third. That was fine with me. I did not want to deal with the third issue anyway. He said I was to find a woman to take me through the book when I left to go to college. Because I did not plan to leave to go to college, I was okay with this idea. He said I was not to call or visit him at his home. We would talk after the meetings. I was okay with his parameters.

I did not learn until three years later that his wife was highly uncomfortable with me talking with her husband. When she found out about our working relationship, she quit talking to him. I knew that he was going through a hard time that fall. I had no clue how hard. She did not talk to him for three full months. When Thanksgiving came and went without so much as one word, I think he almost drank. But he did not give up on me or on his marriage.

After a few years his wife got over her issues with me and I was welcome in their home. I enjoyed visiting with her. She was supportive of his sobriety until the day she died. Not many alcoholics are so blessed as he.

Once, when Bob and I talked in the car after the meeting, I asked him why was it that I always did as he told me to do, but I rebelled strongly when other people told me what to do.

He said, "I never tell you what to do." He further explained, "I let you hurt bad enough until you ask for help. Then I give you a few suggestions. I let you decide if you want to go on hurting and maybe take a drink or if you want to try some of the things I suggest. It is your choice. But I never tell you what to do."

Fifteen years later we visited, he said, "Have I ever told you what to do?'

"No."

"No, I never have. And I said I never will. But, I am going to tell you what to do today."

I was shocked. I listened and obeyed him the one time he told me NOT to do something. He has never told me what to do again. Only that one unforgettable time did he ever tell me what to do.

A few years after our initial start, he called me when I was in college. He was in town for some business training for his job. We met and visited. I proudly told him how well I was doing both in school and in my sobriety. He patiently listened to me ramble on and on.

When I finally paused to take a breath, he said, "What about your isolationism?"

Damn. He had me. When I did not have anything to say on that subject, he continued.

He said, "When we first met you had such a gigantic wall built around yourself. You've been working very hard at taking down the bricks. But instead of throwing the bricks away you have built a shorter, thicker wall. Others can see you now, but you are harder to reach."

I did not know what to do differently at that time.

Over the years whenever I went through town I stopped to see him. I may not stop to see family, but I always tried to look him up for a visit.

Even more years later, I sought for another woman to guide me on this way of life. I could not find one I felt comfortable with. I talked to Bob about it.

Bob said, "You know, I never fired you."

He went on to remind me that my main relationship is with God. I was not to look for an easier, softer way by trying to rely on others too much. He said I had to have trusted people in my life with whom I am accountable, but not to rely on them for spiritual guidance. I learned about spiritual guidance from God when I took the steps necessary for my life to change. Other people were in my life to discuss issues and to discuss where I thought God might be leading me. God speaks first to my heart and then in English through others.

I have never found the need to seek for another person to guide me. Bob still has not fired me or I him. We talk a few times a year. I try to remember to call him on his sobriety birthday. I stop to visit him whenever I am in town. Whenever shit hits the fan in my life, I will call him. Usually the first thing he says is, "Have you prayed about it?" He lets me know of momentous changes in his life as well. We send emails to each other every few months.

I believe I owe my life to this man.

He disagrees. He says I have done the work needed to change my life.

True. But. If it had not been for him during that first year of hell and throughout the years with him being my kite string as I bounced off invisible walls and flitted to and fro on the winds of confusion, then I cannot imagine how my life would have turned out. Certainly, my life would not be the life of love and joy it is today had it not been for the man who loved to help drunks get sober enough to endure three months of his wife's anger in order to help me.

For Bob, I am eternally grateful.

College

Soon the folks at the meetings asked me when I was going to move away and attend college. I had no plans to do so. Thirteen months later the boys and I moved to Bozeman for me to attend Montana State University (MSU).

I knew MSU did not have the degree in conservation that I wanted. But I did not want to attend the University of Montana in Missoula. I met a gal, Steph, at the "transfer student" orientation; she suggested I talk to the Assistant Dean of the College of Agriculture about my dilemma.

And so I met Clayton Marlow, who became one of my greatest mentors.

Dr. Clayton Marlow

Dr. Marlow, whom I call Clayton, told me of a new degree the college staff had thought about offering. I was the first student to enter the Rangeland Watershed Management course work. It turns out that I was the only student to graduate with that degree. In my junior year, the college hired a new dean. He changed the requirements for the degree; soon the offering of the degree was canceled.

Clayton became my advisor in college. I followed his direction with suggested course work. I told Clayton of my determination to not be on welfare, to be employed. He hired me as his "assistant." This meant that whenever a graduate student came to him in a panic about their deadline and their research, he would "give" them his assistant to succor the grad student. For me this was great. The hours were flexible. More importantly, I had the opportunity to work on almost a dozen different research projects during my time at MSU. I love research.

In a lab one day with one of the graduate students we visited about his research project. He had just finished telling me the weak aspect of the research when my brother Levi walked in. Levi and I attended MSU at the same time. Levi asked what we were doing. The grad student briefly outlined the project. Levi said, what about ... some aspect of the research. Levi had immediately identified the weak spot in the research. Later the grad student told me that none of the professors on his committee had noticed the weak area. Levi has no natural resources background. The fact he recognized and nailed the flaw in the research so quickly is a testament to his brains.

Outside of my Auntie Diane, Clayton has been probably the second greatest "cheerleader" in my life. He encouraged me continuously and tremendously. Through his reassurance and reinforcement, I thrived in college like I had never done so before. Clayton was my advisor, my boss, my dean, my friend. I hold him in the greatest of respect.

Once when I had left his office and walked down the hall of the college, the thought went through my head, "man I love that man." I damn near tripped! I do not "love" married men! But as I thought about it, about what love is — respect, thoughtfulness, admiration, kindness, caring, concern, "to think highly of" ... yes, I love that man. He was and is very important to me. Never was my "love" for him in a "physical" or "sexual" manner. It was never in a way or manner that would cause jealousy or problems in his marriage. It was simply the love of one human being for another — true "brotherly love."

Throughout the years, whenever I plan a trip to Bozeman, I contact Clayton ahead of time to see if he would have time for coffee when I am in town. Except when he is out of town conducting research, he has always had time for me. He asks about my sons, I ask about his family. He tells me of his research, I tell him of my writing. He continues to encourage me. I continue to hold him in the highest respect and admiration.

There were other professors who encouraged me greatly as well. One from whom I never took a class.

Dr. John E. (Jack) Taylor

I met Dr. John E. (Jack) Taylor a month before I got sober, fourteen months before I headed off to college.

I participated in the organization of the annual Range Days. This event is held throughout Montana in a different county each year. At one of the organizational meetings, I informed the group that the master of ceremonies (MC) for the banquet had told me he would not be able to be the MC for the event. Then, needing to use the restroom, I left the room. Returning to the meeting, feeling much relieved, I learned they had voted, in my absence, for me to MC the banquet.

I no longer felt relieved.

I had not done any public speaking since high school. I had been in a marriage in which I allowed my self-esteem and self-confidence to become worse than eroded; damn near destroyed. I doubted my ability. I thought I was in no way capable of MCing the banquet.

Having learned to pause when doubtful to pray, I began to pray. I was not secure enough within myself to tell jokes, as many MCs do. I asked God for inspiration. I wrote a ballad about sagebrush. At the banquet, I "read" the ballad.

Afterward, Jack approached me. I already knew he was a Professor Emeritus from MSU. Being retired is one thing, being an emeritus is quite another. I was in awe of him and somewhat intimidated at, what I perceived as, his greatness. As the years passed I grew in understanding what a great man he truly is.

That first night, after the banquet, Jack told me how much he enjoyed my poem. He asked me for a copy.

I almost could not speak. Here was a man who had taught at the University level for thirty-six years, who had taught hundreds of students, and who had read thousands of papers asking ME for a copy of a simple ballad I had written.

I probably nodded dumbly as was my custom when I felt too overwhelmed to speak.

He asked me if I were a student of Stegner.

Who?

I had not heard of, let alone read, of the Pulitzer Price winning author Wallace Stegner. Since then, I have read all of Stegner's works. I do not think I write in the style of Stegner but if Jack thinks so — great. Stegner was one of the world's greatest authors.

Jack also asked me if I had thought about attending college. I told him no. He encouraged me to go to MSU and to look him up when I got there. I thought he was kind but not serious with his invitation to "look him up" and that he did not know how impossible it would be for me to "compete" with all those young, bright minds at the university.

That conversation lasted maybe all of ten minutes but changed my life forever. That conversation gave me hope.

Once I enrolled in college, I ran into him in the halls of the College of Agriculture. Jack no longer taught much at the school, but he did advise a couple of graduate students. He seemed genuinely disappointed that I had not sought him out upon my arrival at the University. He had been serious in his invitation to look him up once I arrived! We started occasionally, about once a month or six-weeks, to meet for coffee.

Surprisingly, we had quite a bit in common. He spoke German and played the tuba in a German polka band. I love to polka. He was on the Symphony Board. My birthday gift to myself every year I was in college was season tickets to the symphony. He frequently floated the Missouri River through the Missouri Breaks south of where I was raised. I love the "Misery" Breaks. He was an avid student of the Lewis & Clerk Expedition. I love history.

His beloved wife had died (they had had a "storybook" relationship and marriage by Jack's account), his children did not live close by, and he no longer had a full teaching load. Then he had a heart attack. He had a second heart attack in the hospital and died. They revived him. I phoned him while he was in the hospital; he did not fear death, he did not want to die; yet, there was a sadness in his voice. Basically he was lonely.

Shortly thereafter, he was introduced to a woman who lived an hour and a half away. They fell in love and were married. He moved to her city. Because of his heart, he did not know how much time he had left on this earth. They decided to celebrate monthly anniversaries instead of annually.

We lost contact.

Some ten or twelve year later I drove 90 miles in -40 degree weather one cold winter night to hear him speak. I was not sure he would even remember me. We made eye contact across the room and he immediately made his was over to shake my hand.

In the course of our conversation, he told me they were still celebrating their wedding anniversary monthly. He added, "do you know how difficult it is to find a 135th anniversary card?"

When I told him my first science fiction novel had been published, he grinned from ear to ear and said he wanted an autographed copy. He told me he always knew I was as good of an author as Stegner — all I had to do was write a novel and find a publishing house to offer me a contract.

It was another six of more years when I contacted him again. By this time, I had a radio show, *Coping With Life*, about human triumphs over life's traumas and tragedies. My shows corresponded with days, weeks, or months of celebration such as American Heart Day. I phoned Jack to see if he would allow me to interview him. Of course he would.

This man has an indomitable spirit. I believe love is what makes him the strong man he is. Leading, there was the love with his first wife. Then there was the near heart-breaking time alone. Now, there is the love with his second wife.

I wish I could have or would have spent more time with him. I think Jack could have or would have taught me much, much more about love and life than he ever taught about range plants and natural resource conservation.

Dr. Bret Olson

Dr. Olson and I did not start off bonding as did Jack and me or Clayton and me. I had met Bret around the halls of the college and knew who he was before I took a class from him. I do not know how many classes I took from him over the course work and four years of college, there were several.

In the first class, he stated that we students were not to come to his office to complain about a grade. He said he would never change a grade once he set it; do not come to him whining about the grade.

On a test, I answered a question correctly how he taught the answer in class. Then I added a post script based on my experience, the post-script was somewhat different than the precise, exact, and proper answer.

He marked the answer wrong.

I went to his office. I pointed out that my answer in the space for the answer was exactly as he had taught in class. Yes, but, he pointed out, I added my post script.

He did not change the grade.

One thing I detest about schools is the lack of teaching for students to use their head, to use their experience, or to digest the information. Students are force fed information and then expected to puke it out on paper exactly as it was fed. No digestion, no assimilation, no internalization. No wonder we raise generations of robots.

A recent conversation with my college-attending nephew, Levi's son, reinforced my conviction of a generation not capable of using their heads to think. My nephew went to visit his parents for the weekend. There was sink full of dishes in the house he shares with other engineering students when he left. The dirty dishes were still in the sink when he returned, although, now they soaked in a sink full of cold icky water. My nephew asked his roommate why the roommate had not washed the dishes. The roommate told Levi's son the sink was plugged; that he, the roommate, had done everything he could think of to unplug the sink and nothing worked. The sink was unequivocally stopped up.

My nephew reached his hand into the grimy water and pulled the metal plug from the drain.

Need I say more?

Returning to the story of my college years, one day Dr. Olson asked me to come to his office. I was in his Ecological class and there were a couple of quite disruptive classmates in the course. I knew Bret did not like being questioned in class, and I had done so. The most disruptive classmate had begun to raise questions as well, but his were of off-color comments for the laughter of the class.

What did I do now? I wondered as I trudged my way to Bret's office. Clayton had already informed me that I had attained quite the "controversial" reputation among the professors. I questioned, I played the devil's advocate, and I challenged their teachings. I wanted to be forced into thinking and I wanted my fellow classmates to think for themselves as well. Perhaps Bret wanted to ask me to back off with my challenging questioning.

My father always said, "You have a brain, use it."

So I do — or at least try to.

Arriving at Bret's office, I noticed one of my papers on his desk. He greeted me, thanked me for coming, and indicated to the paper.

"You have potential as a writer," he said, looking me in the eye. "But you lack grammatical knowledge. Have you taken the required English courses?"

Yes.

He looked at my paper on his desk. "I will help you with your grammar, if you are interested in learning how to write better." He looked up at me again. He waited for my answer. I think he expected a negative response.

But that is not what I gave him.

I think I am, in part, the writer I am today because of Dr. Bret Olson. I am forever in his debt.

I started to write technical papers. He started to give me "outside" writing assignments. He would discuss with me his edits and what I needed to do or to change in order to write more concisely.

Bret's wife, Kathrin, also worked at the college. She was a researcher. Clayton had me work with her on a couple of mapping projects — thanks to my background as a cartographic aide. Kathrin is one of the most intelligent, capable women I had ever met. I learned to respect and admire her greatly. She encouraged me in my love for research. She was one of the few people who comprehended and respected my sobriety. Most normal people cannot totally get a grip on the necessity for me to abstain from alcohol. Kathrin had a brother who was an alcoholic; she understood my new way of life.

Bret and Kathrin were the new, modern type of couple. They were dedicated to their careers, passionate about their research, and hungry to learn and to dispel what they had learned to others. They did not plan to be the traditional type of couple who settled down to raise a family. Children were not in their strategy for their life - ever.

Then Kathrin got pregnant.

The Animal and Range Department of the College of Agriculture held a baby shower for them. By then, Clayton had given me my own office and I was nearly considered staff. I was invited to the shower.

At one point, Bret and Kathrin struggled with figuring out how to use or put together some baby contraption. I do not remember what it was. It could have been a car seat. Modern car seats are a study within themselves of belts and buckles. I did not fully pay attention to with what they struggled. I was musing in my head about the change in the direction of their lives.

I giggled.

Bret shot me a look.

After the shower was over, he and I walked down the hall. Bret was several yards in front of me. Suddenly, he turned.

"Why did you laugh at me?" he asked. "Did you laugh because you thought it was funny that two PhDs couldn't figure out how to put a … (whatever it was) together?"

For a second I did not know to what he referred and then I remembered my giggle during the shower. By that time, I had caught up with him in the hallway.

"No Bret," I said as I fell into step along side of him. "I did not laugh because of that. I laughed because you will know love like you have never known love before. I find that funny; it is funny in a good way."

He gave me a quizzical, blank look and turned down the hall toward his office.

I went on my way.

A few days later, he saw me in the hall and summoned me into his office.

"What did you mean by that crack the other day," he asked, "about me knowing love like I never had known it before? Do you mean I will love Kathrin more after the baby is born?"

I laughed.

"No," I said. "If that were true, I would still be married to my children's father." I grinned at him, knowing there was no way for me to explain to him something he had no conception of or had not experienced prior. I continued, "Believe me when I say, you will know love like you have never known love before."

Grinning at the idea of stumping a professor, I left his office.

When I graduated from college, Bret and Kathrin attended my graduation party. They were the only staff from the college to do so. I did not see Bret again for three years.

I ran into Bret at a Range Convention or Workshop in Wyoming. As is the custom, following the day long meetings, everyone gathers at the bar in the evening to chat. I found myself sitting next to Bret at a table. It was our first opportunity to visit all weekend.

He started the conversation. "Do you remember what you said to me?" he asked.

I knew instantly exactly to what he referred.

"Yes." I grinned.

He was totally serious when he said, "You were right. When our son was born, I learned love like I never experienced love or knew love before."

Kathrin was pregnant with their second child.

I smiled.

Children can and do teach parents about love. I know my sons have taught me about love in a manner I would have never learned had it not been for them.

I have seen Bret one time since, at a Society for Range Management meeting in Canada a few years later. I have never seen Kathrin again. I think of them often in warm memory of their help to me as a "young" college student. I remember Kathrin's delicious broccoli pizza and her welcoming warmth as another professional woman. I remember Bret every time I edit my writing.

Chemistry

This subject deserves its own space in this manuscript.

I never took chemistry in high school. I did not take chemistry in the two bible colleges or the community college I attended. I had an unreasonable fear of chemistry.

My first day in chem class I was so overwhelmed that I walked out of the auditorium where it was held, I walked to Clayton's office, and I convinced him I had to drop the course. He allowed me to do so with the admonition, I could not graduate without three chemistry classes. I had to take chemistry, no matter what, the next two quarters and during the summer session. The University changed from quarters to semesters. I was out of time. No more procrastination.

I took chemistry the next quarter. Toward the beginning of the quarter, I told the professor, a man whom I will call Jim, that all I knew about chemistry was that NA stood for Narcotics Anonymous and table salt.

He laughed.

I did not think my comment was that funny. Apparently he did.

I studied diligently. I learned. Yet, I still had a fear.

I cheated on the final.

I had gotten the answers to the final from another student who had been allowed to take the final early. I quickly memorized the questions and the answers. I had studied my ass off so I knew the material. The final was a composite of all earlier tests. I finished the final in less than twenty minutes. When I turned my paper in, I thought Jim had a funny grin on his face. Maybe he knew I had cheated. I could not maintain eye-contact, knowing I was guilty of the only time I cheated in college.

The following week I attended a different meeting for the gathering of alcoholics to help one another stay sober. It was the first time I attended this particular group.

There sat Jim, my chemistry teacher.

Shit.

I had to make amends for what I had done. All week my duplicity had haunted me. I had to admit to what I had done. I had to face and accept the fact that, with the knowledge of my cheating, he could very well flunk me from his class. I could even be expelled from school. I also knew I would not stay sober if I did not practice honesty in all aspects of my life.

I approached Jim after the meeting.

"I need to talk to you," I said.

He nodded.

"I have to tell you that I cheated on the final in your class."

I do not remember exactly how the conversation went. My fear and nervousness at the time hinders my memory now.

Jim asked if I could have passed the final had I not cheated.

Yes.

At some point he asked me, "Did you learn anything in my class?"

Oh yes. Jim had the ability to dissolve, if not completely at least partially, the fear I had of my possible inability to learn chemistry. His teaching caused the elements on the periodic table to be understandable; his teaching caused the atoms, neurons, electrons, particles — everything about chemistry — to make sense. His teaching caused chemistry to be alive, interactive, fascinating, and the knowledge thereof to be attainable and desirable.

I did not tell him all of that. I simply said everything I knew about chemistry, I had learned in his class and I had learned a lot.

He concluded that conversation with a statement that if I had learned, that was his goal for his teaching — for the students to learn. He would let the fact of my cheating go.

And he said for me not to cheat in any class for the rest of my college years.

Over the next two years I saw him frequently, he never asked me if I cheated in any class. He trusted my word that I would not cheat.

I did not cheat again. My continued sobriety is more important than passing a class.

The next semester class times conflicted and I had to take my second quarter of chemistry from a different professor. He was a good teacher as well, but he was not Jim. I took my last quarter of chemistry from Jim. It was a very tough class, but I passed with a "B" which was a low grade for me.

Many other professors at the university made strong impacts on my life. There was the soil professor, with his gentle spirit he referred to soil as beautiful. I am four credits short of qualifying as a Soil Scientist. I like soil. But I did not want to spend day after day alone in the field mapping soils. Soil Scientists do NOT refer to soil as "dirt." Dirt is misplaced soil such as a weed is a misplaced plant. I did teach a soil lab for this man. I was the only female soils lab teacher. My students averaged higher grades in his class than any other lab teacher's students. I learned I loved to teach.

I became friends with one of my students in my soils lab. He had phoned me at home, had heard my children playing and laughing in the background, and had said he missed his kids. My sons and I called him "Mountain Man Larry" because he dressed in the fashion of the fur trapping days of rendezvous and mountain men of a hundred and fifty years prior.

Larry had a tough time with the concept of friendship with a female. He asked me out once; I told him I did not date my friends. He insisted; I relented. After an awkward time listening to music at a bar, he took me home. I invited him in. He refused. He had been in our apartment many times. I asked him what-the-hell was going on. He confessed. He was seeing a therapist; the therapist suggested he learn to go on a date with a woman without having sex. Larry said he knew of no one with whom he would trust himself to go out with without sex except me. He said I was "safe" to date.

Thanks. Yes, I am a safe woman for most men to be around. Maybe Bob is still right; maybe the walls are still there.

Years later I ran into Larry in Kmart near where I lived. He had a temporary job on the hi-line for a few weeks. I invited him for breakfast on a Sunday with a drive to the Little Rocky Mountains, my mountains, in the afternoon. As I drove on a narrow mountain trail Terry said he wanted to thank me. He said I had taught him how to be friends with women. He had met a woman and became her friend; they were engaged to be married. He thought he would not have been in the relationship he was now in if it had not been for me and our friendship.

It was not my intention to teach men how to be friends with women; it was my intension to have sex-less coed friendships with men. Larry was not the only man in my life who told me I was their first female friend. He was the only man who then thanked me for teaching him how. Being friends with the opposite sex is important to me and I am happy I helped Larry learn how to be friends with women.

While teaching the soils lab, I thought about continuing my education and becoming a University professor. I did not wholly embrace the agency for which I worked. There were and are some philosophy differences that I struggled with. I was accepted for a fellowship at the University of Maine — Orono.

I actually did not qualify for the program in Maine. The program was for engineering or physics students. But the Dean of the

Engineering College was involved with constructed wetland research. My background in natural resources provided the experienced for me to get accepted. I had applied for the fellowship knowing I was not eligible but, what-the-hell, why not shoot and arrow up into the sky and see where it lands?

I think Dr. Chet Rock really did not want to be involved with the program. I heard later that he had had trouble with the female summer research student the year before. I do not think he realized I was female, due to my name, until we met at the orientation. I did not understand the look of shock (or was it disappointment?) on his face when he was introduced to this gal wearing a dress as his next research assistant — me.

In spite of his initial surprise, Chet and I got a long greatly. Toward the end of the research season, he told me that I had accomplished more that summer session than the grad student on the project had completed in two years.

Due to that research, I was asked to participate in writing a chapter in a college level textbook on constructed wetland research. I am proud of that accomplishment.

It was during the wetland research there that I began to search for a university for graduate school. Chet offered me a grad student position but I did not want to continue with bio-engineering. I feared I would fail miserably with the math aspect of engineering. I was accepted into graduate school at the University of New Mexico in Las Cruses. I wanted to attend Oregon State University, but was not accepted there.

I went to talk with another professor in the college of agriculture. I do not remember his position in the college at that time. I think he had the responsibility to interview graduating seniors. I told him of my future plans; I told him of my acceptance into grad school; I talked to him about my sons. I told him I was not 100% satisfied with a career with USDA. We talked about the fact that graduate school is often 80 hour work weeks. My sons were nearing the end of their grade school years. I knew their approaching teen years would take a lot of my time and energy.

He told me that he put his career ahead of his family. And, although he had a stellar career as a range professional, his son hated him. By putting his career ahead of his family, he had lost his relationship or damaged his relationship with his son so greatly he feared his son would never forgive him. He feared they would never have any type of good, loving relationship. He told me to not follow in his footsteps. He strongly suggested I stay with the government, with my established career, and concentrate on maintaining and retaining my relationship with my children.

I listened. I turned down the offer for grad school; the professor who offered to mentor me in grad school said he would keep the offer open to me for ten years in case I changed my mind. A ten year offer is quite the offer.

I never made it to grad school. I often wonder how different my life would be had I moved to New Mexico way back then. It is futile meanderings in the mind to ponder that scenario. Yet, I do — even to this day. I do not regret the path I took. Nevertheless, I do think about how my life could be different had I not stayed with USDA and had I not contracted my illness.

I also think that I would not have neglected my sons in my pursuit of a different career.

I turned my focus on my federal government career only to have my supervisor in the state office recommended that I not be retained in employment after college graduation.

Study Partners

As in the previous three colleges, the university was tough for me. With the pride of the way in which I was raised, I did not want to accept "welfare" in order to go to school. Grandma Doll raised ten kids without welfare; I should be able to raise two children without welfare. At times, I had up to four part-time jobs.

Having the fear of "not being good-enough" I thought I had to be an honor student in order to be "good-enough" to attend college with "kids" at least ten years my junior. I graduated with a 3.45 GPA. I got one "C" in my college career and Clayton is the professor who gave it to me that last miserable semester.

And I had two young boys to raise. Nothing was more important than being a "good mother." I had to cook hot breakfasts, I had to take time to do fun things, and I had "be there" for them when they needed me.

There were times I had my days scheduled into fifteen minute intervals. If a person was not on my schedule, I had no time to talk to them.

I did not know I had established a reputation with my classmates. It was not until my senior year when I studied with a class mate that I learned how "stand-offish" others viewed me. While Juniper and I studied, she would say things such as: so-and-so wants to know; such-and-such asked me to ask you; someone wants to know the answer to . . . .

Finally, jokingly, I said to her, "Why doesn't so-and-so or such-and-such ask me themselves?"

With a shocked look on her face, she said, "Because they are afraid of you." As if I would know that.

I have never understood people being afraid of me. I am afraid of THEM. How could they be afraid of me?

I have come to understand that in my insecurity, I portrayed an attitude of hostility, of indifference, and of a basic dislike of others. These are not true. I LIKE people, even then — I just did not know how to approach them. I feared they would not like me so I shied away from going up to others, of being the first person to reach my hand forth in friendship. I was quiet. I could be preoccupied with all the things on my mind of all the things I had to do. But, I, in no way, felt hostile toward others.

Not all classmates viewed me with aversion. There was one young study partner who asked me to be the "best man" at his wedding. His future mother-in-law put a stop to that idea. After her reaction, I felt lucky to be invited to the ceremony.

I am a kinetic learner. I have to be able to touch something to learn about it. That is one reason studying plants, water, and soil was perfect for me. Abstract concepts such as is found in subjects along the lines of math or philosophy are difficult for me. To learn I have to see, hear, touch, and sometimes taste what I am learning. I cannot simply listen and take notes. I cannot read my notes and retain. I have to talk it out and talk it over with other people. I have to have study partners in order for me to learn.

In every class, I sought out people with whom to study. When I was successful in securing a like-minded student, I would get an "A" in the class. Most of my grades were "A's." I found a great study partner, a younger married man. He had a double major, both Range Science and Animal Science. He was as focused as I was, he was as smart as I was, and he was "safe" because he was married.

After graduation I visited with his wife and thanked her for never having a problem with her husband and me studying together.

She did not look at me. "That is not true, you know," she said, busy at the task in front of her.

No, I did not know. I have a tendency to be quite oblivious to what is obvious to others.

I learned that an idiot in our class teased her husband about me so much that she became jealous. She demanded he quit studying with me.

He did not. He told her to get over her stupid jealousy. He told her that I was the smartest person he knew in our class and he was going to continue to study with me.

She left him.

I knew she had gotten a job in Idaho, but I did not realize it was a "temporary separation."

My beloved Grandfather, Papa, died. I was out of school for nearly a week to attend his funeral and family gathering. When I returned, I bumped into my study partner in the hall.

"Where have you been?" he asked.

I told him. I also told him that Papa died of cancer and of how prevalent cancer was in our family. I told him how a friend suggested I start annual cancer exams beyond the normal yearly female pap smear.

He told me that cancer was widespread in his family as well. Maybe he should think about annual exams. In fact he had this lump … his hand strayed to his throat.

Dammit, get to the clinic and have that thing checked out.

Funny, that is what his wife had suggested as well.

Well, then, DO IT.

He went to class.

Later he told me that throughout class he kept thinking about his wife and my urging him to have the lump on his neck examined. After class, he went to the campus clinic.

That was on a Tuesday. The staff at the clinic biopsied the lump near his adam's apple that day. By Thursday he had the diagnosis of thyroid cancer.

He ran into me in the hall and told me the news. He was twenty-five years old.

"What do you suggest I do?" he asked. "Should I stay in school and get treatment here or should I leave school and get treatment near where my wife lives?"

Go to your wife was my advice.

So he did.

That was when and how she learned ours was truly a relationship of study partners and friends, not of potential lovers. That is when she began to outgrow her mistrust of me.

He had surgery, treatment, and returned to school a few short weeks later. To my knowledge, he has never had a reoccurrence of cancer. But I do not know.

I do not think she ever fully trusted my relationship with her husband. He and I had much in common with our love of agriculture, especially cows and natural resources. She was a grade school teacher who was allergic to many things out-of-doors. His and my ease of conversation and our closeness was difficult for her. We lost contact over the decade following graduation.

I had been told, when the rape-task force paid for me to attend therapy, that I use humor as a defense. Hmm. This is true. I also use humor as my social dance and outreach. I love to joke. I tease everyone I like. And, I like most people. It is difficult for me to not tease someone I like. But I have met a few people who do not like teasing and joking. These people are hard for me to be around much. It is hard for me to watch myself, my humor, and my tongue.

Toward the end of my freshman year, in one of Bret's classes, we were out on a field trip. I joked around. One of the "older guys" (meaning he was near my age) in the class told me I was offensive.

Shocked, I replied, "don't you mean obnoxious?"

"No," said Stuart, "I am obnoxious, you are offensive."

My feelings were hurt. And I decided that I did not like Stuart.

The next fall, we were in a class together again. In this grass seed identification class, another classmate, Judy, complimented me on my coat.

"This old thing," I said. I was not gracious in my acceptance of her compliment. My coat was grey and pink; my ex-husband had a matching one in black and grey. I told her so.

Stuart interrupted our conversation. "You hate men." He stated.

"No I don't."

"Yes you do."

"No I don't."

We continued this two-year old argument behavior for several rounds.

Finally in exasperation, I hotly stated. "NO I DON'T HATE MEN! I have two sons whom I love very much and that proves I do not hate all men!" I stalked from the classroom.

Later that night, when I reviewed my day, I realized I owned Stuart an amend for the way in which I talked to him.

I phoned him and apologized. I do not remember the conversation. He does. He was surprised I would apologize. Admitting when I am wrong is a habit I try to foster; I do not remember every time I have had to call or talk to someone to try to correct my idiotic behavior. I try not to engage in idiotic behavior; I do not relish admitting my mistakes. Eating crow — or humble pie, is difficult for most people; it is no fun for me either. I do not always realize when I have offended someone or made a mistake. I try to examine my behavior and right wrongs I have made.

A week or so later Stuart phoned me.

It was my turn to be surprised.

He said he would not pass the grass seed id class without my help. Would I consider being his study partner?

Yes.

We met every Wednesday night from 8:00 to 10:00pm at my house. My sons went to bed at 8pm. As the weeks progressed, I invited Stuart to join us for supper on Wednesdays. Nope, he would not. He would arrive at exactly 8 o'clock pm; he would leave at exactly at 10pm. The only times in which this differed is when we had a big test that week. On those weeks we would study every night from 8 to 10 and on the night before the test, we would study until two o'clock in the morning. I got a "B" in the class; Stuart passed with a "D." He was happy.

During that semester Stuart became my friend. At one point, before we graduated, he commented that when he died he would have to be cremated because he did not have enough friends to carry a casket. It takes six people to carry a casket. Stuart had three friends; Bill, Caine, and me.

He is now friends with a family he refers to as "The Olsons." I have never met them. Holding people away from himself is a learned behavior started back when he was young. He never gave up the habit. I think, the only reason Stuart does not make friends is because he thinks he is dumb and he does not want other people to know. He is not dumb! He has severe dyslexia. It took him seven or more years to make it through college. He graduated with a Range degree. During our last year, Clayton talked Stuart into getting tested. Stuart tested at a first grade level of reading.

Not very many people can graduate from college reading at a first grade level without special help. Yet Stuart did so. Day after day I would see him sitting in the student union building studying. He studied and studied and studied. NO ONE studied and worked harder at studying and passing classes than Stuart. I admire him greatly. His tenacity may be greater than mine.

In college, after we became friends, Stuart started to tell me that I was too intense. I had to be intense. The standard I held myself to — honor student, sons, jobs — to maintain that level of functioning, I had to be concentrated and determined in my time management. It started to irritate me when he would tell me I was too intense. Once, when we were sitting in the hall waiting for the professor to come and unlock the door to the classroom, he told me again that I was too intense. I had a comeback.

I told him that an intense person was a very passionate person. And I was very passionate. Stuart was dumbfounded into silence. Caine was there. He laughed.

Years later, Stuart and I went to Bozeman together. I stayed with Peggy while he stayed with Bill. We met Caine for coffee. I left the table to go to the ladies room. Later Stuart told me that while I was away from the table, Caine said he almost did not know me — I did not resemble the young woman he had attended class with. I was no longer intense.

Gratefully, Caine was correct. Unfortunately I had to learn the hard way to lighten up.

Stuart and I had our careers with the same USDA agency. Our paths have crossed many, many times over the years. Our friendship went beyond college and careers. Both retired now, we still talk frequently on the phone and visit often to share a meal and a movie. Both of us take our friendship with each other earnestly.

Other Important People I Met During College

Stephanie

I met Steph at transfer student orientation. We were an unlikely couple. Steph was from Auburn, Arkansas. But the fact she was a southerner did not cause our friendship to be odd. She did not comb or brush her hair, or so it looked. She wore stretched out sweatshirts and holey jeans. I normally wore dresses and braided my hair daily. We were quite the "Thelma and Louise" pair. She wore Burkenstock sandals; I wore boots (not with the dresses, I wore boots when I wore jeans). She worked in a bar and was known to "tie one on;" I did not drink. She was a tree-hugging liberal; I was a down-to-earth conservative.

Yet we became instant friends. Her parents were both from Montana. Her mom was from the south east corner of the state, ranching country; her father was from the hi-line region of north central Montana, farming country. Steph was closest to her father's family. His youngest brother stayed on the farm, farming it. She thought very highly of that uncle.

Clayton advised both of us. He did not know we were friends.

One day, I accompanied her to his office. While she talked to him, I waited patiently. When he finished their conversation, he turned to me and asked me what I needed.

"Nothing," I said, "I'm with her."

He did not hide the shock on his face.

She got pissed.

Her tirade against people in agriculture lasted clear out into the parking lot across the street. She loudly ranted and raved about how they ruin the land and she used the f-word over and over again.

Finally, I yelled back at her. "Do you think that your fucking uncle gets up every fucking day with one fucking thought in his fucking mind of how the fuck he was going to fuck the earth again that fucking day?"

Normally I do not use the f-word, at least I use it very infrequently. That day, my over use of the word and the reference to her beloved uncle got her to finally shut up. It was that day she finally got through her thick skull that people in agriculture do not ever intend to spoil their livelihood by purposefully harming the land on which they raise their families. The land they love. The land they wish to pass on to their children.

I told her I would buy a pair of Burkenstocks if she would buy a pair of Ropers.

I did. She did not. Every time I wear my "burks" I think of her, my fiery red-headed hot tempered friend.

George

One day I was in an on-campus meeting of the gathering of ex-drunks when an older man, clearly not a student, entered the room and started to greet people. He would say, "Hello Darling," and give them a hug. When he was near to me in his circling of the room, I suddenly blurted out. "I want to meet you."

He stopped arms outstretched mid-way toward a hug with someone else and looked at me with a quizzical expression on his face. "Why?" he asked.

"Because I want to be called "Darling too," was my uncharacteristic response.

We became friends.

George would call me and say, "I'm coming to pick you up for a meeting."

I would respond, “I’m not going to a meeting tonight.” Then I would list my reasons: I had no babysitter for the boys, I had to study, I was tired, I had to get up early in the morning, etc … .

He would not listen to me. He would repeat that he was on his way to get me for a meeting and for me to get ready. Within minutes George would arrive at my door. I think I always ended up going with him. I had a neighbor down the hall of the apartment building who often babysat for me. I babysat for her when she needed a babysitter. I think George knew this.

When the boys and I moved to an old farm house in the country during my senior year in college; George lived in a trailer not far away. He was a frequent visitor to our home. The group of ex-drunks out in that area got together on Sunday afternoons, nearly every Sunday, to play cards. I learned how to play pinochle. The annual Super Bowl Party was a wonderful event and day of fellowship.

I was devastated when my supervisor at the government agency recommended for me to not be allowed to continue my employment with the agency once I graduated. I had worked and sacrificed a lot during those four years to be denied employment. Plus, I had given up my graduate school offer. I did not know what I had done for her to recommend termination. I thought I was a stellar employee; I got more done than other employed students. I learned later that by excelling above others, I did not “fit” in the company. We were expected to be lemmings and I was not. We were expected to be sycophants and I was not. This is not to say all federal employees are mindless robots; there are many outstanding people in federal service. They have learned to fly under the radar, to be content in their position, and to not irritate their superiors or co-workers. Three qualities I never acquired. To be denied my goal was hard for me to swallow. To say I was devastated was an understatement.

I sat in my recliner unable to deal with the pain of the threat of losing my job and what I had decided was my career. For three days I sat there in my pajamas totally at a loss as to what to do.

George came to visit. His nose involuntarily wrinkled at the odor of my for-three-days unwashed body. I immediately felt very embarrassed due to my body odor. He suggested I get up off of my ass, shower, get my ass to a meeting, and get the phone numbers of other women in the organization.

I listened and did what he said.

One of the first women who responded to my request for phone numbers and reached her hand out in friendship to me was Margaret. I had seen Margaret around campus but had never talked to her. She was from California. She was a blond "surfer girl" whose hair looked like it had not seen a brush in weeks, and she wore stretched out sweatshirts, holey jeans, and sandals — a lot like Steph. I did not think we had anything in common.

Another woman suggested I ask a woman to work with me on the program. She suggested Norma S. There were two "Norma S's" - she meant one and my mind went to the other one.

The Norma I talked to was a maintenance person on campus. I had seen her around with her tool belt and had visited with her occasionally.

Norma and Margaret would soon make a big difference in my life.

Back to the story of George and his influence on my life.

George came to my graduation party. We sat, side-by-side, watching a game of volleyball.

He commented, "Ya know, when I first met you, I thought you were gay."

Shocked, I turned to him and said "Why?"

"Because you didn't have anything to do with the guys in the program."

"Do you still think that?"

"No."

"Why not?"

He reiterated an experience we had. He drove taxi. I was walking from the bus stop home to my apartment when the boys and I still lived in town. Thinking about something that I am sure that was important, I did not pay attention to my surroundings. Crossing the four lane street, I heard a horn beep. Looking up, I saw George waving at me from his taxi cab. I ran over to him, kissed him on the cheek, and finished crossing the street at a jog.

He continued, “That’s when I realized you were not gay, you were just afraid of men.”

I did not think my fears were evident.

The idiot in my class (who teased my study partner about me) once said to me, “Brain, bucks, and beauty, why the hell aren’t you married?”

I responded, “Because “A” comes before “B”.”

The idiot looked at me dumbfounded.

So I explained to the idiot, “ “A” for Attitude comes before “B” for Brains, etc … .” Then I walked away from him.

I guess I had quite the attitude.

George was one of the few people who looked beyond my attitude and continued to befriend me. When he told me to get the phone numbers of other people in the program, I had his number and one woman’s phone number. I was just too damn busy for friendships. And Steph had moved away after our first year in college together.

I was not informed when George died. In fact, I hardly ever saw him again after the boys and I left Bozeman. But the unconditional love and acceptance that man held for me is unforgettable.

Norma

My last semester in college Norma and I met every Saturday morning for her to help me get my head out of my ass. It worked. By the following autumn, my life had changed so dramatically I can clearly draw the line between “before” and “after.”

One of the things I hated about myself was the fact that I yelled at my children. I hated it when my parents yelled at me and I vowed I would not yell at my kids. But I did.

I agonized over it, I prayed about it, and I redoubled my efforts not to yell. It did not happen; I continued to yell.

Sometime after Norma quit working with me, I came home from my job one day. The boys were emptying the dishwasher.

Matthew, the oldest and the one usually delegated to talk to me, said, "Mom, Andrew and I noticed something."

"What's that?"

"You don't yell at us anymore."

I stopped to think. He was right. I could not remember the last time I had yelled at them. After my pause to think, I grinned and said, "You're right. Do you miss it? Do you want me to yell at you again?"

"NO!" they both responded quite emphatically.

I needed no further proof that my life had changed and it has continued to change for the better as I apply the principles of love, tolerance, acceptance, kindliness, and patience of the program to my life.

Margaret

I only got to know Margaret the last semester I was in college. She was an English Literature major. Besides not wanting to drink again we really did not have anything in common. She was much younger than me. Her father was a world-renown physicist; my father is a rancher. She was gay; I am straight. There was nothing in our backgrounds, our experiences, or our planned personal futures that were at all alike, let alone similar.

We started to phone one another and to talk with each other. Our discussions centered on recovery from alcoholism. She helped me make it through that last tough semester.

Margaret wanted to write books, such as I do now. She had another year of college left after I graduated. She applied to and was accepted in graduate school at Oregon State, the very college I had wanted to attend. That summer, following her graduation and prior to moving to Oregon, she took a trip through the southwestern states with a friend. She was killed by a drunk driver. There is a memorial scholarship in her name at MSU.

The scholarship is to go to people who are like Margaret. Not to women who are like how I was. The scholarship is to go to women who are excellent students yet have the balance in their lives to "be there" for others. Young women like Margaret.

Clayton had suggested I quit school and take a semester off. He did not understand I could not take a break from college. I was out of time and money. When the boys and I left Bozeman, the propane tank to heat the house was empty, the stack of firewood for the wood stove was gone, and I was exhausted from pushing myself so hard for four years. I could not go on. I was so fully at-the-end of my rope.

The agency decided to retain me in spite of my supervisor's recommendation to let me go. The woman who made the decision to keep me employed also decided to give me one more chance to prove myself a "team player." She sentenced me to a penal colony in the agency, the office in Chinook.

Post-Graduation

When I learned I was sentenced to Chinook, I did not take the news well. In the previous seven years, I did not visit the town in which my baby had died and in which my divorce had taken place. Be damned if I wanted to move back there to live!

I bawled, I squalled, and I beat the roof of my car with my fists. I was willing to do anything but to go back there. When I had exhausted myself of tears and bargaining with God I finally said, "Not my will but Your Will be done."

I went into the house and had smoked salmon on crackers with the boys. Smoked salmon was a rare and special treat in our family. My Uncle Herb would bring jars of home-smoked home-canned salmon to Montana from Alaska when he traveled between those two states. I would get a jar or two a year. The boys did not know what the occasion was that night I opened our only jar of smoked salmon; I am not sure I knew what the celebration was for. I think now, it was for the submission of my will.

So we went back. We moved to Chinook.

We stayed in a motel while I worked and looked for a house. The boys locked themselves in the motel and would not leave the room.

I became angry at them for doing so. They could very well walk to the town swimming pool and meet some kids before their dad came to take them to Tennessee for the summer.

Matthew explained to me why they could not venture out of the motel. "Mom," he patiently started to enlighten me, "we can't go to the pool."

"Why not?"

"Because, Mom, if we do that, we will meet some kids."

"Well, good! That is the whole point to going — to meet some kids before you start school here this fall."

"No Mom, it would not be good."

"Why not?" For the life of me, I could not think of why meeting other kids in town would not be a good thing to do.

He continued, "Mom, when we meet other kids, some kid will ask me to go to his house. When I do, his parents will ask me who I am and who my parents are. I will have to tell them … and then they will know."

Shocked, I had no idea that the traumatic summer of the baby's death and the divorce had affected him so strongly. As the years went by in this town, I would learn more of what my oldest son remembered.

I knelt down to look him in the eye. I placed both of my hands on each of his shoulders. "Matthew," I said, "we have nothing to be ashamed of."

It was his turn to look at me with shock.

Eventually they left the motel room, went to the pool, met some kids, one boy invited them over to his house; they went without talking to me about it first. That night I came home to a very excited young boy.

"Mom," he said, "it happened! It happened!"

"What happened?"

"What I told you about."

I gave him my full attention because I had no idea what he was talking about. I asked, "What did you tell me about?"

With all the patience of a twelve year old, he said, "Mom, I told you that if Andrew and I left the motel and went to the pool we would meet some kids and some kid would ask me to his house."

I nodded.

"Well, it happened. I met this kid named Brent and Andrew and I went to his house with him."

"And … ." I prompted.

"And what I told you would happen happened. His dad asked me who I was and I told him."

"And then what did the dad say?"

Matthew grinned from ear to ear. "He rubbed my head and said, 'oh yeah, I think I remember them.' He welcomed us to Chinook and he told us to have a good time at his house. Mom, he didn't say anything about the divorce or anything else!"

My son began to grow out of a shame I did not know he had.

My Sons

No one and nothing has affected my life for the good like my sons have. I love them with every beat of my heart. I love them with every breath I take. When I told Dr. Bret Olson that he would know love like he had not known love before when Kathrin was pregnant, I knew what I was talking about. My sons have taught me more about love; no, they taught me love. They taught me how to love, how to give love, how to receive love, how to experience love, and how to express love. I have no greater joy than the joy of the relationships between my sons and me.

At this time they live in the same city as each other. Their lives have dramatically different courses, yet, they remain very close. When Andrew attended college, he lived with Matthew for over two years and Matthew paid the rent. When Matthew went through a hard time, he lived with Andrew for over a year and Andrew paid the rent. When Matthew had kidney stones and no insurance, Andrew gave Matthew some of his college money to help him with the medical expenses; Matthew paid Andrew back over time.

That is what families do; they help one another in whatever supportive roles are needed.

Matthew

Matthew was born on September 18th. I woke up around midnight of the night of the 17th unable to sleep due to back pain. I did not know I was in labor; I thought I needed to go to the bathroom. Around 1:00 in the morning, I woke my husband up because the pain had gotten substantially worse. I asked him to call the doctor. The doctor suggested we wait a couple of hours and if the pain had not subsided, to come to the hospital.

I think the doctor wanted more sleep.

A woman in pain is not one to argue with. I told my husband shortly afterward that we were going to the hospital NOW. We called my father a little before 2AM to let him know we may not show up for work in the morning. Dad insisted he drive us to the hospital some 120 miles away. It was the nearest hospital that delivered babies. The hospital in the town closest was little more than a glorified emergency room at that time.

We met Dad on the gravel road into his place. Bumpy gravel roads are not comfortable for a woman in labor! I was not in the mood to argue with my dad.

For some unknown reason, my husband rode with me in the back seat of the old LTD Ford we had. He should have ridden in front with my father. Within 50 miles, my husband was car sick. I think the shocks were going out of that old car added to the undulating ride down the highway. My husband puked in my bag of ice. No more ice for me. He threw the bag of puke out the window.

Yes, he littered on the highway.

The old LTD had its horn around the steering wheel. To honk the horn, all one had to do is squeeze the steering wheel.

Unbeknownst to us, I went into hard labor. I am not quiet when I am in hard labor. The more I screamed the heavier Dad's foot got on the accelerator and the faster he drove. The more I screamed the tighter Dad's grip got on the steering wheel and the more he honked the horn.

We barreled down the highway with the horn honking frequently. The speed may or may not have been a good thing, but the horn honking repeatedly was probably a good thing.

In September, in Montana, herds of deer and antelope are on the move. It is dangerous to drive at night. When Dad would round a corner or top a rise at 120 mph to find a herd of deer or antelope in the middle of the highway, he would slam on the brakes and the horn would honk as his grip tightened.

I would tumble to the floorboards of that old car, screaming in pain. Dad would hit the accelerator again in reaction to my screams. The horn continued to honk.

I do not remember if my husband said or did anything but puke. Maybe he moaned but his moans could not equal the volume of my screams.

At one point I yelled, "Stop this damn car and let this baby be born NOW!"

Dad depressed the accelerator to the floorboards and the car sped up.

My father never has listened to me much.

I think with Dad's experience in birthing calves, he would have done just fine assisting in the birth of his first grandchild. I do not think my husband would have been of any assistance what-so-ever. Green-around-the-gills nauseated people should not be allowed to assist in anything.

Somewhere north of Lewistown we caught up with a speeding ambulance. Dad got between the ambulance and the carload of worried family members that followed the ambulance.

Following the ambulance, we raced through Lewistown to the hospital. The ambulance turned to back up to the emergency room door. Dad barreled our car straight up to the door — any closer and I think he would have driven INto the hospital.

ER staff hurried out to tell Dad to move the car. He was already out of the car and yelling at them that he had a woman giving birth in the back seat of the car.

I got into the hospital before the woman in the ambulance who had a heart attack. I heard later that she survived.

The ER staff had difficulty getting me off of the back seat/ floorboards and out of the car. Matthew had crowned. It is not easy to maneuver one's self when there is a head between your legs.

Finally some medical person with authority looked between my legs, saw the baby's head, and ordered a wheel chair for me. They wheeled me into the delivery room.

Dumping me onto the table a nurse got into my face from the left side.

"Push!" she demanded. She had VERY bad breath.

I was not about to push until I got some pain medication!

The doctor was by the bedside within five minutes.

"Push!" he demanded.

"NO! NOT until I get some pain medication!"

He explained it was too late for pain medication. The baby was here. I had to push NOW!

I pushed hard … twice.

"Push again," said the doctor who concentrated on what was happening between my legs.

I pushed again and out came a perfect baby.

Later the doctor told me that he never gives a perfect score of whatever scoring medical personnel give when babies are born. Babies always have a discoloration or some reason for not obtaining a perfect score until the second time they score a baby some ten or so minutes later. Matthew got a perfect score both times.

Matthew arrived a perfect pink skin color. He had to be slapped on the ass to get him to cry — a silly practice to … what? Ensure a baby's lungs worked correctly? To ensure they begin life traumatized?

Matthew was born at peace with the world; he was at perfect tranquility with life. His mother, his father, and his grandfather calmed down.

The new baby and the new mother needed to rest. The new father and the new grandfather got in the old car and headed back north to the ranch. They did not get 40 miles when the car broke down; it never ran again. They had to hitchhike to the ranch, get another vehicle and a tow bar, and go back for the dead old beast of a car.

I am grateful the car did not die in the middle of the Missouri Breaks that night! I am not sure how the two men would have handled that. The baby and momma probably would have been just fine.

Of course, the news of the new baby spread rapidly in the community. Dad had to tell everyone about my husband puking. Although Dad made it sound as if the sounds of my labor was what made the young father sick and not my dad's driving.

Matthew truly was a perfect baby. He did not get colic. He did not cry much. He took to nursing well. He was a very content little man.

When he was a month old, we moved back to Tennessee.

My husband had a twin sister. She gave birth to a baby daughter the same month in which Matthew was born. Some of my most precious baby pictures are of those two as toddlers when I babysat my niece.

Matthew liked for me to sit him up on an apple tree branch. When my husband found out, he cut the branch off. I thought the baby was safe; he apparently did not think Matthew was safe in a tree. It was not an issue we discussed. Matthew was angry; so was I.

I remember when Matthew made his first lego airplane. I was so proud of him; I wanted to take a picture of him and his creation. He got angry. HE wanted to take the picture of his toy airplane. I love that picture of him scowling up at me as he sat next to his little lego airplane.

Matthew's "Pa'paw" Ralph was especially close to the little boy. Ralph took Matthew for his first hair cut — an honor I thought I would get to do. Ralph took Matthew with him often that second and third year of Matthew's life.

Our move back to Montana was probably as hard for Matthew, and as confusing, as the move to the ranch was for me at a similar age. I did not realize how much Matthew missed his Pa'Paw until we visited my Great-aunt Violet and her husband. Matthew, not quite three years old yet, lit up and exclaimed "Pa'paw!" He sat on Uncle Lawrence's lap for the duration of the visit, happy and content he had found a Pa'paw.

Once we settled down in Billings to look for a job, we started to talk to Matthew about the new baby in mommy's tummy. We told him he would soon have a little brother or a little sister with whom to play.

As children do, he took us literally. When we brought Andrew home in a Christmas stocking at nine hours old, Matthew promptly threw a football at him. The football bounced off of the baby's head.

Before I could admonish Matthew, he said in complete confusion, "What's wrong with the kid? Can't he play ball?"

He wanted a playmate right then and there. He did not realize Andrew had to grow for several months before the baby could be any type of playmate.

Andrew

Andrew's birth was as traumatic and not ever as funny in retrospect as Matthew's birth. He "dropped" on December 5th. His heartbeat became very faint. I was monitored. Birth seemed eminent. Yet nothing happened. My husband and I were out of money. Dad planned to come get us and our stuff the week after Christmas. My nurse mid-wife planned her wedding for the week after Christmas. The baby HAD to be born!

The midwife scheduled the day to induce labor, December 22. I thought, induced labor was done via injection of some sort of drug. Nope. She broke my water.

I went into labor fast and furiously. Within two hours, Andrew was born. I did not get any drugs for pain that time either; it happened too fast. Again.

Andrew was born screaming his ever-loving head off and the most god-awful purple color I have ever seen in my life. The hospital staff whisked him away immediately. They took him away almost before I caught a glimpse of my purple, angry baby.

His coloration filled me with fear.

The hospital personnel who stayed with me tried to reassure me that everything was okay. But I had seen the tiny purple people-eater. I knew babies are not supposed to be born purple!

The staff who took him away returned to me. They explained that the umbilical cord had been wrapped around his neck twice and around his chest once. It was so tight around his neck, that they recorded it as around his neck once at first. They advised me to watch him closely over the first year of his life in order to catch any obvious signs of brain damage. This advice was so we could get the help needed to deal with whatever would be the effects of his brain damage. They acted sure that my tiny purple monster would have brain damage due to over two weeks of reduced blood flow to his brain.

It was a miracle he was alive and without brain damage. To have lived in vitro for nearly three weeks with a reduced oxygen supply is amazing to me. That kid had a heck of a will to live.

Needless-to-say, Andrew did not get a perfect score when he was born. In fact, he got a very low score. But the second time hospital staff "scored" him, he got a perfect score. He had gone from purple screaming should-have-been-dead baby to a perfect newborn within minutes. Andrew was as perfect as Matthew.

I had been told that if your first baby was a "good" baby, meaning easy to care for and not a crier, the second child would be the opposite. Matthew was born so placid and easy-to-get-along-with that I feared the second child would not be so easy. When Andrew was born screaming his little head off, one thought that went through my head was *oh no, I'm going to have a brat. How am I going to do with a screaming child?* I remembered how difficult my sister had been as a baby! I dreaded going through THAT again!

I needed not to have worried. Andrew was as perfect a baby as Matthew was in every way. I was one lucky momma to have had two easy to care for babies. About the only difference between them was Andrew did not nurse as often as Matthew, but he nursed as long as Matthew had nursed.

For some reason I had a tremendous craving for eggnog when I was pregnant with him. Perhaps that is why I gained so much weight? To this day that man loves eggnog. We called it "Christmas milk." Recently he sent me an email, it said, in part: "I'm sitting here drinking a glass of Christmas milk, ah the memories … ."

I agree — ah, the memories. Almost all of my memories of my children are fond, good memories. They are the joy of my life.

The only time I remember Andrew getting angry with me as a baby is when I caught him eating cat food. He had crawled over to the cat dish and was eating like a cat; his fat little face was right in the dish. He was not happy with me when I took his cat food away!

Both Boys and Me

The boys were five years old and two years old when we began our lives of just the three of us. Most children sleep through the night within weeks of birth. Not my children. In fact, Matthew had seldom slept through the night by the time their dad left us. Andrew had never slept through the night. Within a week after returning home from the domestic violence shelter, both of my sons slept through the night. THAT fact alone was proof enough for me that there had been more stress in the home than I was aware of, that my children as young as they were felt the stress keenly, and that life was bound to be more peaceful in the future for us.

Because of the divorce, learning to walk again, and all the moves, I did not start Matthew in the first grade until he was seven years old. He struggled in school from day one.

I should say he struggled with classroom teaching. He thrived on the playground and socially.

One day he came home with the proud announcement that he could run faster than any other kid in the first grade.

A week or so later he came home with another announcement. He had learned a new game. It is the game in which the girls chase the boys and when a girl catches a boy, she gets to kiss him.

"And you know, Mom," he added with extreme seriousness, "I can't run very fast."

WAIT a minute … I thought he said … just last week … .

He was the only boy in the second grade to take binoculars to the 5th and 6th grade basketball games so he could watch the cheerleaders.

But I knew before then that he liked girls. When he was five years old he asked me about kissing girls.

I determined to always answer my children's questions honestly. Matthew started to ask questions early in his life.

He was eight when he asked me what sex felt like.

We had been at my father's place, where we had watched a "James Bond 007" movie. Matthew had gone down stairs and announced to my stepsister that we had just watched a movie about sex. We were on our way home when Matthew asked the question.

My answer may have been a bit evasive. "Um … uh … good?"

Then he asked what sex felt like for a guy.

Ah-ha! A question I did not know the answer to — I was not a guy.

He was persistent. Okay, then, who could he ask.

That stumped me. Certainly he could ask neither my father nor my brother. I was certain they did not approve of my open relationship with my sons.

For many of Matthew's questions, Andrew was present. Andrew, my quiet son, did not ask many questions. He did not have to. He had an older brother present to ask anything they wanted to know.

I prayed a lot.

Children are not born with "How to …" manuals. There is not a "How to raise THIS child for Dummies" book. And some of the so-called experts in child rearing, in my opinion, have their head so far up their ass that either they never raised a child themselves or their children are screwed up.

I had no more idea on how to raise these two little tow-headed boys than I knew how to rebuild a car motor.

All I knew is that I was going to communicate to them that I loved them no matter what.

I thought about the things my parents did that I did not like. Yelling. Okay, I was not going to yell at my children. Hmm, that took over a decade. Not much talking. There had not been a lot of chitchat bullshit sessions that I remember in my home growing up. That trait was easy for me to establish with the boys. I vowed to be available to them whenever they wanted to talk and to talk about whatever they wanted to talk about. I vowed to be approachable. No hugging. That attribute was very easy to me to change in my own home. I hug a lot of people all the time anyway. I like to hug. Hugging my sons was the easiest thing to do.

Hugging was not always easy for me to do. I remember hugging my sister once when she was five and I was fifteen. I felt so guilty for "spoiling" the child.

I thought about the things my parents did that I liked.

I enjoyed the Sunday night at the movies on TV that we watched as a family. My children and I had a movie night and still frequently watch movies together.

My folks took us camping almost every year; the boys and I went camping a lot. Our little six midgets (it was advertised as a six man tent, but there is no way …) tent almost got wore out we went camping so frequently. We got so we could almost stake up the tent in the dark. Levi would give me MREs (military meals-ready-to-eat), I would save them for our last day at camp so the boys would want to go home to have real food. That did not work well. Matthew, especially, really liked the MREs. Both boys liked finding out what kind of dessert was in their pouch of MREs.

One time in the spring we rented a Forrest Service Cabin outside of Livingston. We had to hike three miles to get to it. I had planned on skiing cross county to the cabin, but the snow was too melted for skiing. The sun was almost set when I saw its rays reflect off the window of the cabin. Without the sun's guidance, I am not sure we would have found the cabin that night. We were all very cold. I got a fire going in the little wood stove in the cabin and we ended up having a peaceful night.

My family of origin had a lot of time doing things together. So, with my sons, we cleaned house together; we weeded the garden together.

Wait, the boys and I did fun things together, too. We went camping and hiking together. We target shot .22s together; we got long bows and target shot with them, too. I took my boys hunting just like my father had taken me. I took my sons to cross-country ski lessons every Saturday when we lived in Bozeman. We went down-hill skiing as often as I could afford it. We played outside as often as we could. We read together and discussed what we read. I did not play Intendo though.

One time I was playing in the snow "Fox and Geese" with my sons when a schoolmate, who had been a few years ahead of me in school, stopped his vehicle on the street and stared. I guess not many Moms played in the snow with their kids the way I did.

My last year in college, they brought to me our "fun fund." This was a glass jar in which I put change. Matthew asked, with Andrew standing next to him, if we had enough money in our fun fund to go to Disney Land.

Yes.

There was $37.00 and some change in the jar.

I took out another student loan. We went to California for Christmas that year.

There was one rule in our home. Be kind.

That's it. Six letters, two simple words yet it was as difficult for the boys to learn as it was for me to practice. Yes, our household rule applied to me as well.

I obtained this "rule" from the Bible. The verse is longer than two words; the entire verse was too much for young boys to remember. "Be kind" was hard enough to practice without memorizing the entire verse.

For example, the boys did not have a curfew. We would discuss what was the kindest time for them to return home: too late and I would worry, that would not be kind of them to me; too early and they would not get to spend the amount of time with friends that they wanted, that would not be kind of me to them.

Years later I learned Matthew would try his hardest to come up with a scenario in which "be kind" would not apply. I admit there were times I had a hellova time finding an application for the rule. We both remember that I was always successful in finding an application.

We also had a philosophy in the home. I taught them that families worked together and played together. They helped with all aspects of house cleaning and home caring. When Andrew bought his first home, his girlfriend was surprised at the number of "handy man" things he could do — especially because he had been raised without a father.

I admit I went over board at times. Once, when we were still living in Bozeman, Matthew came home with a joke.

"How many men does it take to clean a toilet?"

"I don't know, how many?"

"None, that's women's work."

I did not clean the toilet for YEARS. Andrew wondered why HE got punished for the "joke" as well and had to alternate cleaning the toilet with Matthew. I remember, by then, we had two toilets. I cleaned the main floor bathroom and they took turns cleaning the upstairs bathroom. But, I could be wrong and he could be right.

I was adamant in my conviction that they would learn to share in household chores; they would not have the attitude such as their father had about roles in the home. I may have gone overboard on this as well.

Many years later Matthew lived with a gal. She became pissy toward me. When they visited me, she asked me why I never taught Matthew how to wash dishes or how to clean house. I was shocked. I looked at him; he grinned at me.

Just because someone knows how to do something does not mean they will chose to do it once they have the freedom of choice.

I am not real keen on the commercialism of modern Christmas. The boys would often sneakily unwrap and then rewrap their Christmas gifts so there was no surprise on Christmas morning. And considering Andrew's birthday was only a few days before Christmas, I did not go "all out" buying gifts for that holiday. Instead, I would buy gifts whenever I saw something I thought the boys or someone would like. For others, I kept the gifts until Christmas. But with my sons, I would give them "I love you" gifts throughout the year.

Once when Andrew's bike was stolen, I said, "Let's get in the car." He did not know why but he obeyed. I drove to Havre and bought him a new bike. It was the only brand new bike I have ever purchased. Andrew was surprised. It was not his birthday, it was no holiday. When he asked me why, I simply said it was an "I love you gift."

We still give "I love you gifts" to each other. It is always a joy and a surprise to see what they come up with. Once Matthew gave me a bag of rubber bands — why? Simply because he knew we did not have any. Another time he gave me a set of Pyrex cooking and bakeware; my favorite cookware. Andrew's gifts are more apt to be more practical in a way. For example computer related items such as an external hard drive or expensive software. Their gifts are beautiful expressions of love.

Back to the struggle of their school years: When we moved to Bozeman for me to attend college, Matthew entered the third grade. Within a week the school phoned me and recommended he be retained back into the second grade as he was not ready for the third grade. Andrew went to day care.

Matthew did okay the second time in second grade. The male teacher he had was excellent. But, he had a hellova time in the third grade the following year.

There was a war going on at the time. My son had an extreme anti-war passivist for a teacher.

Shortly after their father left, my sons started to insist in wearing "army clothes." Matthew was much more militant about the decision. He would not wear jeans, only fatigues or camouflage print pants. He insisted on equal types of shirts. They played army games. I did not think this was odd. My brother spent his entire childhood playing army man.

My sons built booby traps.

Once Matthew helped the younger kids at Andrew's babysitter's build a booby trap at the babysitter's house. He showed them how it worked. The babysitter called me. I immediately went to her house. My oldest son had gotten hit in the mouth by a flying brick. His mouth bled profusely. Yes, the booby trap worked just fine.

On the drive home afterwards, I said, "I have something I want to tell you."

Matthew sullenly said, "Yeah, and I know what you're going to say."

His tone of voice irritated me. “Oh yeah,” I said, “and what am I going to say?”

“No more booby traps.”

That was exactly what I was going to say. But I was not going to have him think he could read my mind so I said, “No, that is not what I was going to say.”

He looked at me.

“I was going to say that I want you to make a booby trap as soon as we get home.”

He looked at me with surprise and I realized I had said the right thing. Like riding a horse, a person has to get back on after getting bucked off in order to not become afraid of trying or of riding.

He made a booby trap near our front walk, with Andrew’s help. As far as I can remember, that was the last booby trap they ever made.

But the military style clothing continued. His third grade teacher was very successful in communicating to him that he was unacceptable.

He started to say things to me such as, “When I go to prison, Mom, will you visit me?”

“When? Don’t you mean if?”

“No, … when.”

He quit school

“You cannot quit school at ten years old.”

He looked me straight in the eye and said, “Wanna bet?”

I called my father in total exasperation, frustration, and desperation.

He said … “God’s revenge.”

And then my father hung up on me.

I sat in my chair at a total loss. My father called me back and suggested I call the nuns in North Dakota and ask them to pray for my son.

I did. I did not know what else to do.

Two things happened.

First, Matthew got sick. I sat on the floor indian-style and held him.

He finally looked up and me and said, “You really do love me don’t you?”

“Of course I do.”

"Dad said you didn't." He relaxed. No wonder Matthew struggled with self-acceptance at such a young age when he was taught by his father that his own mother did not love and accept him! How a parent could do such damage to their children is beyond my comprehension.

After that bout with the flu, Matthew's attitude and behavior toward me changed.

Second, my talks with his teacher did not avail to any change. I went to the Principal. The last week (or day) of school, Matthew's teacher gave him a book about Colin Powell, one of Matthew's hero's. That simple gesture on her part communicated to him that interest in things military really was alright.

I had asked the Principal, several times, for Matthew to be tested. I knew he did not lack in intelligence, yet, his struggle in school was horrific. She, the Principal, would not do so — she gave the excuse of the cost to the school district and to the budget.

A new school opened in Bozeman, The Wilson School of Technology. This alternative grade school was to be ungraded and "unclassed" — meaning there would not be strict "A, B, C, D, F" grades and that children would not get solely lumped together with other children their exact age. The students would advance when they were ready and would spend two years in one classroom. I enrolled the boys in this new school. Andrew started the first grade; Matthew started fourth grade. Matthew's teacher also transferred from his former school, so she was aware of Matthew and his struggles. Matthew had her for two years; she was a great teacher. He learned under her teaching style.

When we moved to the country in November of my senior year in college; we moved to a different school district. I asked this teacher of Matthew's for her advice. She suggested we just not say anything and for me to keep the children in the Wilson school. I did.

The teacher at the one-room school house in the country heard of us living in the school district and she turned us in. She needed more students in her little school and she wanted my sons enrolled there.

The Superintendent of Schools contacted me and informed me that my sons had to leave the Wilson school and attend the country school.

I went back to Matthew's teacher for advice. She simply said, in her opinion, because we would leave Bozeman in a few short months with my pending graduation and because of Matthew's difficulties in school that it would not be in Matthew's best interest to start in a different school.

I informed the Superintendent of Schools that I was now homeschooling my sons. I learned a lot about my sons during those six months of homeschooling.

I learned that, although Andrew is above average intelligence and is probably a genius, he had inherited my inability to spell. I gave them writing assignments and would take their spelling words from what the spelled incorrectly on the assignment. I think Andrew went to college spelling "this" as "thes." Maybe he graduated from college spelling the word his way, I do not know.

I still have the gift Andrew made for me during those first two years of his formal education. I display the back side of it on which he wrote: "Dear Mom I lave yu with my hrt Mom plez cep thes mother ba pesit. And dot for git, I lave yuu, Mom Andrew" The translation is: "Dear Mom, I love you with my heart. Mom, please accept this Mother's Day present. And don't forget, I love you Mom. Andrew" The front has a nicely printed poem and his hand print. But it is his hand written message of love on the back that I display and that I cherish. It is one of the best "I love you gifts" I have ever received.

I also have the book he wrote in the second grade. His teacher found a publishing house in Colorado that would print a copy of a book students wrote. His was, by far, the best made up story of his class. It is a story of a young woodpecker bird who liked to get dirty and not wash.

Andrew had a lot of practice making up stories. We all did. We would each take turns embellishing a story line. We quit this after a few years though because Andrew would always say the same thing, "and there was a bunny rabbit hopping down the road." Matthew and I would try to create a story in which Andrew could not add those words. It did not work. I would start a story with something such as "Once upon a time (all good stories begin this way and all of our stories began that way) there once was a man who lived in a huge industrial city … ." Matthew would continue the story line "The city was at war and the man was a soldier … ." Andrew would add, "and there was a bunny rabbit hopping down the road."

Now how did that bunny rabbit get into the war zone in the city?

I also learned that my sons still liked for me to read to them. So we revisited that childhood habit. But they were older now, so we would discuss the book I read to them. We began to discuss the books they read as well. By the time we moved to Chinook, we frequently had two hour suppers during which we would discuss what we read.

One morning, my supervisor at work in Chinook was a bit peeved at me. I had missed an important evening meeting with some dignitaries form Washington DC the night before.

"Just what" he wanted to know, "were you doing that was so important that you forgot the meeting?"

I had dramatically read "Hop Frog" by Edgar Allen Poe to my sons. A "dramatic reading" is interpretation while acting out the reading. So, yeah, I acted out "Hop Frog" for my sons when I should have been hobnobbing with big shots.

I told my supervisor what I had done the evening before.

He never said another word. He simply stared at me. In the upcoming weeks, I would catch him staring at me with the same dumbfounded, confused look on his face that he first looked at me with the day I confessed to a two hour supper of reading and acting Poe with my sons.

My supervisor was not the only person dumbfounded by the open, talking relationship I had with my sons. A co-worker once asked me if I had worked on a computer program at home the night before.

"No," I confessed.

Why not, she wanted to know. She had recommended, had told me to, work on it at home.

I continued my confession. Andrew had wanted to talk. He and I ended up talking for two hours.

She looked away from me and was silent for several long seconds. Finally she said in a strange voice, still staring off into space not looking at me, "I cannot imagine talking to one of my kids for twenty minutes let alone two hours."

I thought to myself, *Yeah, and that is why your kids are the way they are.*

Andrew wants to talk when Andrew wants to talk. He does not always want to talk when someone else wants to talk. He does not want to talk often. But, when he wants to talk, he wants to talk. I have learned to set aside whatever I am doing whenever he wants to visit.

Once after a 19 hour day for me, Andrew wanted to talk. After two hours of trying to stay awake and totally present in order to listen to him, I finally said, "Honey, I need to sleep. Can we continue this conversation when I am in your town in a few days?"

I do not think he was totally happy with me, but he agreed. He was an adult by this time.

A couple of days later we talked for nine hours straight.

A person has to pay attention to Andrew or risk missing what was going on in his life. When he was little and sick, he would wake me up in the middle of the night.

"I'm sick, Mom."

I would immediately start to get out of bed.

"No, you don't have to get out of bed. I'm going to sleep in the bathroom in case I need to puke in the night."

"Honey, I'll get blankets for you and make you a bed."

"I already did that, Mom. I just woke you up to let you know in case you can't find me in my bed in the morning so you don't worry about me. You can go back to sleep now."

Once when Mom came to Bozeman to watch the boys while I flew somewhere to speak, Andrew had an accident. In his vocabulary of an eight year old, he said a little girl "indicated" that she wanted to kiss him. He climbed to the top of a swing set and fell off; he landed on his right arm. Andrew complained to Mom that his arm hurt. For two days, he would mention, somewhat frequently, that his arm really did hurt a lot.

Mom had to take Matthew to the doctor for a scheduled visit. To appease Andrew she asked for an x-ray of his arm. The ulna was broke up near the shoulder. Mom felt so badly about not taking him to the emergency room right away after the accident. But that is the way Andrew is — he does not cry, whine, pitch a fit, or throw a tantrum. He simply, quietly, and determinedly states what is going on in his life, what he wants, and what he thinks. And he expects people to listen to him.

Within six weeks or so of breaking his arm he began to have seizures but we did not know they were seizures at the time. Within three months of him breaking his arm we were living in Chinook and I had taken him to the emergency room because of what looked like convulsions when he had the flu. The ER staff could not find anything wrong with him. He did not seize in the ER.

The boys' father came to Chinook to pick them up for the summer. It was hard for me to move back to Chinook with all the memories. I guess it was hard for him to think of us moving back to Chinook as well; he had memories, too. Neither of us had many good memories of when we lived in that town years prior.

In August I looked forward to the boys' return. I had bought our first house. Mom and I painted it and I had moved in. The house was ready for occupancy by the three of us.

Their dad called and said he would leave Tennessee on such and such date. I waited. They did not show up. I feared an automobile wreck somewhere along the highway. I did not know if they were hurt, dead, or where they were. I was in a panic!

At one point a woman said, "Well at least they aren't dead."

But I did not know if they were dead or not. Missing children causes more of a fear and dread in a parent than deceased children. Dead, a parent knows they are no longer in harm's way. Missing, a parent knows only their nightmares and the horrific stories of sadistic abuse to abducted children. Not knowing is worse than knowing.

I started to phone my ex-husband, no one answered; I started to phone his parents. They did not have much to say at first. After a few repeated calls, my father-in-law confessed that my ex was still in Tennessee with the boys, that he had enrolled the boys in school down there, and he had filed papers against me.

The next day the local police served me papers. It was a restraining order. I was not to phone anyone in my ex's family. And there was a court date set for change in custody hearing for the day after my upcoming birthday. There was a claim that I did not provide for my children proper medical care and that Andrew suffered from epilepsy.

Later I learned after a person develops a seizure disorder that seizures can be brought on by stress, inconsistent sleeping patterns, and/or inconsistent or poor eating habits. On the trip to Tennessee Andrew's seizures increased exponentially. A doctor in Chattanooga diagnosed the seizure disorder; he got to witness Andrew's seizing.

I made arraignments to fly to Tennessee for the hearing. My mom went with me. We stayed at the home of my former roommate,Thea.

Thea secured a lawyer for me. She said he had a reputation of winning his court cases. I walked into this office to meet him. He was Afro-American. He must have thought I reacted to his color. But Thea also had told me he was Black.

He said, "If you are not comfortable with me, I can help you find a different attorney."

I had not reacted to his race and I said, "I don't care if you're Green as long as you help me get my kids back." I sat down in a chair across the desk from him.

We went to work.

One thing I requested was to be allowed to be with my sons on my birthday. Thea had driven Mom and me out to where my ex-husband and his second wife lived. We had spied on them from the road and we had seen the boys outside the house. I knew they were okay. The lawyer said not to do that again.

My ex did not want to allow me to spend time with our sons. The lawyer told me that my ex said he feared I would take off for Montana with them. I promised my lawyer I would not do so. My lawyer said that if I had not heard from him by noon of the day of my birthday, that he would have been unsuccessful in obtaining permission for me to see the boys.

Noon came and went on the day of my 34th birthday. In the afternoon, Thea and Mom drove to town while I stayed at Thea's house to watch her children.

At 4:00 my attorney phoned. I could pick up the boys at 5:00 and they could hang out with me until 8:00.

I did not have a vehicle at my disposal. This was in the days before cell phones; I had no way to contact Thea.

At 4:45 Thea and Mom arrived. I quickly told Thea what was going on. She allowed me to take her car and drive to the meeting place, my lawyer's office.

My ex showed up with the kids. The boys acted a bit shy. As soon as we were alone together in Thea's car they began to ask questions.

"What are you doing here, Mom?"

"We didn't think we would see YOU in Tennessee."

"We're in school here. It's okay, but we go to a different school than (their step-brother and sisters)."

"Why are you here?"

They had no idea what was really going on. Their father had told them that I had a new boyfriend and that I did not want them anymore.

I feel the anger again as I write this. To tell children that their parent does not love or want them anymore has got to be one of the most traumatizing things to a child that a parent can say. I did not want the boys to know how pissed off I felt. I tried to answer their questions casually.

At Thea's house we had birthday cake and ice cream. The boys played with Thea's two kids. I felt a little miffed that they were not happier to see me. But they were content and at peace being with me so they played with other children such as happy children will do.

When it was time to take them back to their father, I was again, alone with them in the vehicle. We talked about the possibility of returning to Montana with me or staying in Tennessee with their father.

I asked them what they would prefer. I feared their answer. They were my life. I had no desire to live without them. By this time I had lost four babies. I always wanted six children (why, I have no idea

— raising children to be responsible, well-adjusted, interdependent adults is the toughest job in the world); well, I had six pregnancies and two live births. My two living sons were and are more important to me than anything else in life.

Andrew, like many bright, imaginative kids, had an invisible friend. He said his friend flew along beside the car as I drove. His friend was somewhat like a honey bee. He asked his friend what the friend thought.

Andrew told me that his friend said to return to Montana with me.

Matthew concurred that it would be good to go back to Montana with me also.

I prayed about the hearing outcome.

The next day, the judge told the boys' dad that if he wanted to contest the custody of the children, he would have to file suit in Blaine County Montana, where the divorce was issued. The judge also told me that I had to have a pediatric neurologist for Andrew or be in violation of his order.

There was one pediatric neurologist in all of Montana. Andrew went to him for several years. In my opinion the man was an idiot. As soon as we could, we found a neurologist who specialized in seizure disorders. Unfortunately that doctor has since left Montana but for the years Andrew went to him, he was encouraging to Andrew.

Andrew's seizures are not common. But like the specialist stated, if it looks like a duck, quacks like a duck, swims like a duck, and walks like a duck — let's call it a duck.

Andrew and I discussed the possibility of never being allowed a driver's license, of the possible need to live where there was public transportation, and of living a regular life. I never told him he could not do something due to having seizures. He swims, he drives, and he plays paint ball wars.

I did not realize that I had the option of trying to shelter him and his life until he met a friend in college who had cerebral palsy (CP). That kid's dad allowed him to fully live and experience life as well. I have a friend with CP. His parents did not fully accept and support their son; he is one messed up guy.

I read once that we all have different abilities. Instead of using the word "disability" we should simply say "different abilities." If there were 700 different abilities available for us to choose and we could choose 300, there would be three hundred things we could do well. Yet there would be 400 things we could not do well. Humanity's different abilities is what give life and friendships such a rich savor. Different abilities give life and friendships complimentary skills. Perhaps this is why it is said that "opposites attract."

Matthew's class had read Homer's Odysseys in school. Matthew acted out for Andrew and me, at home, the stories. Yet, he flunked the test in school. I knew he knew the material. I finally succeeded in convincing a school district to test him; he was in his second year of High School. Yep, I was correct. He has two different learning styles. I will not label them learning disabilities.

One, learning difference Matthew has is hearing comprehension. This means he does not totally comprehend what other people say when they do not allow him to interact with them in conversation. We had other odd names for common items besides eggnog being Christmas milk. We had a dirty clothes "hamster" in our house. We rode up to the top of tall buildings in an "alligator." One of our favorite meals was "Cuban Snake" which is simply cube steak. One time, when we lived in Bozeman, Matthew asked me what a "homeless sexual" was. I had no idea. Maybe someone who slept under a bridge and … . Some kid at school had called one of my sons some name that sounded like … oh, he meant "homosexual." There were clues Matthew did not understand the spoken word well.

Two, the other learning difference Matthew has is written expression. This means he cannot write down what he knows in his head.

Together this means the traditional way of education: lectures, note taking, and written testing, is truly impossible for Matthew to do. Matthew did not learn how to read until he was in the fifth grade; by seventh grade he read at a full adult level. Talk about a bright kid once his learning style is enacted! He learns through his eyes, through reading. He shares this knowledge through his mouth, through talking or discussing.

School personnel met with me and we devised an "individual education plan" (IEP). They did not, would not, follow their own plan. I continued to hound the school on my son's behalf. He turned eighteen the beginning of his junior year. The Principal told me my son was now an adult and I could not fight for him in the school district any longer.

Matthew quit formal education. Within weeks he obtained his GED; the woman who gave him the test said he scored higher than anyone else had ever done per their records.

One of my greatest difficulties as a parent was to encourage Andrew's acumen while not appearing to insult Matthew's struggles. It was challenging to hearten Matthew while not hindering Andrew's proficiency.

Andrew had a great sixth grade teacher who assisted me. His fifth grade teacher did nothing to challenge Andrew. Andrew was an easy student, not making waves or difficulties in the classroom (unlike his brother). His fifth grade teacher basically ignored him for a year.

But his sixth grade teacher, who lived next door, came to my house over the summer and told me she would have Andrew in her classroom that fall. Was there anything she should know about him?

Yes.

I told her about his quietness and how, due to his seizures, he did not like direct attention. I asked her to arrange for him challenges. I said I believed he would rise to any challenge she had for him.

She challenged him in the classroom. Andrew rose to every challenge and excelled.

They had another "life touching" experience together as well.

We had a tree with a rope swing in the back yard. One day, while I was still at work, Andrew climbed the rope and somehow fell and got tangled in the rope at the same time. He hung there, upside down, calling for help.

The teacher, our neighbor woman, heard his cries.

That menopausal woman leaped the chain link fence that separated our yards, lifted my son up, and helped to untangle his legs. How she was able to do so at her age is only a testament to the power of an adrenaline rush.

Matthew told me about it. I discussed this with Andrew. I did not tell him to never climb the rope again but to be careful. He wanted to do something special for our neighbor woman. I gave him some money; he went to the floral shop.

She came to the fence while I pulled weeds in the garden. She wanted to let me know what happened and how he could have died had the rope tangled around his neck instead of his legs. I kept glancing down the alley. I did not say much to her. I already knew the story and I knew what would have happened if the rope had tangled differently. She was quite upset about the whole ordeal.

I saw Andrew walking up the alley. I turned to her and said that I knew what happened, that the boys had told me, and that I knew what would have happened if the rope had tangled differently.

Andrew neared.

I said I wanted to thank her and that Andrew had something to say to her.

Andrew handed her the flowers and solemnly said, “Thank you for saving my life.”

She immediately got tears in her eyes, turned, and fled to her home. She never mentioned the incident again.

Because Andrew feared the embarrassment of having seizures in public, he avoided the public or direct attention. Yet, he wanted to be a part of the “high school scene.” He joined pep band. The High School had a great pep band those years Andrew was able to contribute. Pep band truly allowed him to participate in High School.

Matthew did not have any trouble with public attention, both in school and in the public. Once in the same newspaper edition, his picture was on the front page for selling lemonade on the street corner. Later in the paper Matthew, unnamed, was listed as someone who the local police had been called about shooting off fireworks or fire crackers inside of the city limits.

Matthew worked in the local grocery store. With his extroverted personality, I think everyone in town knew him. When he left home Andrew got a job at the same grocery store. People would come up to me and ask, "What's wrong with Matthew? He is not as friendly as he used to be."

I would explain that Matthew no longer lived in town and that it was my younger, not so gregarious son, Andrew, who now worked in the store.

Often they would look at me in shock. "You have TWO sons?" they would exclaim.

This was after living in Chinook for at least six years. Chinook is a town of 750 households. Basically everyone knows everyone. Yet my younger, shyer, quieter son few people realized existed.

Part of the reason people did not realize I had two boys is the fact my sons looked very much alike. Many people commented on my "twins." Matthew, more than three years older than Andrew, did not like this much. Often, when people saw Andrew, they assumed he was Matthew.

The other reason people did not realize I had two sons is that Andrew used to be very shy and quiet. He never got in trouble in school or in the community. He was more the studious bookworm type of child. He, I think, was also sneakier about the things he did than Matthew was. It was obvious when Matthew would do something; it took close observation to notice when Andrew did something.

Teasing takes place a lot in the family. One time, Mom teased Andrew that if he kept drinking milk, he would grow up to be bigger than Matthew and he would not fit in the family. Andrew is the only one who likes to drink milk. Matthew and I both dislike it greatly.

Andrew looked at his grandmother and remarked, "Don't worry, Grandma, I'll still fit. I'll still be weird."

He was maybe ten years old at that time.

I encouraged individual thinking and honoring one's own unique personality. We called it "being weird" when the boys were young.

When Andrew was in junior high he made a comment in his English class about his family being weird. His teacher got after him, unaccepting of his term for his family. Confused, he came home and asked me what was wrong with being weird.

"Nothing," I answered, "why do you ask?"

He told me what his teacher had said.

Knowing his teacher, Matthew had her as the junior high English teacher as well, I said, "Tomorrow, tell her your family is eccentric with a few idiosyncrasies."

"What does THAT mean?"

"It means that we're weird."

He did not do it.

My niece, Lesley, celebrates quirks as well. When she told her new boyfriend that he was weird, his feelings were hurt. Oh no, no, no … to be told from someone in our family that you are weird is a compliment. Later, this same boyfriend was to become her husband. They are fantastic people.

We celebrated not being "run of the mill." We did not have television; we had a TV for movies but no prime time, cable, or local viewing. EVERYONE else had TV, or so my children said.

My father once said that if I got TV, the boys would watch sports, would get interested in sports, would want to play sports in school, and then, Matthew would get better grades. I asked my sons if they would watch sports if we had a TV. Their answer was no, they would not be interested in sports and had no desire to watch sports on television. We did not get TV.

Instead of watching mind numbing shows, so frequently of people hurting other people, we read instead. And we talked about what we read. I read all the books my sons read. They would quiz each other about characters and events in different series of books. I did not remember all the characters and events in each individual book. Their retention of the storyline was amazing to me.

My home was open to all young people.

Andrew came home from grade school one time and asked if he could bring a certain kid home with him.

"Of course," I answered. "You know any one is welcome in our home, why do you ask?"

"Mom," he said, "this kid needs you to teach him how to act."

"What do you mean?"

He sighed. "I'll bring him home, and then you'll see what I mean."

He started to have this kid over after school. It did not take me long to understand what my son had meant. This young man had been sent to his room to watch TV or to play video games for his entire life. He had no idea how to interact with others, how to interact within a family, or how to be polite.

I began to slowly, subtly teach the young man such simple things such as how to say "please" and "thank you," how to chew with his mouth closed, and how to eat what was set before him.

One of the many times when he said, "Ew, I'm not eating THAT."

I said, "Yes you are. Try one."

After trying one, he ate the whole jar of pickled green beans. My home-canned pickled green beans are one of our family's favorite condiments.

Another time Andrew came home from grade school and said, "Mom, will you talk to (a friend of his)."

"Sure. Why? What's up?"

"He has a problem. He tried to talk to me about it but I don't know what to say to him. I don't know what it is like to have the problem he has. I told him when I had a problem I talked to you about it. He can't talk to his parents about his problem. He asked if he could talk to you."

Sure.

Matthew, on the other hand, talked to me about things for his friends, often with his friend present. I knew the information was actually for the friend when the friend lurked in the other room as I answered my son's questions.

I often agonized about the viewpoint I was giving these children — other parent's children. It turns out that many of them were very grateful for my help and advice. Even some parents who know of my talks with their children were grateful. Today I am more relaxed with the idea that I influence people with my writing.

One thing my frank discussions about all topics under the sun and open door policy did was communicate to the young people who hung out at my house that I cared for them. One young man, in particular, was a very difficult young man.

We met him when we looked for a place to live; his parents had a house in the country for rent. He was in Matthew's class. The first day of school, he came home to our house after school with Matthew.

Later that evening I received a phone call from a woman who lived completely across town on the other side of the little city.

She said, "I understand you allowed (this child) in your home today."

I was surprised she knew. I should have known that in small towns "everyone knows everything about everybody." I answered her, "Yes, he was here after school for a while."

"Well, if you want to be accepted in Chinook, you will not have children such as (his name) in your home."

That was not something to say to me. I said to her, "Any and all children are welcome in my home, including (his name). I don't give a rat's ass if I am accepted in Chinook or not. BUT any child is welcome in my home." I hung up the phone. For the ten years I lived in that town that woman never so much as acknowledged me, let alone spoke to me again.

No problem. I know some of her history and she would or should be embarrassed if I told it.

At times it was difficult to have this child in my home. He was the town bully. There were times my sons would ask that I not allow this child in my home. But, he was always welcome in my home.

As he grew into a young man, whenever I saw him I would give him a hug. He, like many young people, did not always make very wise choices. I think he learned from his mistakes.

Years later I was asked to develop a made-for-television documentary about my young adult novels and to have interviewed adults who I influenced (for the good) when they were children. I went to where this young man worked.

He greeted me with a hug and stated the fact he was no longer on probation, no longer in trouble with the law. Then he said hello. He agreed to be interviewed. I was a little surprised at some of his answers on how I influenced his life. And he was correct; I cared for him and always try to "be there" for him. He has moved to a further western state to follow his dream of being a helicopter pilot. I hear he is doing well.

Another young man did not come to our home often. He was in Matthew's class. Every time I saw him, I would greet him enthusiastically, "Hey (his name), how ya doing?"

He asked Matthew, "Man, your mom always is so friendly to me. She's not like that with other guys in our class. Do you think she knows I'm high when she sees me?"

Matthew remarked dryly, "Yeah, I think she can tell."

Duh.

This young man is still in my life. He has tried several times to clean up his life. He struggles in doing so. I continue to greet and to hug him whenever I see him. He knows I love him and am always "there" for him.

Young men have been an important part of my life's ministry as far back as my own junior high years. When I was in junior high, I volunteered at a "Day Camp" for younger kids. I think it was a 4-H thing. There was a young boy in that week long day care that touched my heart. I do not know if Michael had birth defects or mentally different abilities; I know he was a little unlike the others. He died in a trampoline accident when he was a teenager.

Shortly after meeting Michael, I decided I wanted to work with children in my life. I volunteered as Junior Leader at 4-H camp, I was a Camp Counselor at Bible Camp, and my major in Bible College was recreation and education. I knew I did not want to be a teacher; I did not want to be between administration, parents, and students. But I knew I wanted to help children not to feel the way I felt when I was young.

I became a Youth Pastor after Bible College. A position I held in all of the churches we attended until Aaron died.

With my drinking out of control, I did not think God could use me to positively influence children once I sobered up. Surely churches did not want an ex-drunk as a Youth Pastor.

After a little over a month of sobriety, the local teen group for young people whose parent's drinking had affected them voted me in as the adult facilitator of their group. Most of the attendees lived at the Christian Youth Ranch where years before my first dating boyfriend, Mike, had worked. These young men changed my life. The Ranch, as it was referred to, was home to at least a dozen young men. My take on it is that these young men were "too bad" for foster care, yet "too good" for reform school.

There were about six to eight of these young men in the group I facilitated, plus about four young people from the community.

One of the young men from The Ranch asked me if he could borrow my car. He had a driver's license. I let him take and use my car.

Later someone in town asked me about my wild, dangerous driving. At first I did not know what they meant. We traced down the day and time and I realized it was when this young man had borrowed my car.

The next week at group I brought up the topic of honesty. I picked people to share on the topic; I waited for this particular young man until last.

Finally I looked at him and asked him if he had driven my car in an erratic manner.

He boldly stared into my eyes.

One of the other boys from The Ranch piped up and quickly said, "No, he didn't."

I turned to that boy and said, "(his name), I did not ask you, I asked (the driver's name)." I returned my eyes to the driver.

He continued to stare into my eyes as he answered, "Yes." The way he answered felt like a challenge.

I thanked him for his honesty and closed the group.

Later that evening, when enough time had passed for those boys to have returned to The Ranch, I phoned The Ranch and asked to speak with him. I was still fuming angry with him but I really did not know what I wanted to say to him. All I knew is that I wanted to talk out what had happened.

"What do you want?" he asked.

"I want to talk to you."

"You're going to say that you regret letting me use your car and you will never do that again." His voice was defiant.

"No, that is not what I planned to say. What I want to say to you is to thank you again for your honesty. I appreciate it very much."

There was silence on the phone.

"If you want to borrow my car again, you may - if you give me your word that you will drive in a responsible manner. Because of your honesty tonight, I trust you will not drive recklessly if you say you will not."

There was more silence on the phone. But I could sense something was happening in this young man. I waited in silence as well.

Finally he choked, "Why?"

"Because I love you."

More muffled chokes.

"(His name), you don't think you are lovable do you?"

No answer.

I was exasperated. "(His name), I love you."

"Why?" he sobbed quietly.

"(His name), love is a choice. I love you because I have love to give and I chose to give it to you. You act as though you are unlovable, but … inside of you I can see such a wonderful person. I know you have been through a lot of shit in your life. But, (his name) you are a lovable person and I love you."

He hung up the phone but not before I could hear him give way to his tears.

He never asked to borrow my car again. In fact he barely ever spoke to me again. But I would catch him looking at me in group with a strange half-grin on his face.

I lost contact with most of the young people from group when I left for college. One guy, who did not live at The Ranch, and I stayed in contact for nearly a decade. When I graduated from college, he got me in touch with the young man who had spoken up (and lied) in the driver's defense and who had lived at The Ranch. This wild young man and I have stayed in contact throughout the past decades. All others I have lost contact, including the one I had stayed in contact with for many years at first.

This wild young man, with whom I have retained our friendship, told me that after my phone conversation with the driver that the driver changed. He went from being super sullen to simply being quiet. Although the driver rarely spoke to me again, he was the first to remember what night group was on and to get ready for the trip into town. The last I heard is that the driver had gotten a job as an electrician at Disney World in Florida and was married. I hope he is doing well.

I only know of three of the young men from The Ranch whom I knew during that period who did not end up in prison: the driver, his defender, and the defender's brother.

There were a few years during which I lost contact with the wild young defender. I had gotten sick and lost contact with many people.

When Andrew first attended college, he worked in the grocery store in the university town. He told me of a co-worker who taught him how to spot shop-lifters.

One day when I went into the store to visit my son, I ran into my old buddy, the young wild defender of crazy drivers. We stood in the aisle hugging. He asked, "What are you doing here?"

In the embrace, I answered, "I came here to see my son."

"Who's your son?" He relaxed his embrace and looked at me.

We both noticed a shocked faced young man standing next to us.

"Mom, what are you doing hugging him?"

"Andrew is your son!" He laughed. "I can't believe he is your little boy all grown up! How can he be YOUR son, he is such a good guy!"

"Mom, how do you know him?"

Andrew knew the story of this young man and his brother, but he did not know that his co-worker who taught him how to spot shoplifters was one in the same person.

This young man also agreed to be interviewed on the documentary. Again, what he said surprised me. He said that he and his brother had been in twenty-three different foster homes in a ridiculously short amount of time — a year, two years, I do not remember. They each had a garbage bag of clothes and "stuff" that they had learned not to unpack.

In the interview he said what I did that made the largest difference in his life is that … I trusted him.

I did not know I was not supposed to trust him. All relationships are based on trust. Looking back, I can see with his long dark hair, black clothing, and defiant attitude why people were afraid of him and afraid to trust him.

This young man learned I trusted him when he asked to spend the night at my home. He was granted permission. He hung out with other local teens until the appointed time to be at my home.

For some unknown reason, I woke up at 5:00AM. I never wake up early. I got up and checked the house. This young man was gone. I did not smoke in the house, but it was too cold to go outside in my pajamas so I went into the bathroom and turned on the fan.

I heard a noise. It was this young man returning to my home. He joined me in the bathroom for a cigarette. The young men who lived at The Ranch were not supposed to smoke, but I never stopped them from this infraction of the rules.

We did not talk much, sitting there in my bathroom — me in my nightgown and he with a smirk on his face. I did not know if the smirk was to dare me to say something about his behavior or if it was about smoking in the bathroom in my sleeping attire.

I had to think about what to do. Per the rules, I was to turn him in for sneaking out during the night. I knew what I was supposed to do. But, I had snuck out many, many times as a teen. Sneaking out at night, I think, is a common, normal part of the teen years. At least in my life experience it was normal behavior. At least one of my sons also took to sneaking out at night.

I decided not to turn him in. I talked to him about letting me know if he wanted to stay out later at night if he was granted permission to spend the night in town again so I would not worry about him.

He learned I trusted him. I learned he was a normal teenager who had lived an abnormal childhood.

A couple of years ago his grade school aged son was asked in a newspaper interview for whom he would vote for President and why. "My dad." he said, "because he plays football with us in the street."

My wild young friend made the commitment that his children would not have the childhood he had. He sticks to that decision. I am proud of him as if he were one of my own sons.

And I am immensely proud of my sons.

New Life

The boys and I settled into our new life in Chinook. The boys had their friends and school; I had my friends and work. I thoroughly enjoyed what I did for a living. I valued the conservation practices I assisted landowners in developing and implementing on their land. I established good working relationships with the producers with whom I worked and assisted. I had the opportunity to spend a lot of time with Vinee. For three years my life podded along well. Then tragedy hit again.

The boys and I went camping for nearly a week over the Fourth of July weekend. We borrowed horses from Vinee and rode off into the Missouri Breaks.

A rancher I had worked with on a stock water pipeline project out near the Missouri Breaks had shown me a Kid Curry Hideout. The boys and I rode to the famous outlaw hideout and puttered around in the canyon. We did not camp there. We camped at an old sheep shed and corral so there would be a small pasture in which to turn out the horses at night.

It rained. We moved our tarp and sleeping bags into the old sheep barn.

I unexpectedly got my period. Having not planned for this monthly visitor to show up on our camping trip, I was unprepared. I simply used "yesterday's socks" for pads.

Apparently I caught a virus by using the dirty socks.

Within two weeks I suffered severe headaches. A week or so later I finally went to the doctor.

This jerk was also an alcoholic. He had been to treatment several times for his disease. He had lost his practice in Havre due to his drinking and for some unknown reason the clinic in Chinook hired him. I know of people in Havre who think that he, in his drunken stupor or alcohol affected brain, contributed to their loved one's demise.

My blood tests showed high liver enzymes. One indication of high liver enzymes, such as mine, is that the person is a daily drinker and got drunker than a skunk the night before.

He knew what was wrong with me. I, as he did, tried to hide my drinking while attending meetings geared to help people not to drink alcohol.

Wrong. I was eight years sober and was not drinking alcohol, let alone drinking nightly.

The asshole, er, I mean doctor, would not listen to me. He tried to treat me for excessive alcohol consumption. He sent me to a liver specialist in Great Falls who was quite rude and very rough in his taking of a blood sample. The Specialist said that he would not treat me until I became honest about my drinking.

Dammit, I was honest. I did not drink alcohol.

The headaches persisted. I began to miss a lot of work. We headed into our busy season in the agency. Later I calculated that I missed 40% of my work week, yet was expected to do my job as a Soil Conservationist, plus the extra autumn responsibilities of, what we called "crop cop," residue management on summer fallow fields that reduces wind erosion. In addition, I had received specialized training through the Army Corps of Engineers and had become a Wetland Specialist. As the Wetland Specialist, in our four-county team, I was expected to drop everything in my office to answer the requests from other offices for wetland delineation or wetland evaluation.

When I went to work I pushed myself unmercifully. I had a job to do and I had to do it. At home I crashed in the recliner as soon as I got home from work — on the days I actually went to work. I barely functioned at home. I wore clothes I found on the floor to work. The boys began to help cook supper … help … hmm … they began to cook supper. Laundry and house cleaning waned. I continued to seek medical advice. I saw a therapist weekly to try and deal with the stress at work. I went to any and all medical specialists recommended. None of them could diagnosis the cause of the headaches and growing fatigue.

Under stress, the weakest link breaks.

Unbeknownst for several years, I had a post-traumatic stress disorder (PTSD) breakdown on the job.

During the violent rape ten years previous, the assailant had grabbed the hair on the back of my head and bounced my face off of the dash of his truck several times. I was knocked unconscious. When I came to, my head was between my knees under the dash board. You know what end was up. I had my period; he did not bother to take the tampon out. I began bawling and squalling, begging him to quit.

He just laughed.

When he finished, he opened the pick-up door and kicked me out on to the snow bank, with my crutches.

I did not call the police. I felt too ashamed to do so. I had known this guy for almost my entire life. I was the one who called him to get together while I in town to check out the college. We were drunk when the assault occurred. I felt as if the assault was my fault.

I did get therapy for the rape through the domestic violence program rape task force. They paid for three sessions with a woman who specialized in such therapy. After one session, she cut her price in half and scheduled a total of six visits. But that was not enough for healing of the abuses and victimization patterns that developed over the years of devaluing usage of my person that had occurred. Her counsel had only been a beginning. There was no diagnosis of PTSD.

I had a couple of friends who were Viet Nam era veterans. One is 100% disabled due to PTSD; the other also suffered from PTSD but he maintained full employment. They had been telling me for three years prior to the incident on the job that I had PTSD. Admittedly, I had some of the symptoms. I was hyper-vigilant but I passed that off as simply enjoying watching people. I was very fear-based, but I passed that off as my normal personality.

What happened at work was that I had been called to do a wetland determination in the southern part of a county. My supervisor, who was not a Certified Wetland Specialist, had made a pre-determination using only aerial photography. This was the agency standard practice prior to training Certified Wetland Specialists and infrared aerial photography can be quite accurate. Wetland Specialists make the delineation on the ground by evaluating the soil, the water movement, and the vegetation surrounding the site.

My supervisor told me to find the site in concurrence to his determination.

I would not agree to do that. I said I would make the determination per the soil, vegetation and water.

He started to raise his voice at me.

I began to feel tense and upset. I tried to tell him, that in all probability, my determination, based on the actuality of the site, would probably not differ much from his determination.

He did not listen but talked even louder about how my determination had to concur with his.

A co-worker laughed at our "fight" as this was the first time in three years that the supervisor had raised his voice to me. He did so regularly with the other woman in the office, who yelled back at him. It was their standard of communication. But not mine.

I broke.

Instantly I was transmitted back to the rape when I was highly upset and he laughed. Suddenly I wanted to smash my supervisor and the man who had laughed in the head with a baseball bat. In my mind's eye I could see blood and brains dripping off of the walls onto the computers.

I fled the building shaken. I am not a violent person. I do not ever hit people. I have never defended myself, as an adult, in a fight or abusive situation. To envision, let alone do, what I had seen in my mind's eye was unthinkable.

Besides, neither I, nor my sons, owned a baseball bat.

I went to the floral shop. This was the most tranquil place in town. The beautiful store owner not only had it tastefully decorated, the scent of flowers and incense was extremely calming and sedating. I stood and pretended to search for a greeting card. I could not wrap my head around what I had just felt like doing. That was not me. That was not like me. I could not fathom where that thought or those thoughts had come from. I went home.

The next day I worked in the field all day and did not return to the office afterward. Normally, I was the first person in the office every day. I did not see any of my co-workers that day.

Two days after the incident, I had a doctor's appointment with a psychiatrist. She told me I was depressed and that I needed hospitalization. I phoned my therapist to ask her advice. I did not feel depressed. The therapist, who had not made any headway in my treatment, said, yes I was depressed and that maybe hospitalization would help me.

Shaken, I agreed to be hospitalized.

It was a waste of four days in my life.

The intake nurse, whom I had known for years, would not note the rapes, although it was some of the questions she asked as part of her professional intake forms. I never did like her and I still do not like her nor do I respect her in any manner.

I was given anti-depressant medication and I slept. The headaches went away for a few days. With the forced relaxation, my body finally crashed.

That hospitalization started my association with shrinks.

This first shrink sucked. She was an ego-maniac who loved being in control of other people's lives. I got to know other people with diagnosed mental illness; we made fun of her. She was crazier than anyone with a mental illness diagnosis I have ever met. She loved to prescribe drugs and create compliant zombies out of people. She and Jeffry Dalmer would have gotten along well.

Her experimentation with me and my body and with drugs has caused continued side-effects even all these years later. It seemed she changed my medication every few months or weeks. She was not medicating me for the proper diagnosis, so of course, the medication did not work. One medication caused me to gain 50 pounds in six months. I have never been able to lose that extra weight.

My fortieth birthday was one of the best birthday celebrations I have ever had. Ludell worked as a traveling (legal) drug salesperson: she sold veterinarian medicine and supplies. She was in the area in which I lived at the time of my birthday. Ludell and Jen got together and came out to my place with black balloons, gag gifts (I still have the psychedelic reading glasses they gave me), and a wonderful chocolate pie. I cannot express how wonderful it was to surprise me and join me for a day of celebration and fellowship. But they kept asking me what was wrong; why I did not express the joy I said I felt.

I was too overloaded with medication.

Two days later I got into a verbal altercation with my shrink over the medication he had me taking. I think Dr. H. was a competent Psychiatrist, but like so many, he did not listen or give respect to his patients. I am not a doctor, but I know myself and my body.

I did not learn for ten years that I was not depressed. So all the years of different shrinks and different anti-depressant medication only messed with my body's natural rhythms and systems.

I will admit I became depressed at times. After the physical and mental crash and the four days of hospitalization I have never been able to return to work at any job full-time since. I can do anything for a day or two, but, due to the constant fatigue, I cannot consistently show up for anything on a continual basis. For years I was able to do something for a day, and then I would need to be in bed for two days afterward. I have had two part-time jobs in the past dozen years. I was scheduled to work from eight to fifteen hours a week. Neither time could I consistently work at my appointed job. I could work maybe ten hours a week rather consistently, but not consistently enough. Forget trying to work fifteen hours a week consistently, that is impossible for me to do. I could not remember things; the simple things I could not remember how to do got me fired from the first job.

It is, or can be, depressing when a person's body does not function in what had always been a normal manner. It is, or can be, depressing when a person does not or cannot accept their new way of life. It is, or can be, depressing when one's tenacity had gotten them through situations before but was to no avail in a new limited lifestyle.

When my body finally got permission to stop and to rest … it did. I would sometimes sleep for up to twenty hours in a day. One doctor told me not to worry about it; he said that a person's body healed while they slept. Apparently my body needed a lot of healing because I sure did sleep.

Often my sleep was full of dreams of war-like settings with bombings, fire, flying bullets, and fleeing people screaming. I lived my nights in violent action-movie type dreams. If others in the dreams were responsible for the murder and mayhem, I would have a restless night and be tired the next day. If I was the one in the dreams who created the chaos, I would become afraid to go to sleep. Not sleeping preceded other hospitalizations. My doctors have all been very concerned with my getting sufficient amounts of sleep.

The first shrink prescribed a medicine so I would sleep without dreaming. I did. I slept so deeply I went into a drug-induced coma for a couple of days. I remember almost coming to consciousness to hear Matthew say things like, "Mom's sleeping, we'd better make breakfast and go to school." And "Mom's still sleeping, I'm hungry, let's make supper." I got my period. I knew I was menstruating but I could not wake up enough to do anything about it. When the drugs finally wore off enough for me to wake up fully and get out of bed, I went back to the doctor and she took me off of that medication right away.

By this time the boys were teenagers. Not an ideal time for a single parent to be so sick. Andrew turned thirteen the day I got out of the hospital. Matthew had already turned sixteen. They had to take over the house-hold. They did absolutely everything that was needed to be done. They did laundry, they went to the post office, they cooked, and they cleaned. I put Matthew on the checking account so he could buy groceries and pay the bills. He paid all of the bills: the mortgage, the utilities, the phone, the vehicle payments, and whatever else needed to get paid. Matthew drove the car.

I would get lost when I drove, even though it was a small town and I knew my way around. My head just did not work. I would "come to" on the familiar highway 2 and not have a clue where I was. I would look around and nothing I saw was familiar although I had driven that highway all of my life.

Within a couple of months I was well enough to do one thing a day. I could either cook a meal or I could take a shower. I could not do both things in one day.

Once, as I sat at my desk, I looked at the clock, I had two hours until the boys got home from school. I thought I had better go to the couch in the next room and lie down to rest before they got to the house so I could be there for them when they got home. I did not make it to the couch. I lay on the carpeted floor for the two hours and was still there when the boys came through the door. They ran to my side.

"Mom! Mom! Are you okay?"

Not wanting to alarm them, I said, "Yeah, I'm just looking at the carpet fibers. Have you ever looked closely at carpet fibers? They are fascinating. Why don't you go get the magnifying glass and look at carpet fibers with me?"

Being teenagers, they were not interested in a child-like fascination with carpet fibers. They went upstairs to their room. I drug myself to the couch and lay there worried about my fatigue. By this time, the headaches were no longer a daily occurrence but fatigue immobilized me. I was too tired to think, I was too tired to listen, I was too tired to do anything. I learned how much energy it takes to listen and to speak. There were times I could not speak; I was too tired to do so.

Surprisingly, my sons did not take advantage of having a nonfunctioning parent … at least not too badly. Ask Matthew about some of the shenanigans he did. Andrew did his share of tomfooleries during this time as well.

I feared the state might take my sons away if anyone turned me in for not being able to care for my family. I could not have borne the stress of another Child Protection Agency investigation. I did not want anyone to know truly how sick I was. At times, I feared I was dying. Part of the secrecy was also the fact I did not have a diagnosis, no one really knew what was wrong with me, and I was embarrassed at not being able to function normally.

Laziness is considered one of the greatest sins in my family of origin. Here I was, unable to get my ass off of the couch or out of bed too much of the time.

Over a year into this nightmare, my new life, I was in Lewistown. As was my custom, I got a hold of Bev Ophus for a visit and supper. After we went out to eat, we sat in my car outside her home and talked. I told her I felt "lazy" because of my lack of ability to function normally and to work.

Bev snorted out her nose. "YOU are NOT lazy," she said.

She did not say anything more and I was shocked into silence. To this day I can still feel the relief I felt then when she voiced those words. I will always regret not being healthy enough to attend her funeral.

The end of February, over two years after the incident, I received paperwork from the government; they retired me on January 15th — six weeks prior. I contested the retirement and did not sign the papers for over five years. I do not recommend a long, drawn out court case with the federal government. An individual never wins against "Big Brother." But, due to my stubbornness, I was not about to give in and give up. Besides, I wanted to work at my chosen profession. I hated not being a contributing member of society. I liked playing with plants, water, and soil!

I continued to search out an answer to this strange and debilitating health issue. I found a wonderful Naturopathic Doctor freshly graduated from college in her first medical practice. She worked with me like none other. Yet, in her inexperience, she did not find the answer either. But she did find many things breaking down in my body as my body fought the virus I had obtained four years prior. Under her care, further breakdown was arrested. Under her care, some aspects of my health were dealt with and improved. Eventually she left the state.

About a year and a half into this nightmare, I came down with fibromyalgia. Pain became my constant companion (compainion? Hmmm … I like my newly discovered misspelling of a word) as well as the fatigue. At first it was just my right shoulder, now it is over my entire body. I will not live my life wigged out on narcotic pain killers. I deal with and live with pain on a daily basis. I have become quite creative in my pain management. The things that help me are stretching exercises, water aerobics, walking in a stroll, massages, acupuncture, keeping stress at a minimum, and herbal teas. Vitamin and mineral supplements have helped as well, especially mega-doses of vitamin C and liquid vitamin D.

Three and a half years into this life of ill-health, I contracted cytomeglio virus (CMV). In researching CMV, I learned that 75-80% of Americans will test positive for antibodies for having contracted the virus. Most people do not know when they contracted it. Symptoms are similar to a bad cold, or flu. In severe cases it is sometimes misdiagnosed as the Epstein Bar virus (mononucleosis). CMV is relatively harmless to most people. But for people with an already compromised immune system, this nasty little virus can be fatal. There was not a lot of information available about the virus when I was diagnosed with it. I started to read the Gay Man's Journal on-line to learn about CMV. When people with AIDS die of pneumonia, they die of CMV. CMV affects the eyesight and the lungs.

Several years later I had the opportunity to spend Christmas Eve in the emergency room due to breathing complications. The doctor told me good news and bad news. The bad news was that the damage caused by CMV to my lungs was irreversible; the damage would just get worse. The damage to my lungs had nothing to do with smoking cigarettes although smoking was not beneficial to my health. And he told me that I would probably die of pneumonia. The good news was that at the end of my life, medical personnel could give me enough morphine to make the passing from this life into the next without pain.

I punched the air with my fist and exclaimed, "Bring on the morphine!"

He looked at me as though I had lost my marbles.

I like morphine.

I do not know when I will die, but I know how … that is, unless I get hit by a Mac truck tomorrow or something else happens.

Most people would not think it an opportunity to sit beside someone as they die. But I got the opportunity to sit with my cousins as my Uncle Jess passed away. I had thought people who die from not being able to breath would fight for air and that they would struggle, gasp, and turn blue. Not so with Uncle Jess. He simply, quietly, and slowly breathed less and less until he did not take in another breath of air.

I look forward to dying in the manner of my Uncle Jess — surrounded by people who love me and to go peacefully.

Uncle Jess was a big man. My childhood memories of him include him sitting at the kitchen table with a cup of coffee and a cigarette. He made the best home-made butterscotch pudding I have ever eaten. He made the worst oatmeal I have ever eaten; he put salt in his oatmeal. I do not like salt in my oatmeal. I think of him every day as I eat a bowl of oatmeal in the morning to combat high cholesterol.

When Uncle Jess was in his older years, and on oxygen, he still smoked cigarettes. Auntie Diane would give him hell for this. She had quit smoking years before. When I visited them, I would say, "Uncle Jess, are you ready to have a smoke?"

He would unhook his oxygen and we would go outside to visit and have a cigarette. Auntie Diane did not give him hell when I smoked with him. We bonded then like we never did when I was a kid and stayed at their house. When he moved into the nursing home, I visited him every time I was in town. Uncle Jess knew how to visit. I think he taught me how to sit and chat. Visiting is a great skill that causes other people to feel welcome in a person's home or to feel important in a person's life. I miss my Uncle Jess.

The summer of shedding the CMV virus was terrible. If I thought I had been fatigued before, ha! That was nothing like how I felt now. It would take me a full ten minutes to put on my shoes. I would put on one, and then would have to rest for ten minutes before I could put on the second shoe.

It would take me at least twenty minutes to empty the top rack in the dishwasher.

It would take me an hour to walk to the chicken coop to feed and water the chickens, pick the eggs, and walk back up the hill. This was a distance of maybe a half of a city block. Maybe.

Way too frequently I would not be able to drive down the driveway to pick Andrew up from the school bus ¾ miles away. He was not happy with me when he had to walk home and find me lying on the couch. Matthew had moved away.

By this time, we had moved into the country to follow my life-long dream of owning my own ranch. It is extremely difficult to ranch while lying on the couch unable to speak or move due to incomprehensible fatigue.

It was not until eight years into this seemingly impossible to overcome new reduced functioning life did I find a doctor who was able to diagnose the stealth virus that had attacked my immune system. Similar to the HIV virus, a person's guard cells cannot see this "invisible" virus — so the body begins to attack itself. To me, it is a little bit like the childhood game of "Blind Man's Bluff" … eventually the blindfolded begin to swing their fists at anything and everything within reach.

Had I been treated with antibiotics immediately upon going to the first drunken fool of a doctor, the virus would have been killed. But, by not treating the virus, it was allowed to mutate into two additional forms that would not respond to antibiotic treatment. One form affected my head. At one point in the first year of my new life in hell, the first shrink had me neurologically tested. The psychologist who did the testing told me that my IQ was intact but I had suffered some brain damage. They thought at the time the brain damage was due to the intensity and duration of headaches. The headaches could have been due to the mutated virus, I do not know. Occasionally I stutter; I never stuttered before in my life. I do know that I do not have the memory I once had. I can remember minute details from prior to getting sick. I have a hellova time remembering anything since contracting the stealth virus.

Once I was irritatingly searching in the refrigerator.

Matthew asked what I was looking for.

I snapped, "My ashtray."

Undaunted by my peevishness, he asked, "In the refrigerator?"

"Well, I've looked every other goddamn place for it!"

I have put the milk on top of the refrigerator and my ashtray inside of the refrigerator before. I thought I might have done something like that again.

"Brain fog" is also common in people with fibromyalgia. I think I have it double due to the "brain damage." Some people with fibromyalgia can joke about brain fog. It is not always a joking matter. It is very frustrating to have "blackout-type" memory lapses. Hmmm … my drinking was arrested but my blackouts continue. Only now the blackouts are more frequent, for shorter amounts of time, and not near as scary — but more irritating.

I have to have specified places for things or I do not know where they are. I have to put my keys away immediately upon entering my home or I will not be able to find them. I cannot be asked, "Think about the last place you saw … (whatever it is I need to find)." It does no good. I cannot "think" about the last place I saw something. There is no memory whatsoever.

My sons joke that I am preparing myself for dementia. Or that I already have it. They also joke that they are searching Montana for the worst nursing home in the state to put me in when I fully cannot remember anything anymore. I tell Matthew that he is the oldest therefore it is his responsibility to take care of me when I am old. We both joke with Andrew that he makes the most money so he is the one who will be able to take care of both of us when we are old. May we never get old. No worries, "old" is an attitude … I do not think we will develop that attitude.

When the stealth virus attacked my immune system, it attacked my liver the most. Eventually my kidneys "thought" they had to take over for my liver. Kidneys are not livers, but apparently they may be slightly co-dependent. I started to have kidney problems. Early, my endocrine system was affected, especially my adrenal glands which exacerbated the fatigue. My digestive system was affected and I started to develop food sensitivities. I developed an allergy to gold and stainless steel; I was told no one is allergic to pure gold. Hmm, call me "no one" then. A lot of the physical problems and breakdowns were caught by the first Naturopathic Doctor and addressed. I think I would be dead if it were not for her health care and the start of living a healthier life-style. I continue to need to build my immune system on a daily basis. This ol' Grey Mare just ain't what she used to be!

I now have lived for well over a decade with constant fatigue, pain, and the persistent threat of headaches. In the beginning I would think, I overcame so many things in my life; surely I should be able to overcome this debilitating disease. As with alcoholism, my "will power" is not enough for me to heal from the effects of the virus. I have had to learn acceptance and adapt to a new way of living.

Some family and friends still do not understand my hindered way of life. It is okay that they do not understand. There are times I do not understand it either. Sometimes they get irritated at my inability to be present or to do things. There are times I get irritated at myself for my inabilities as well. I have accepted my ill-health and my life. For those who do not accept me for the way I am — I figure those who love me love me, and those who do not love me, don't. And, well, there just is not anything I can do to change their mind. The writing of this book proved that, again, to me.

I have not so much accepted my illness as to do nothing about it. I have accepted the fact that I have it. And that I have choices on how to deal with it. I choose to fight for my life. I choose to decide to enjoy life no matter what, to live each day with joy and happiness, and to have the attitude that I play with pleasure in all that I do no matter how I feel physically.

There have been blessings with the new life-style as well as living with the curse of it.

One blessing is the new ability to "stop and smell the roses." Prior, and a good example was the way I was in college, I did not have time to stop and do other things. Early in my illness, I noticed for the first time how beautiful the hairs on a geranium plant leaves glistened silver in the golden sunlight streaming through a window.

I now had the time to spend hours visiting with other people. I did not have the energy to get up and do things. I always knew that love and people were more important than things. I was just too damn busy for most people. Needless-to-say, I did not have many people in my life. Today, I am amazed at the number of people in my life. I have many people in my life who I truly care about and who truly care about me.

In my self-imposed isolation of working and of not socializing, I puttered away my life mostly alone. I am not the social butterflies my mother and sons are and I never will be. It is not in my character. But when I want to be around friends or to have someone to talk to it is easy to pick up the phone and find someone to talk to or to hang out with.

This new ability to express the love I have for people is greater than the loss of the ability to consistently be occupied or busy doing something for double digit hours a day.

Early in my illness, when I was well enough to do so … maybe after the first year or so, I read a lot. There is not much one can do while lying on a couch. Reading was one thing I could do. I could read up to five books a day. Not children's books either, I read adult level reading books.

Inconsistencies in a book irritated me. For example, when a character had blue eyes in one chapter and the same character had brown eyes a few chapters later. I thought about becoming a proofreader. Certainly many new novels did not have good proofreaders! I had no idea how to pursue this occupational idea.

I thought about writing. I had continued to write professionally and technically when I still worked for the government agency. Writing was something I could do when I felt well enough to do it and I could do it while lying down if need be. I sold my first article. Free-lance writing is a difficult occupation when there is no other income. Waiting six months for the payment of a $100.00 is not a living wage for a half of a year. I could not dedicate hours a day to writing; I had a ranch to run.

There are few occupations one can make a living while lying on a couch.

I saw an ad for a school in Connecticut for persons interested in writing children's books. I answered the ad thinking it might be an avenue for networking on how to become a proofreader. To my surprise, I was accepted into the school to learn about writing. They claim they only accept 26% of applicants. I did not think I would be in this percentage.

My mom gave me the money to attend the first class as a Christmas/ Birthday gift. It was one of the many things she did over the years to support and to encourage me.

Where my body quit functioning normally, my brain did not stop functioning. I think all of the time. I have a vivid imagination. I do not mind solitude and am comfortable with being alone with myself. These are good qualities for a writer to have.

When Matthew was in the seventh grade, he brought home a book from the school library with sodomy in it.

He brought the book to me. "Mom," he asked, "are these two guys doing what I think they are doing?"

I read the section. Yep. Ah, let's not read this book.

Seventh grade is too young for that type of adult literature. Although I am not sure a person can refer to semi-porn as literature.

Later I learned he read every book written by that author that the school library had, he just never brought home another book by that author. I have read much of what that author has published as well, that first book I read was the only book with sodomy rape in it.

It was very difficult to find decent young adult literature for young men, especially when Matthew read at an adult level.

I decided I would write novels for young men.

My instructor at the school advised me not to do so. She said that publishing houses do not like to contract manuscripts geared toward young men. She said that only 11% of young men liked to read, whereas 86% of young women like to read. Therefore, if I planned on writing books and hoped to be offered contracts on my manuscripts,

I should write for young women. She also suggested I get established as an author by writing articles first.

I have written many articles for a variety of publications. I do not fully enjoy this type of writing. I prefer to create and develop characters in relationships with one another throughout a story line than to write a short article about some topic. Writing articles reminds me too much of the technical writing I did years ago. Technical writing is not fun for me, and I try to have fun on a daily basis.

I tried to write for young women. In fact, I started a "Vacation series" with two young teen girls as the main characters. The first book in that series did receive a contract for publication. I have started two additional manuscripts in that series and have never finished them. I spent my life helping young men, I raised two outstanding young men, and I was raised as a "tomboy." I know very little about young teen girls. It is very difficult for me to get into the minds and actions of a normal teenage girl.

But, my science fiction war survival series for boys has done well. Both boys and girls enjoy reading the books. What has surprised and delighted me is that adults enjoy reading the sci-fi series as well. My fans are male and female and are ages from 9 years old to 90 years old.

Once I spoke to a group of older adult women. Afterward one little old lady, she is at least four inches shorter than I am and I am short, came up to me and said, "My mom is your greatest fan."

I thought to myself, *your mom is still alive?*

She told me that her mom, at age 92, read my first book, *The Seekers*, and announced that I had become her favorite author. She told her daughter - if her daughter was ever to meet me, to tell me that she had decided she would stay alive long enough to read my second book. After she read my second book, *Alisa and Leah's Amtrak Vacation*, she told her daughter that she doubted if she would still be alive when my third book came out and to tell me to keep writing no matter what. She lived long enough to read my third book, *The Marauders*. She died the year my fourth book, *The Overcomers*, was published many months prior to publication. I mourn the death of a woman I never met; a woman who touched my life and encouraged me greatly.

Another time a woman bought a copy of *The Seekers* to read to her son who was between his third and fourth year in grade school. The family planned a several hundred mile family vacation. She wanted a book to read in the car while her husband drove so their son would not get too impatient with sitting in a car for long hours at a time.

By the time they returned home, she had not finished the book. Her husband asked if she planned to finish reading the book to their son.

"Yes," she replied. "I plan to read it to him at night while he is in bed."

Her husband sheepishly said, "But I want to listen to you read it, too. I really like the story."

She read the book to both guys in the living room of their home.

A month or so later, I spoke to a group of school librarians. The librarian from the young man's school was in attendance. I shared the story of the young man from her town.

I, with the help of a librarian and a sixth grade teacher, had developed an Accelerated Reader test for the book. The Accelerated Reader program is a reading program of accumulated points to encourage children to read. The teaching professionals gave *The Seekers* a rate of 6.0. This means children who can read at a sixth grade first month level could comprehend the story.

The librarian, who heard me speak, went back to her school and asked the boy, whose mother had read the book to him, if he would like to take the test. The boy had just entered the fourth grade and did not read at a sixth grade level. He took the test. He got nine out of ten questions correct so great was his attention to and retention of the story. This was three months after his mom had read to him the book.

Young adult novels are considered for readers ages 13 to 18. That age group is the only age group that does not seem to enjoy my novels. There is not enough sex and violence in my novels for them. In fact, there is no sex and violence in any of my young adult novels.

Sex

When I was nine years old, my mom and I were alone in the car. Mom "gave me the finger" and said, "Do you know what this means?"

That was the start of her conversation with me about sex. I do not remember the rest of the conversation; I was so shocked she flipped me off. I already had a "playground education" about sex. A playground education is misinformed children discussing what they think they know about such adult issues during recess in grade school. Thanks to a playground education, I thought I already knew everything there was to know about sex. Nothing I learned on the playground was even close to accurate.

Somewhere in my early teens, my father called me down to his office for a similar conversation. I do not remember much about that talk either. I know that he said to stay away from beds and boys, that all boys wanted was "one thing," and that he would kick me out of the house if I ever became pregnant. I believed him on that last point.

When I was sixteen, again alone in a car, with my grandfather when he said, "Has your parents talked to you about sex?"

Sheesh, Papa, I AM sixteen! I thought. Many of my friends were already sexually active. I did not want to have THE conversation with my grandfather. I squirmed in my seat. I did not know how to answer him.

He said, "Well, I don't know if they taught you right nor not. So I'm going to talk to you about sex."

There was no escape.

I remember vividly, although not exactly, what my grandfather said and it is his advice that has guided my sexual activity most of the time all of my life.

He said, in essence, that to decide whether or not to have sex with a guy is a lot like buying a bull for your herd of cows. And then he went on about bull selection. By phrasing the conversation about cattle instead of humans, I could listen without embarrassment and I could understand the jest of what he said better. I knew about cows and bulls so I easily understood his illustration.

He said that when you consider buying a bull for your herd, you take into consideration whether or not it was a good expenditure of funds, whether or not the bull would improve the herd, and whether or not you really needed to commit to buying another bull.

He said it is similar with men and sex. He suggested I ask myself a similar set of three questions. He suggested I ask myself if I was willing to risk pregnancy and a baby (and later in life, sexually transmitted disease possibility) in order to engage (expend the funds) in the activity now. He suggested I ask myself if the act was only for pleasure or for relationship (improve the herd). He suggested I ask myself if this guy was a guy I would want to spend a lot of time with, maybe the rest of my life (commitment of purchase).

Papa said all major decisions in life should be written out with "pro" and "con" lists. He suggested whenever I had a major decision facing me that I consider the pros and the cons of the situation. He suggested when considering having sex with a guy that I write out why I wanted to have sex with this fellow and why I should maybe wait either for another time or for a different fellow.

Selecting a bull for one's herd of cattle, one takes into consideration other attributes of the bull as well, such as scrotal circumference. Papa did not suggest I ask the fellow about size of his testicles.

The only thing Papa somewhat mislead me on was, I understood from him that women were similar to cows … coming into fertilization every twenty-one days and only wanting or only available to accept a bull's service at that time. I enjoy "accepting service" more often than once a month, as do most women I know.

Using Papas method of evaluation potential herd sires and fearing my father's wrath had I become pregnant, I did not have sex until after I was married. Many of my classmates were sexually active and I did lie about having sex with a few friends. As much as I drank and partied, many people thought I was sexually active. But, I was not.

I did not have sex for the first time on my wedding night either.

Mom had loaned us her house and her water bed for our wedding night. Finally alone, we had just barely got started with kissing when the phone rang.

I could not concentrate on the pending act with a damn phone going off near my head, so I answered it. The caller was Uncle Jess; he inquired if my cousin Wyatt was there.

Ah, no, no one else is here … we are on our wedding night.

Embarrassed, Uncle Jess hung up the phone. I looked around for my new husband.

He had gone into the bathroom to masturbate. Finished, he came back to bed, laid with his back to me, and went to sleep. I lay there staring at the ceiling wondering what the hell I had gotten myself into.

Our sex life did not get any better, ever.

My sexual development was slow. I was not a horny teenager. All I wanted to do during my teen years was to drink.

I only had one "serious" boyfriend in high school with whom I "went steady." He gave me his class key to wear. Cary was a great guy. He, like me, really liked to drink. And drink we did. When we made out, as soon as the car windows started to fog up, he would quit kissing me and say, "It's getting hot in here." Then he would reach for another cigarette and for another beer. We did drink a lot of beer together. Our favorite parking spot was on the railroad tracks. Neither of us thought we would live to age thirty and making-out in a car on the railroad tracks could have been exciting had we not been so drunk. Thank God a train never came through when we acted so stupid.

I learned years and years later that we both named our first born sons, Matthew. I have not talked to Cary in nearly half a century, yet I know where he works and in what town he lives.

When I tried to get sober and in my first year of sobriety, I would sometimes spend the night at a sober fellow's house. We would talk late into the night. My sons would have fallen asleep on the couch. So I would go to sleep on the couch with them.

I never thought this was strange. I would wonder why neighbors of his would come over for coffee in the morning and grin at us.

Nearly twenty years later, I had a nasty rope burn on my hand and was at his home. He suggested I spend the night because he had an ice maker and I would need ice for my hand. I did. But I was highly uncomfortable. As I lay there on his couch, I thought back to all the times I had spent the night in his home years prior without ever feeling uncomfortable. Yet here I was pushing twenty years sober and I was uncomfortable sleeping in my friend's house.

Suddenly I had an epiphany.

Adults do not have sexless "sleep overs" with the opposite sex.

As I lie there on his couch contemplating this new and startling revelation in my life, I realized more things about myself. I realized I had the physical maturation of an adult; I had the chronological age of an adult; I had the emotional maturity of a child when I had spent the night at his house before. And children do not have sex when they have a sleep-over. Now that I was (finally) an adult emotionally, I was uncomfortable "sleeping over" at his house.

It is often said in the circles of sober drunks that a person's emotional development is stopped when an alcoholic begins drinking. For years I had the emotional development of a three year old. My body had continued to grow but my inner self had not grown up. No wonder I had such a problem with fear; I, and others, expected me to act and feel like an adult when in reality I was still a child inside. Children cannot function at an adult level. Trying to live as an adult when one is truly a child is a frightening endeavor.

The concept of emotional immaturity of an alcoholic is so wide spread that my sons knew of this awareness. As a teenager, Matthew would often tell me that he was more mature than me. I would argue that with my first three years of life without drinking and my seven years married to his father without drinking, I was at least ten years old emotionally when I sobered up. He was seven years old when I sobered up. Therefore, I reasoned, I was at least three years ahead of him in emotional maturity. Some days I am not too sure my assessment was correct. I think there were times in which he was correct in his evaluation.

I think my emotional retardation is the reason I did not struggle with hormones until I was in my thirties. By that time, I was sober and learning to live a life of spiritual principles. It is not a spiritual principle to be promiscuous.

I was invited to my brother's 30th birthday party. It was held in the home of people I did not know. In fact, I knew no one at the party except my brother and sister-in-law. The hosts played the movie, "The Urban Cowboy." Toward the beginning of the movie there is a marital spat during which the husband states something to the effect of: well, you would be grumpy too if you hadn't had sex in xxx years!

At this point, my sister-in-law turned to me and said, "Is that why you are so grumpy all of the time?"

Before I could answer in my shock of public embarrassment, the hostess said, "Oh is this the one who does not like sex?"

"No," my sister-in-law answered in front of a room full of strangers, who sat with rapt attention to her discussion with the hostess, "the one who doesn't like sex is (she named a relative of hers). This is Levi's sister, BilliJo. She likes sex, she just never gets any." Then she turned to me and asked, "When was the last time you got laid?"

"Last night," I said.

She did not expect that answer.

Whether or not my answer was truthful, the topic ended with my remark.

Teasing and joking about sex and getting laid is very common in the family.

With my fear of men and not being attracted to women in that manner, I have spent most of my life celibate. At times being celibate has been frustrating; at times being celibate has been okay.

George was not the first or only person who guessed incorrectly that I was gay. My roommate in college in Tennessee asked to be moved from our room because she was suspicious of my orientation. I brushed that off because she was from Brazil. When the boys' father and I divorced and I did not welcome midnight callers from local men, the rumors began again. These rumors have continued to resurface now and then over the years.

To deal with false rumors, I began to "collect" lesbian jokes.

The first one I heard: "Did you hear of the new tennis shoes for lesbians? They're called Dykies. But they were recalled, do you know why? They're tongues weren't long enough."

When I told Jen the joke, she did not laugh. Instead, she seriously said, "Do you know what they're saying about you around the county?"

Yes, I had heard. That is why I collected a multitude of jokes around the issue.

Years later I realized why the rumors flew. First, because I did not welcome men who wanted so "service me." Second, because I was "in touch" with my masculine side.

Single women ranchers are not extremely common, although I know of a few. Most of whom I do not consider as masculine. But apparently others do.

Because I am capable of doing male-type jobs, I was suspect of enjoying an alternative sexual orientation.

Men who are "in touch" with their feminine side are heralded as "sensitive" men. But women who are in touch with their masculine side are labeled gay. I do not understand this. I think it is wise for both genders to try to or to attempt to understand the opposite sex. When we are sensitive to the opposite sex's characteristics we can understand each other better. I also think it is good for both genders to know how to do the things considered the "role" of the other gender.

I believe my sons understand the importance of being indulgent of the female gender's peculiarities. I have this believe due to what I have seen and how they treat women. I am proud of their sensitivities.

My sons also know themselves.

When Andrew was about eleven years old he said to me, "Don't worry, Mom, I won't be like Matthew." He is not. Andrew has matured to be much more confident than he was as an early teen. We agree his attending Boys State was a turning point in his life. He is now as social as Matthew was when Matthew was young.

Once when Matthew was in junior high, a female friend of his gave him a condom for potential use with his girlfriend. I did not know this until he came out of the bathroom with the condom in his hand.

He handed me the condom and said, "Here Mom, take this. You might need to use it before I do."

"Thanks, *I think.*" I said and thought as I accepted the condom from his outstretched hand.

I was not sure if he had my protection or my pleasure in mind. Not often do junior high aged boys give their moms condoms.

Actually I think he knew he was not ready to need to use it at that time. I think I gave it back to him a few years later.

This frequent long-term celibacy is not to say that I have not had my share of lovers. I have. I am grateful for the man who helped me get over my hang-ups in bed. Many years my senior, he had the patience and self-control to stop when we were thus engaged in the activity and hold me when I would begin to freak out. Sexual healing is of utmost importance for a rape victim if the victim is to live any semblance of a healthy life. I do not mean solely a healthy sex life; I truly mean a healthy life.

There are three acts in the human existence that can visually appear similar but are not what-so-ever alike. They are: rape, sex, and making love. All three acts involved human genitalia. Rape, on the far bottom end of the bell curve, is a sadistic, selfish act of brutalization, terror, and domination. Sex, on the top of the bell curve thereby signifying the most common and frequent form of genital interaction, is similar to what animals do. They simply "do it." Many people simply "do it" for the pleasure. Making love, which is on the opposite end of the scale from the first mentioned act, is a beautiful, nearly spiritual, expression of commitment between two people who love each other.

I have experienced all three.

Many people who have been raped never heal sexually in order to engage in love making. They can, and often do, engage in sex.

But love-making can be foreign to them. Too often a rape victim automatically disassociates when attempting to make love or to have sex. Because in all cases, rape, sex, and making love, the genitals are involved; there is often a trigger, usually a touch but can be a sound, smell, sight, or taste, that transports the victim back to the assault without the partner ever meaning to trigger the victim. Thus engaging in the act in a withdrawn manner and simply engaging in sex. When this disassociated sex occurs often enough, the victim eventually loses their ability to even engage in sex with any measure of pleasure and often ceases to have sex all together.

Many rape or molestation victims become promiscuous as if frequent sex with multiple partners will somehow prove something, at least to themselves. Too often the victims quit having sex, much to their partner's sorrow. The partner is not to blame. The assailants years prior are the cause of the "sexual hang-ups."

But the victim has a choice. To remain in the "victim mode" as an adult, or years later, is to volunteer to be dysfunctional. Many choose this choice. It is easier to roll over and shut down than it is to face the fears and deal with the issues.

No one changes, or choses to change, until the pain of staying the same is greater than the fear of something new (change) or the fear of going through the healing process. There is a lot of snot and tears in the healing process. There is terror in the healing process. BUT it is all worth going through to get to the other side.

I thank God I had the determination to work through the fear to find a joyful, loving, giving sex life.

Ranching

When I was married to my sons' father and did not own cattle, I missed the ranching life tremendously. Although we often lived in the country, living in the country and ranching are not the same thing. My whole goal in attending college was to get a job where I would make enough money to be able to ranch.

Before my Grandfather died, he called each one of us grandchildren to come have a one-on-one conversation with him. I visited with him when he was in a motel while receiving cancer treatments. He wanted to make sure and clean up any wreckage of his past or damage he had done to others before he died.

He said, "Honey (he had shortened my mom's nickname for me, Honey Bee, to simply calling me Honey years before), have I ever done anything that has caused a problem between you and me?" He gestured between his chest and mine.

"No, Papa."

"Come on now, Honey, you are in your thirties now. Surely there was something I have done that has hurt you."

I thought back. I thought of his advice on sex. I thought about how he taught me to read. I thought about his advice on financial management. I thought about all the times we spent together. There was nothing I could come up with.

Then I thought of something else. I said, "Well, you never supported my desire to be a rancher."

He said, "Honey, do you understand why I did that?"

Only slightly did I nod my head.

He continued, "Ranching is a hard life. It is even harder for a woman alone."

"I know, Papa, but it is all I ever wanted to do."

He looked at me intently for a moment. Then he said, "Do you forgive me for that?"

"Oh Papa, I forgave you years ago. I hold no resentment over it."

He said, "Would you like to buy some of my cows?"

My grandfather made arrangements for me to buy several head of cattle from him. He also made arrangements for cousin Rolly to run them for four years. That amount of time, he reasoned, would give me sufficient time to graduate from college, get established, and find grass on which to run the cattle.

It did not work out quite that way. After four years, I had not been able to secure pasture of my own. I started to rent grass and run my cows with other people. This went on for another four years before I was able to buy a place to run my cows.

With my inheritance from my grandfather and my retirement from the government, I was able to put a down payment of an irrigated mud farm. Or was it an irritated pasture ground? When the agency "retired" me, they also forced me to withdraw my retirement fund.

I did not know until then my sons thought that "cows" was a four letter cuss word; that "farm" was a four letter "f-word;" and that "ag" rhymed with "gag" for a reason. Matthew lived with us on the property for less than a year.

It was too late in life to realize my dream to raise my sons similar to how I had been raised.

Still, it was the life I loved. Why I love cows, the big doe-eyed monsters, I do not know. I just do. These toothless (on the upper jaw) beasts give me a sense of well-being when I am around them. I also really like chickens. I find mirth and merriment when I watch the feather-covered creatures run around. And I agree that the outside of a horse (riding) is good for the inside of a man (person); I would happily ride all day long if I could. I love the solitude and quietness of the country. I love the peacefulness and tranquility of living where there are only the sounds of nature: the birds singing, the wind in the trees, and the howl of the coyote at night.

Another thing my grandfather did was to will me his horse. When Papa was in his early 70's, he was selected to be a drover on the bicentennial cattle drive. Each county had two representatives, drovers, to herd the longhorn cattle from Round-up, Montana to Billings, Montana. Papa bought a new horse for the week long drive.

Papa said his new horse, Buck, was too rank (wild) for a woman or a child to ever ride. Papa also was over a decade into his fight against cancer. I did not know if this horse would be safe for my grandfather to ride.

Visiting his ranch, I went out to the corral to capture, saddle, and ride this five year old hot-energy horse. Papa saw me from the living room window as I rode across the yard. He rushed out to stop me.

Assuring him I was only going to ride in the summer fallow fields, he allowed me to ride away.

Later he remarked about what a good cowboy I was to ride such a rank horse. When Papa died four years later, he gave me the horse.

I do not like the name "Buck" for a buckskin dun horse. The horse's registered name was Tardy's Gold Dollar, I called him Dollar. I kept that fine old beast until he was sick with face/head cancer. Like my grandmother had done nearly a century before, when Dollar died I had his hide tanned.

I have my grandmother's first horse's hide and my grandfather's last horse's hide.

The therapist I saw for seven years determined my major mental problem was a low ability to deal with stress. She suggested I eliminate, as much as possible, stress from my life. She thought that by living out my life-long desire of ranching that I would heal from whatever tormented me faster.

She was partially correct. I do need a tranquil life-style.

I wanted to augment my ranching habit with an organic herb farm. But I did not have the energy needed to do all of the weeding necessary. And I got no help in that endeavor whatsoever.

I had been convinced, by someone who held great influence in my life that I could not ranch alone. There was a man with whom I shared pasture for our horses; he also helped me ride on my cattle. He was a good man, he did not smoke, drink, chase women, etc … and he was a hard worker (later I learned this attribute was only when he wanted to do something). So we got married without the words "I love you" ever being spoken. Any physical relationship we had ended when we got married.

There were two apartments in the ranch house — the upper and lower floors each had separate complete living spaces. Within months we lived on separate floors. I did all of the cooking, cleaning, and laundry. He had no idea how to do these things. When we married at age forty, his mother still did basic household chores for him. I once handed him a carrot and a potato-peeler and asked him to scrape the carrot for me. Minutes later, having not heard a sound, I turned to him. He stood there still staring at the carrot and the peeler, having no idea what to do with them or how to begin to do what I asked.

He had lived with and worked for his maternal grandfather prior to that man's death. This grandfather said that "the city boy" could not run machinery, even though he was in his early thirties when that old man died. He refused to learn how to run machinery when we were together. He did, finally, learn to run the tractor to move snow.

When I walked into a room where he was, he would walk out of it. He was not good to my sons. The legal contract we signed can never and should never be referred to as a "marriage."

The day we got married, prior to the service, he said, "I never wanted a fat wife who smokes."

We should have called the whole thing off right then and there. Hell, we should never have gotten that far to begin with!

But I was sick and not in my right head. I did have a moment of clarity before that date when I knew that if I were well, I would not marry this man. But I was not well so I married him.

It had taken me a quarter of a century to save enough money to buy a ranch. It took him three years to break me. The man had holes in his pockets — big time. Where or how he spent all of the money he spent

I do not know to this day. He had a full-time job in town so he was gone all day. He was afraid of the dark and would not go outside after dark no matter what. If I had trouble in the night with a heifer calving I either had to deal with it myself or take her to the veterinarian in town. To avoid me, he did work outside on the place, mostly fixing fence or corrals, on the weekends. Although most of the time he spent outside was knapping arrowheads.

I do not regret my five years of owning my own place. I had developed a fine herd of cattle over the previous years and continued to improve my herd when I owned the place. I heard through the grapevine that my father once remarked that no one had finer cattle in the county than I had.

Ranching is damn hard work for damn little pay. It is a lot like writing, only writing is not near as difficult physically. Through ranching, one can learn the art of delayed gratification. A skill needed in order to write.

With ranching, it is the life-style that attracts those who ranch, not the income.

When it was over and the place was up for sale, we had the boys out for supper. By this time Andrew was in college and lived with Matthew. The four of us went through the house and amicably divided things and decided who would get what. Then we had a nice cordial dinner.

The rancher, who had phoned my husband and said that he would give my husband a job if we got a divorce, then called my husband and said that if my husband took me to court to try and get my inheritance from my grandfather and my retirement from the government, then my soon-to-be-ex-husband could run cattle on this other man's ranch. What gets me is that my (now) ex-husband hated this other rancher until this man asked my ex to go to work for him. Suddenly they were the best of buds. Although this ex-husband no longer works for this rancher, they continue to go hunting in the fall together.

The amicable divorce turned ugly. The man walked into the legal contract with very little money; he walked out with one hundred times more money. Not one hundred percent more, that would only be two times more money. I truly mean one hundred times more money. Plus he had assets we had gotten together that he took with him. Prior to the legal contract, I had over a half of a million dollars in assets. I did not have much cash, but, with my cattle and property my net worth was well into the upper six digit figures. After the final decree was signed on the settlement, I had substantially under a hundred thousand in assets. How anyone could think the "divorce" was fair is beyond my comprehension.

After it was finally over, this ex-husband took to calling me to ask me advice on dating. We got along fine at that point and we continued to get along until he married again. We have not had the need to speak to one another since.

My mother had a series of mini-strokes. Having nowhere else to go after my place sold, I moved to Glasgow to help my step-father, Billy, on his ranch. I sold most of my cattle to pay for the divorce and settlement, retaining only the best in the herd to run with Billy's cattle.

My first year in Glasgow, I lived in town. It was a very nice house. But, as is normal for me, I was not happy in town.

To meet my neighbors, mostly older, retired people, I baked a rhubarb and raspberry pie. It is my favorite pie. But I do not need to eat a whole pie! I took pieces to the people who lived nearby.

I have a few bad habits. One habit that could be considered a bad habit is that I often do not button my britches after using the bathroom.

With a dish of pie in my hand, I crossed the street to a neighbor's house. After ringing the doorbell, I realized my pants were undone. It was too late to zip my britches, he answered the door. I hoped he would not notice my crotch.

Reaching the plate of pie toward him, I said, "Would you like a piece?"

He looked at my unzipped jeans, shrugged, and said, "Sure, why not, come on in."

"No, no," I said, "I meant a slice of pie. Would you like a piece of pie?"

I trust the plate with a piece of pie on it into his hands and fled.

I never spoke to that man for the rest of the time I lived in Glasgow.

As soon as I could, I moved out to the old farmhouse on Billy's family's property. It was the best built old farmhouse I have ever lived in. It was located in an idyllic setting next to a creek. I loved sitting in the living room and watching the birds, as Billy's father had done before me.

Life was perfect.

I enjoyed working with Billy. He is an easy-going feller who does not yell, scream, or get too wrapped around the axle when things go haywire. I loved living in the country and ranching. Of course, I loved the cows. I had my cattle, two great horses, my dog, a few chickens, and a few cats (to keep the mice away). I cannot fault the life there whatsoever.

It was a perfect life for me, I thought, except for the fact that I had no friends.

When I left that county, I figured I had one friend, a man my mother's age who had known both sides of the family for decades and who was a fellow member of the gathering of ex-drunks.

Two years of living the perfect life I had my second PTSD break. This one was much worse than the first one.

PTSD

The day of my second PTSD break was toward the end of calving in the spring. I had been worked a twenty-three hour a day, I had a kidney infection, I had trouble with my breathing, and I was physically, mentally, spiritually, and financially exhausted. And I was upset about a financial situation.

Billy came into the house. I yelled at him in my anger and frustration.

He laughed.

I understood later that his laughter was the nervous type of laughter of someone who is uncomfortable. I had never yelled at Billy; I had never used the f-word around him either.

But the fact of the matter is when a man laughs when I am agitated, I break. It is my trigger.

I ran to my room to get my gun. No one was going to fuck me again. There was nothing about this situation that resembled the rape — except the laugh. It is the laughing that transports me back into the terror and self-defense or self-preservation when, in reality, there is nothing or no one from whom I need that level of protection.

For twenty years I had slept with a loaded pistol whose holster was snapped to the headboard of my bed. I got my pistol. I pointed the gun at the door and then at my head over and over as though I did not know whom to shoot first, anyone who came through the door or myself.

Anyone in their right frame of mind would know that if a person plans to shoot themselves and another person, one must shoot the other person first. It is normally impossible to shoot another person after one has shot themselves.

That is proof enough that I was not in my right mind at the time.

Besides, I love my step-father and would never want to harm him in any way.

After he left the farm for the day, I fled. I phoned Vinee. I packed my car with important things and headed down the highway.

Fifty miles down the road, I was thirsty. For the first time in my sobriety, I was afraid to stop at a convenience store to buy a drink for fear I would buy booze. I did not trust my mind whatsoever at that instance.

Then I realized that it was Monday. My friend at whose house I used to sleep hosted a meeting in his home on Mondays. I went to his house. After the meeting he and another member spent another hour talking with me. I calmed down somewhat.

I drove onto Vinee's house another hour away.

For the next several days I stayed at Vinee's place. I went to as many meetings as was possible in the next town — on Friday's I could make it to four meetings.

I phoned my case manager, Marna. Marna suggested I see a new therapist at the Center for Mental Health who specialized in PTSD.

I had not had "good luck" with therapists and shrinks over the previous ten years. I was hesitant to see yet another one. But I did not know what else to do. I agreed to see Charlene Schmitz.

Charlene, with her knowledge and training, was able to bring me to the point of recognizing and accepting my PTSD. As importantly, she helped me recognize my trigger. I say that Charlene helped me more in seven months than my previous therapist had helped me in seven years.

Along with meeting the therapist, I met the new Psychiatrist Doctor in town. Needless-to-say, with my experience with shrinks and their condescending attitude and drug-pushing fervor — I did not really want to meet this lady. Charlene told me what I had heard before: mental health treatment works best with the combination of medication and "talk therapy." I listened and submitted to her suggestion.

Although Charlene had suggested someone else to go to for the medical part of therapy, I am glad I went to Dr. Arpon for the medical treatment for my PTSD. Dr. Dia Arpon is the greatest understanding Psychiatrist I had ever encountered. Not once did she ever act or speak in a condescending manner toward me. She honored my intelligence. She allowed me to be a partner in my own treatment. She discussed medication, side-effects, and options. She did not push pharmaceuticals; she was open to the concept of alternative actions to deal with issues such as sleeping and nightmares. She worked with me. She encouraged me. I am eternally grateful to her. She has left Montana and has gone back to the Washington DC area to live closer to her family. I know she will help a great many people with mental health diagnosis in her life time of practicing medicine. The woman doctor who took her place is as understanding and helpful as Dr. Arpon; I am grateful.

Months into therapy, I was awakened in the middle of the night by the sound of a many-chains-on-his-hip wearing young man walking through my property — the property had often been used as a short-cut until I built a fence. I reached for my gun. It was not there. I realized I no longer felt the inner need to sleep with a loaded gun within arm's reach. I continued to listen to the young man's jingle jangle of a walk in complete peace, knowing that I was safe from harm.

I still own guns. I just do not sleep with a loaded gun attached to the headboard of my bed. All guns should be considered loaded at all times, whether they are or not — for safety reasons. My guns are in the other room. I consider them loaded. I have owned guns since my father bought me my first BB gun at age nine. He had me carry that little gun when we went hunting, before I was old enough to truly hunt, in order to have me practice gun safety. We shot gophers and prairie dogs for years together. I went deer and antelope hunting with him more times than I can remember or count. My dad taught me more about gun safety than the hunter's safety classes taught me. I am not afraid of guns. I have been threatened with a gun or shot at five times in my life by three different men. I have pulled my gun on three different men at three different times in my life. I have been told you never point a gun at something unless you plan on shooting it. I know that. And had the men continued to threaten me, I would have shot them. No, the PTSD break with Billy is not counted in this number.

The first time I was shot at was during a house party when I was sixteen. Although my boyfriend, his friend, and I fled when the drunk boy got the gun and threatened to shoot us, I was dumb (or drunk) enough to look out the back window of the pick-up as we sped away. I looked directly down the barrel of that rifle. I saw a male friend of mine knock the drunken boy's arm up as the gun went off. My boyfriend pushed my head down below the window. To this day, my friend knows I think he saved my life that night. The driver of the get-away truck, a wonderful man, and I share a special bond of remembrance of the night we were fired upon. His wife knows the story; I do not think she shares in our mirth about the incident.

The second time someone shot at me was when I was pregnant with Matthew. Two days before he was born, I went on a waddling walk down the creek with my dogs and cats. Tired, I lie down to rest in a dry washout along the creek. Upon hearing gun shots, I got up out of the washout. The land was posted — meaning hunting was not allowed. I saw two bird hunters shooting in my direction. Instantly angry because the land was posted and hunters who violate posting signs are why many landowners do not allow hunting on their land. Hunters should respect the landowner's property. I marched toward them. They did not see me, so intent they were on the pheasants across the road from my yard, birds I later called my wild chickens. They shot again. How they could not see the nine months pregnant feeling and looking like a beached whale woman marching in their direction, I do not know. I started to yell. One man shot again; the other man saw me. He grabbed his friend. They high-tailed it up the road away from my home as fast as they could jump in their truck and speed away.

The other three times were when my son's father thought I killed our baby.

The first time I pulled a gun on a man, I was sleeping in a bunkhouse, on the floor, in a sleeping bag, in the first room of the building. It was summer. It was hot. I slept in the nude. A drunken Indian came in the house hollering that he needed gasoline. Locked doors are not allowed on that rancher's buildings. The Indian had stopped his vehicle on the highway some half mile away. Groggy with sleep, I raised to my elbow to see what was going on. When the drunken fellow saw a naked woman on the floor, he commenced to walk further into the house with a grin on his face. I pulled my gun, pointed it toward him, and told him I had no keys to the gas tanks and had no way to give him fuel for his truck. I suggested he leave. He did.

The second time I had the opportunity to pull my gun on a fellow I did not pick up the gun. All he had to do is see it there beside me to get the idea he was not welcome. Again I was in a bunkhouse. This time I was in college. The research was finished for the day, but I had studying to do for classes. I assume the other researcher saw the light on in the bedroom of the trailer house bunkhouse in which I slept as an invitation. He came bopping into the room with a big grin on his face. He, too, like the drunken Native American, immediately noticed I sleep in the nude in the summer and have a loaded gun by my side. He quickly ascertained that I did not need anything from him and left. I still occasionally see him; he never acknowledges me. I always greet him in a friendly manner, maybe with a bit of a grin on my face. We have never talked about that night.

The third man I held at gunpoint was a friend. All I heard was noises in the house. I had the gun in hand when he opened my bedroom door. What had happened was: I thought the boys were asleep. When this friend arrived, the boys let him in the house and told him to go on back to my room where I was in bed. So he did. When he saw the gun pointed at his middle, he quickly shut the door and exclaimed something like, "Jesus Christ, BilliJo!" To which I responded with something like, "Jesus Christ, (my friend) don't scare me like that." He knew of my rapes and of my fears. I put the gun away and we talked. Neither of us got much sleep that night.

Back to the PTSD therapist and the healing of the fear of another PTSD break.

Two years after I moved to Havre, I had an argument with a man about the fence I wanted to build across my front lawn. He is an obstinate type of man. It could be that I am the obstinate type of person as well. It was my fence and I wanted a flower bed along the bottom of the fence. He argued that it would be more difficult to mow my lawn with a flower bed bisecting the lawn. True, but it would also be pretty to have lilies and calendula growing beneath and up through the fence. I wanted his help in building the fence; I did not need his help in creating the flower bed. He is not the type of man to back down and I started to get peeved with him. If it was his fence, he could build it any damn where he wanted, but it was my fence and I wanted it to bisect the lawn and to have flowers growing beneath it.

At one point he laughed.

I felt the old panic and terror start to rise up within me.

I was able to stop, mentally, and evaluate what was going on inside of me. I realized I was upset and that my friend had laughed. I recognized I had begun to feel the PTSD self-survival mode of self-defense against an incorrectly perceived threat of bodily harm. I did not get to the point of wanting to kill him or to take any action to do so. I calmly suggested it was time for us to take a break from the fence design. He went to his house to do whatever he needed to do; I went inside my home grateful I no longer needed to be afraid of myself and that I might go into a homicidal self-defense mode and do harm to others.

All of us have within us the ability to choose to kill. Most of us chose not to kill other people.

Many years ago there was a television show; I believe its name was China Beach. It was about Viet Nam. In visiting with my supervisor at the time, I told him I went to my brother's house every Tuesday night and watched the show with him. My brother's wife wanted to watch "Cosby" which was on a different station at the same hour. Together my brother and I out-voted his wife.

My supervisor invited me to come to his house to watch the show, to "vote" with him, because his wife watched "Cosby" and he wanted to watch "China Beach." They watched "Cosby" on Tuesday nights.

"Why do you want to watch China Beach?" I asked.

He had been drafted but the war ended before he went to boot camp. He always wondered if he would have killed other people.

Without hesitation, I said, "Yes, you would have."

He was shocked. "Why do you say that?" he asked.

Because he was a good government employee; he did what was asked and what was expected of him.

Yes, but to shoot people.

No problem. Self-preservation and self-defense are great motivators in defending one's life and to return fire.

But, to kill another person, he did not know if he could have done it

Yes, he could have done it. To kill anything, all one has to do is to view the "thing" being shot at as having no living value. He was an avid deer hunter; he understood the taking of an animals' life but he could not associate that with taking of a human's life.

I went on to explain it is why people give the people they shoot at dehumanizing names such as "redskin" and "gook." By depersonalizing and dehumanizing other people, they become easier to shoot and kill. The "enemy" becomes nonhuman.

I do not know if he ever accepted my reasoning. The conversation ended.

I am at peace believing that I will never "break" so much again as to actually kill another human being. All I have to do to continue to prevent another PTSD break is to carry on doing certain things to take care of myself. I have and use a wellness-plan; I am certified to facilitate a particular wellness plan method.

A wellness plan is a written plan of action for dealing with the situations of life. I know of many people with a wellness plan to deal with their mental health diagnosis. I know of people who have a wellness plan to deal with their employment. I have heard of couples with wellness plans for their marriages and of companies who have wellness plans for their businesses.

My wellness plan starts with the concept of what I am like when I am doing well. This is when I am happy, when I laugh easily, when I look forward to time spent with family and friends, when my house is clean (by my standards), when the laundry is done, and when I am at peace with myself in my world.

My written wellness plan includes the things I need to do to take care of myself, mentally and physically, on a daily basis. This includes talking to people daily and even more so when I feel anxious, afraid, tense, or have some other negative emotion going on. The simple act of connecting with other human beings is vital for me to not begin to isolate. Isolation is an ongoing issue for me. By nature, I enjoy solitude and solitude twisted is isolation. A quick cup of coffee, a lunch, or a short phone call is all it takes for me to stay centered. I also attend church and other social functions.

I need to ensure I get regular sleep and to rest when I am tired. Learning to not push myself to get a job done has been difficult for me to learn, albeit, necessary. It is still hard for me to stop working for any length of time.

I need to exercise lightly daily and eat a well-balanced diet. These things sound ridiculously simple. For me, they are not that simple. For example, I do not like to cook for one person. I often eat "non-meals" such as a handful of home-made jerky and some corn tortillas or a handful of dried craisons and a hunk of cheese. While these "meals" are not necessarily "junk food" they are not necessarily well-balanced either. And I usually keep on working (writing or researching) when I eat these non-meals; which, again, is not wise. To stop working to take a little walk around the block or to the store takes concentrated effort on my part to remember to stop what I am doing and to cook a meal or take a walk. I enjoy going for a walk, yet I have to force myself to do so.

When circumstances or my attitude begins to get worse, I need to be aware of the initial signs of stress. These signs are such things as feeling hungry, angry, lonely, tired, sick, or having frequent headaches.

Greater warning signs are when I begin to have nightmares or trouble with sleep. When I recognize these things happening, I need to do more to take care of myself. Unfortunately, this is also when I do not feel like doing more to take care of myself. One of the greatest actions I can take is to brew a calming cup of tea. An old standby used by me and many other people for relaxation is chamomile tea. There are days I seem to drink nothing but tea.

I also need to talk with a trusted confidant about my nightmares. Not everyone is comfortable discussing frightening dreams or ubiquitous feelings of stress and anxiety. There are a few people in my life I trust with these goofy dreams and feelings.

When my stress levels are really beginning to breach a balanced life, when I cannot sleep without nightmares, and when I feel unreasonably anxious and afraid, then I need to see my Psychiatrist. It may be that she will prescribe anti-anxiety medication. Being an alcoholic, I have to be very careful in taking medication. Most anti-anxiety medication is very dangerous to the continued sobriety of people with this disease. Most anti-anxiety prescriptions side-effects mimic the effects of a little alcohol in one's system. For us, when our bodies feel that feeling, we start to crave alcohol. If we give in to the obsession and craving we are doomed to drink. And for many of us, to drink is to die.

At this "pending break down" level, I also need to be around people more, not just talk to them via the telephone. I have to physically be near other people. Often I attend more meetings for the gathering of ex-drunks. Normally, I attend two or three meetings a week; in times of stress and anxiety, I need to attend at least a meeting a day when my status quo is threatened to tilt sideways. Other ways of being near people helps as well. As simple as going to the grocery store is a connection with people that helps to keep me balanced. I need to walk to the grocery store more often when I am overly stressed.

I also know when I am coming out of a near-crisis and what I need to do for myself at that time. I need to communicate with those with whom I have been accountable about my stress levels and mental state. I can tell when my head has relaxed: I have cleaned my house, my laundry is done, and I laugh easily once more. The people I am accountable to do not have PTSD or any other diagnosis of mental disorder and they are not alcoholics. They are people who love me. The guidelines for developing a wellness plan suggested a person has five persons with whom they are accountable. I am blessed; in addition to trusted ex-drunks I trust to talk with, I have nearly double that number. I do not confide with all of them every time I feel stressed. I have no desire to cause them "burn out" with helping or supporting me.

As I learned when I search out the answers to why my family had such difficulties when Lesli Ann died, people get through the tragedies of life in proportion to the support they have when the upheaval occurs. The greater support we give one another, the better chance each of us has to emerge from the dark valley of pain and heartache in a healthy manner. The lesser the support any one of us receives during any catastrophe, the greater the damage and the higher the chance of ongoing issues and problems.

I did not reach out for sufficient help when the brutal rape or any of the other abuses occurred. I know of other women who have been brutally raped and who received help right away. They function well. I now know of the vital importance of talking tragedies through. I am blessed to have people in my life with whom I can confide. I am blessed to be in other people's lives as a person with whom they can confide.

Recently a young man came to my home. We met ten months ago. He is not an alcoholic. He was upset about his living situation; he thought of me and drove over for a visit. It was his 25th birthday. He learned that day he could talk to me and that I would listen.

Three weeks later he arrived on my doorstep crying. He had learned of tragic situations in his family. Upon hanging up the phone with his mother, he thought of me and drove to my house. I have become a confidant for him.

I cannot do much more than listen and offer encouragement when people come to me. But often that is all someone needs. People need to talk out their fears and frightening or angering situations in order to find the answers within themselves.

It is an awesome pleasure and responsibility that people feel comfortable enough to confide in me. That they know, intuitively, that I am a person they can trust.

I have learned how to listen to others.

Havre

When I fled to people who loved and supported me, I realized I could not live the isolated life-style any longer. I made the decision to stay near these people. To live "on the bend of the river" in a coulee, with the creek, the trees, and the birds may be idyllic but for me it was also dangerous.

I started to look for a house in Chinook. This was the town my sons considered as their hometown. When holidays came, they wanted to go to Chinook to hang out with their friends; they did not want to go to Glasgow where they knew only family. I wanted to live where my children wanted to visit.

There was not a house in Chinook for me.

I did not have the money for gasoline to drive back and forth from Chinook to Havre every day. I got caught sleeping in my car.

A man, whom I did not know when I lived in the district before, offered me his apartment to stay in. He spent his nights with his girlfriend so his apartment was a safe place for me to stay. I asked about rent; I had very little cash available. He said that if I would babysit his girlfriend's grandson a day or two a week, I could stay at his place for free. I stayed in his apartment for a month.

It is not often that a new acquaintance will offer a stranger their home. This is especially true in the circles of paranoid clean addicts. Clean addicts have "hockables" in their home. Hockables are items of value worth pawning or hocking for drug money. Yet this man trusted me, someone he did not know. I am forever grateful to him. Every time I see him I tell him I love him. I do not think he is fully comfortable with this because addicts are not often loved people.

I had gone to family members and asked to stay with them. I was turned down. My formerly favorite cousin said he was not comfortable with me in his home. He has PTSD from Viet Nam and has experienced PTSD breaks of violence; I thought he would understand.

I found the perfect house for me. The house truly is perfect; it is not another wishful thinking on my part for the hermit life-style. My new house was in a cul-de-sac within walking distance of downtown. Across the street from my front door is a hill on which, I think, every child in Havre has played on for at least the last three generations. When I look out my front door, I see grass, soil, and the effects of water. To the north of my house is a warehouse which doubles, for me, as a privacy fence. To the south is an apartment complex with very high rent, the renters are quiet to-themselves sort of people. Also, the wall of the building I can see out of my windows has no windows; it is another type of privacy fence. There are large shady trees in my yard, adding to the quiet and privacy. It is almost like living in the country.

However, it has the convenience of living near people. The house has the convenience of living very near people. There is an apartment in the basement and a "mother-in-law" house in the back yard. Both of which I rent out.

When I bought the house, banks would not loan on it. There had been two fires in it in a short period of time. It was considered a financial risk for a bank to offer a loan for this quaint building. It is an older house built at the turn of the previous century. The man who built the back house moved this bigger house to its present location in the 1960's when he was in his 70s. When he died in 1976, his family did not live in the state and yet did not want to sell the family home. It was a rental for thirty years until I bought it. In a hundred years, I am only the second owner of this property. As with most rentals, it had suffered the neglect of out-of-state owners, poor property managers, and the damage and abuse of non-conscientious renters. There had been some updates with the insurance money from the fires, but these updates were mostly cosmetic. It had no yard or garden either.

The previous spring I had finally given up my fight with USDA and my retirement. I accepted retirement and a small settlement. I sold more cattle. I paid cash for the house and paid almost half of its market value. With the work and updates it needed, I was able to secure a loan and a mortgage. I have invested in the house its full market value. Much of the work I have done myself or I have found professionals who will work with my help. My dad taught me how to do many things; he taught me how to work with a variety of tools. My father is left-handed; I am not. I wondered for many years why I felt so awkward doing so many of the things he taught me. I am not naturally ambidextrous but every time I paint with my left hand or do anything left-handed, I think of my father and am grateful for the things he taught me how to do.

In the houses on my property there are two kitchens which have been totally remodeled; the garage and the back house have been reroofed; two bathrooms have had extensive remodeling; my foundation has been dug up and sealed; the back stairs with an addition of an upper balcony have been rebuilt; there is a fence across the front lawn; and there is a beautiful lawn with flower, vegetable, fruit, and herb gardens encircling the property.

When people come to my home, often they exclaim, “It is so peaceful here,” or “I become so relaxed when I am in your house.”

It is important to me to create an atmosphere of peace and tranquility. A stress-free or at least stress-reduced impression is imperative to my health — both physically and mentally. I want a haven of rest for all who enter. A friend of mine made and gave me a wall hanging, it says: Sanctuary — come away to a quiet place and rest … . The framed sign hangs in the entrance to my home.

It is not so much that the house is so important to me. It is that the home is a place of refuge. With the remodeling, color schemes, and landscaping, I want it to be a place where people automatically sigh and begin to unwind when they arrive.

And they do arrive.

On any given day I would have up to five visitors who stopped by for coffee the first year I lived in Havre. Andrew attended the college located in Havre; he was still in school when I moved there. He commented that my house had become a sobriety house. He said he never thought he would see the time when I would have so many people in my life.

I started to heal. I started to heal both physically and mentally.

That autumn, I attended the semi-annual assembly of the gathering of drunks. It had been seven years since I had attended the gathering and weekend long decision making time for the Area. To my surprise, I was nominated for an Area position.

I prayed. I asked God, if it be His Will, if I got elected, then I would trust Him for the strength to do the job. I still needed a day or two of rest after any excursion. Often I needed a day a week to spend in bed sleeping and resting in order to function at a slow pace during the week. I was not sure I could commit to the travel and to the speaking that would be required of me if I was elected.

The vote was in my favor.

I began my two year rotation in Area service. I was able to perform the duties of my position. As each challenge arose for my time and my energy, I was able to find sufficient energy to perform the task. At the end of that rotation, I held another position of Area service.

Near the end of my first rotation in Area service, I joined the Havre/ Hill County Local Advisory Council on Mental Health (LAC).

Mental Health Advocacy

Upon joining the LAC, I became the secretary. Through that organization, I learned of the Service Area Authorities (SAAs). The state of Montana is divided into three SAAs: Western, Central, and Eastern. I lived in the Central Service Area Authority (CSAA). This group met monthly in Helena, where my sons lived. I volunteered to be the Havre LAC's representative at the CSAA meeting. My honest motivation was the opportunity to see my sons, not to contribute to mental health care in Montana. I did not think I had anything to contribute.

I accepted the Board Member Representative position solely because my travel expenses would be paid by the organization and I would get to see my kids occasionally. Or so I thought. God had other plans in mind.

Having had over ten years of negative experiences with mental medical doctors and other so-called mental health professionals, I was dubious of most people who worked in the field of mental health. When I learned of the movement to support and empower people with mental health issues. I was greatly relieved to the point of being ecstatic.

There ought not be any stigma against persons with mental health issues. The greatest minds in history had mental health issues from Einstein to Lincoln to Churchill. The list goes on infinitum. Many great writers also have mental health issues. My long-time therapist once gave be a book about writing and becoming a writer. In it the author, a former publicist, stated something to the effect that if you were diagnosed as alcoholic, depressive, schizophrenic, and the list went on, then you probably would make a good author. Many persons with mental health issues have great imaginations, are above average intelligence, and have the obsessive/compulsiveness to continue to write when there is no income in doing so.

One of the problems in accepting mental health issues, in my opinion, is a lack of understanding toward those with different abilities. Whether one's different abilities are in the physical or in the mental arena. I believe people have come a long way in accepting others with physical differences. But there is still a huge lack of acceptance for people who are mentally diverse.

This lack of understanding has been reinforced through the centuries with bizarre treatment and treatments for the people who are mentally different, with media and movie sensationalism, and with an overall apathy in the general public if the issue does not "hit home." Worldwide the statistics are the same for the percentage of the population who suffer from schizophrenia and bi-polar disorder — it does not matter what country, the stats are the same. With statistics indicating that one out of four people in the United States will suffer from a mental issue at some point in time in their lives … mental illness "hits home" more often than most people are willing to admit. Too often when mental illness "hits home" the person with the diagnosis and the families are ashamed and hide the fact of the illness or diagnosis. Sometimes the family turns away from the one afflicted.

I know of federal and state employees, famous authors, Judge's wives, and successful business owners with mental illness diagnosis. Many people travel out of town to receive medical care. They do not want their friends and neighbors to know they need help. For years I was as silent about my diagnosis; I understand the feelings of shame associated with a mental health diagnosis.

The "medical model" of treatment for those with mental health issues does not assist in breaking the social stigma. This model of treatment, as I see it, is a combination of two aspects. One aspect is to drug the hell out of a person who is different in order to make them become compliant, complacent zombies. The second aspect is to reinforce the idea that persons with different abilities are potentially dangerous nut cases who need constant supervision and medical care. This is the model of treatment that has been, and still is in many incidences, prevalent in the United States for decades.

To this end, when a person with a mental illness diagnosis asserts themselves in their own care and treatment often the police are phoned, the ambulance arrives, and the person is whisked away to the mental ward of the nearest hospital for additional drugs so that they will be compliant to their case manager's (or whoever is in power and control) wishes.

I have been hospitalized against my wishes three times and one additional time when I knew I needed hospitalization. Twice I complied and became willing for the unnecessary in-patient hospitalization. The other time, I learned that a person can be locked up in a "Behavior Health Unit" — the nut hut — for up to seventy-two hours without their consent. If, after three days, the person is willing to sign papers consenting to hospitalization, they will be released. If they do not sign the papers, they get to sit in the hospital until obtaining a court date for a judge to decide whether or not they need in-patient mental health supervision, i.e. hospitalization. This waiting for a hearing or court date can take two weeks to two months. The entire cost of sitting in a psychiatric ward for the duration is the patient's responsibility. Few people, mentally healthy or not, can afford a two month stay in a hospital. Only the very rich do not sign the papers; I have met one such person.

The time I was not willing to sign the paperwork consenting to lock-up, I did sign the paperwork because I surely did not have the financial means in which to spend a longer duration staring at poorly painted walls and twiddling my thumbs. But I let it be known I was not happy about the situation. Oooh. "They" saw me as an angry person, and therefore, maybe dangerous. Maybe to teach me a lesson, "they" lost the paperwork for an additional twenty-four hours thereby giving me a nice little ninety-six hour expensive vacation. I do not like to start my weekends with armed guards by my side, not being allowed to use the bathroom for ten hours, and not being allowed food or drink for twenty-two hours. I have been very careful not to piss off persons who have the authority to commit me ever since.

Not irritating people who have some sort of power and control over others is extremely difficult for me to do. I find most persons with that kind of authority to be idiots. I can let my attitude show.

Case managers, in my experience, are often power and control freaks who thrive on dictating their client's lives. I am lucky my case manager was not like that. Although I think supporting me in my decisions was difficult for Marna at times, she did so always. I am indebted to her forever.

Many, many psychologists and psychiatrists, therapists and social workers share this domination, power and control issues along with case managers. It is not wise for those with a mental health diagnosis to exert one's self and exhort to be considered in the decision making process of our own treatment and care against most mental health care givers. Granted, those of us with mental health issues need support. But we do not need our every thought, action, and decision dictated. Nor do we need to be drugged into submission.

The new model of treatment for persons with mental health issues is driven by those of us with mental health issues. It is called the "recovery model."

The recovery model of treatment is self-directed and self-actuated. We exercise our power of choice and decision. We expect those who support us, especially the professional support who have supposedly been trained in mental health care, to have an understanding of what we are going through. We expect honesty when discussing treatment options and medication options. None of my supporters have PTSD, yet, the people whom I have chosen to be in my life completely give me the backing I need to stay balanced. Some of my supporters are fellow alcoholics; that fellowship has assisted me tremendously in maintaining not only my sobriety but my overall life enjoyment as well.

In the recovery model of mental health treatment, people with mental health issues work with and help support or encourage other people with mental health issues. This is called peer support. A

Peer Specialist is a specifically trained person with a mental health diagnosis who is hired by a mental health organization to mentor, to talk with and listen to, and to encourage other persons with a mental health diagnosis. This method of assisting like-affected people has been used successfully for over seventy-five years. It was first started by alcoholics.

No wonder I took to the recovery model in mental health so readily. Not only do I believe people with mental health diagnosis should be treated with respect and dignity, I know first-hand that the method of peer support to assist people to overcome ailments works. I have over twenty years of experience.

I had the opportunity to watch the recovery model get started and to watch the recovery model become successful in Montana. Implementation, or change, is slow in many communities. Few communities have successful programs. Only the cities with knowledgeable persons in politics and the support of the local mental health clinics have received the backing needed.

There is still a lot of work to do nation-wide to insure the implementation of the recovery model in all states and many, many cities and communities.

The work in Montana is not finished. It was time in my life for me to move on.

Mexico

Ten months after being homeless I vacationed in Mexico. Not a normal turn of events. But when a person turns their lives and will over to the care of God, often events happen that are not common.

Friends had rented a five bedroom apartment in Puerto Vallarta for five weeks with the thought in mind that their six children would come down during that January to visit. None of their children could make the commitment. These friends of mine then opened up the invitation to all of their friends.

I was one of the five people who traveled to Mexico to stay with them for a few days that winter. As soon as they announced the invitation, I started to save money toward the trip. Even a month prior to going I was unsure if I would be able to afford the journey or not. My dad and step-mom gave me money for Christmas; I was able to commit to the spree south of the border.

Why I fell in love with Mexico is only a "God-thing." Puerto Vallarta is a huge city by my standards. There is noise and people everywhere. Yet I absolutely loved the ten days I had with my friends. We spent nearly every day sitting on the beach. We really did not go and do a lot of things; I could not afford to be a full-fledged tourist. But everything I did, everything I ate, and everything I saw I thoroughly enjoyed. I made the comment at the time that when I turned 50 I would live in Mexico.

The following year I dated a man who did not want to go to Mexico that winter, so I did not travel there without him.

I knew I would not want to retire to Puerto Vallarta. As much as I treasure that city, I would not want to live there on a full-time basis. An American man I met while visiting the city the first time had said that if he were to "do it all over again" he would retire to Costa Alegre. I could not find Costa Alegre on the map. Nor, at that time, did a Google search produce anything. I decided to take a bus trip around the state of Jalisco to find somewhere that I would love to live. I had two years to plan the trip.

My mother, having some experience in Mexico, was convinced that Mexican men were bandits &/or wolves, *banditos y/o lobos*. She did not think that I, with my inability to speak Spanish, would be safe traveling alone from town to town on the Mexican bus system.

My step-father's uncle Max was a man my family had known since I was thirteen. We did not know of the connection to my step-father until after my mom and Billy were married. Max had been in the Navy in the early 1950's. While in San Diego, he frequently traveled to Tijuana and engaged in some of the activities in which many young sailors are rumored to participate. He always wanted to return to Mexico but had never done so. My mother suggested I ask Max to accompany me on my trip. I did and he said yes.

By this time I had found the costalegre region of south Jalisco. In the Spanish tradition, the two words had been melded into one word. The term means "Happy Coast." It is a local term for an area such as the Hi-Line is a section in Montana but not found on a map. A Canadian man had created a very informative website for Canadians traveling to Mexico and specifically to the Happy Coast of Jalisco. I included the region in our itinerary.

Max and I spent a couple of days in Puerto Vallarta for both of us to get acclimated to the humidity and to the heat. To go from temperatures of minus twenty degrees to temperatures in the upper eighties takes the body a few days to adjust.

Then we hit the road. Our first stop was Mascota. We had no plan for any length of time in any given town. If we liked the area, we would ask for one more night at the hotel. In Mascota we asked for one more night four times.

Mascota is in a very fertile valley. The term "puerto vallarta" means "harbor to the valley." Puerto Vallarta was the shipping harbor for all the produce grown in the valley around Mascota. In fact, years ago Puerto Vallarta did not have a school. Mascota was the city of the region, not Puerto Vallarta. Children who lived in Puerto Vallarta and attended school had to travel and be boarded in Mascota.

Mascota is not only famous for the vegetables grown there but it is also known for the horses raised in the region and for the cattle. It is an agriculture paradise. I have never seen so many herds of cattle with perfect bags. I was amazed at how all the cows' udders were absolutely perfect. And I do mean "all" — every single cow I saw had a perfect mammilla. The food was great, the people were mostly friendly, the city was very clean, and the country-side was breath-taking.

We met a young Mexican-American who told us of local attractions to see. There are two fantastic museums in that town and another one in a nearby town that we went to. There is a volcano crater lake that is as beautiful as any crater lake I have seen in Glacier National Park in Montana. Max and I spent a full day at the lake.

Even more awe inspiring was the ruins of an unfinished ancient cathedral. Nearly five hundred years ago construction began on what was to be Mexico's largest and most splendid cathedral. With the martyrdom of Catholic priests, which cemented that religion in the country rather than eradicating it, the construction was halted never to be activated again. These ruins are as fantastic, if not more so, than any castle or ruins I visited while in Europe. The grandeur and construction are incredible to behold. Yet the towering arches and walls are not on any tourist website or brochure of places that are a "must see" in Mexico. My photographs do not do the ruins justice so great is their magnificence.

For us to see the rest of the state of Jalisco, it was time for us to move on. I cried on the bus when we left that little town. Both Max and I thought we had found my future hometown.

We traveled to Guadalajara. Guadalajara has one of the best universities in the world. The agriculture college is better than most in the United States. It probably ranks in the top five agriculture colleges in North America. The medical schools in Guadalajara are state-of-the-art and equally prestigious as the ag school.

Max and I got off the bus with the intention of spending a day or so visiting the old part of town with its colonial architecture and to look at the agricultural school for my curiosity sake. We did not make it a block. We turned around to go back to the bus station to get out the hell of that city. I cannot stomach severe air pollution; with my compromised immune system I get sick easily in poisoned air. Diesel fumes are one of the worst. I get nauseated easily. A city of eight million people has severe air pollution, noise, and dirt.

We traveled down to Chapala. This little city is on the banks of Mexico's largest inland lake, Lake Chapala. The lake-side is home to thousands of ex-pats (retired Americans living in Mexico, ex-patriots). With the spring-like weather all year around and the beautiful mountain lake location, Chapala and nearby Ajijic are considered to be prime retirement destination locations.

The hotel I had located during my research was closed. Asking a man on the street, we found an inexpensive hotel close to the town square. I had promised Max we would not stay anywhere where ladies-of-the-street could rent a room by the hour. I had not intended to lie.

Neither of us liked Chapala. The food was poor, in general the people were not as friendly as we had become accustomed to, and there were the most homeless people I have ever seen in Mexico. We traveled on after resting two nights and a day.

Mexico is rumored to have one of the best bus systems in the world. I have not traveled by bus throughout the world; I cannot confirm this rumor. I can say the bus system in Mexico is outstanding. All of the long-distance buses I have rode on have been much more spacious and comfortable than riding on an airplane. Cities buses, by contrast, are a vision in amazement of how mechanics can keep those old wrecks running. The coaches on long-haul buses are comfortable and air conditioned. First class buses have toilet facilities; these toilets are usually in working condition. Many buses have movies. Max traveled well in the buses; he could gaze at the country-side or watch the movies without a problem. I got "car-sick" every time we were on a bus. I do not get car-sick in Montana so I was unprepared for this new physical ailment. Even with taking Dramamine for motion sickness, I would get woozie on the bus trips. I could neither watch the country-side nor watch the movies. I could only stare out the front window and hope I would not puke on the bus.

I was ready to get off the bus in Colima. Looking out the window, I saw no compelling reason to exit the bus. We traveled on. I hoped I could make it to the next major town.

Manzanillo is Mexico's only west coast international seaport. It has been an international shipping harbor for centuries. What I could see of this industrial city was not reason enough for us to get off of the bus no matter how nauseated I felt.

I tried to get off the bus in Barra de Navidad, but our tickets were for Melaque and the bus driver insisted we continue the trip. The four or so kilometers between those two towns felt like four or so hours to me.

Out of the air conditioned bus, the hot, humid air of the southern coast hit me like a punch to the head. We had to find a room and fast.

The nice man who had directed us to the economy hotel in Chapala had also given us a suggestion and an address for a bungalow place in Melaque. Max hailed us a taxi. The taxi cab driver took us nearly to the far southern end of town. The recommended bungalow suite establishment was not for me. There were no seats on the toilets.

Toilet stools without toilet seats are a common feature in many Mexican bathrooms. But I was not going to stay in a room without a toilet seat. When necessary I can squat and hover but it is difficult for me; I do not have the small, hand-held appendage with which to aim.

Max and I started to drag our suitcases back toward the center of town. We got a suite at the first bungalow place with a vacancy. This place was the nicest place we stayed on our trip. Beach-side, it was an ideal place for me to recuperate from the long bus ride.

The costalegre region of the state of Jalisco is not a typical Mexican tourist locale. Instead, it is a destination for snowbirds, most of whom are from western Canada. Even some of the Mexicans here are beginning to say “eh?” at the end of their sentences. A fact I find hilarious. Because Melaque is a snowbird destination, most hotels offer more long-term stay bungalows than individual rooms for the night.

Max and I had a lovely two bedroom, two bath bungalow with a small kitchenette and small living room. The dining room table and chairs were outside under a shaded patio. We paid for two nights right away.

Our days at this bungalow were perfect. After a light breakfast of a smoothie and coffee with maybe a sweet roll, followed or preceded by a walk, we sunbathed on the beach. Afterward we showered and had a snack. Then I wrote. On our three week venture, Melaque was the only town in which I wrote. After writing and a siesta, we would either walk to a nearby restaurant or walk downtown to a different restaurant for supper. Evenings after dark were spent in the town square with a multitude of other people watching the people stroll by or sitting on the beach enjoying the moon-lit waters.

We asked for more nights. The establishment only had two more nights available before people who had previously booked reservations were to arrive. We took the two available nights. We talked about locating another hotel or bungalow in which to stay. We decided to continue on our journey.

Arriving back in Puerto Vallarta, we planned to travel north to San Blas. We did not make it. I got sick whether due to heat stroke of food poisoning, I do not know. Not having the opportunity to venture further north was okay. I had found where I wanted to return to - Melaque.

The man who first told me about the Costa Alegre region also had suggested I spend more and more time in Mexico annually before making the plunge to move to Mexico. Just because a person thoroughly enjoys somewhere for a week or two does not mean they will enjoy the same place for a year or more. I became a registered house-sitter and started to apply for short-terms jobs in Mexico.

I listened to the man's idea not because I thought it was a wise suggestion but because I feared I would not physically or mentally be able to live so far away from my support people. I had done well my first trip but I thought it was partially due to the fact my friends were fellow alcoholics who understood me. The second trip I had done well but I thought it was partially due to the fact I had a traveling companion the entire trip. The following January I booked a three week stay in Melaque -alone. If I were able to stay balanced alone in a foreign country, unable to speak the language, and without established friendships and support personnel, then the following year I would book six weeks. My plan was to slowly, over time, spend more and more time in Mexico and maybe by the time I hit Social Security pension age, I could live in Mexico full time if I wanted to. As it turned out, I got the opportunity to change my plane ticket and stay seven weeks alone by myself instead.

But I was not alone.

I planned a couple days in Puerto Vallarta, two weeks in Melaque, and then another couple of days in Puerto Vallarta before heading back to Montana. It was to be a perfect three week vacation.

When the taxi cab driver dropped me off at the first hotel on my list of possibilities in Melaque, there was a hubbub of activity. Eventually I was given a room another man had rented but he had to return to Canada unexpectedly. His things were still in the room. He was expected back in two weeks. Perfect for me, my two weeks in Melaque. The hubbub was due to the fact the hotel did not have any vacancy but some of the absent man's friends had urged the hotel owners to rent the room to me.

This hotel was home to a group of Canadians, most of whom were from Quebec and spoke French. The lot of them stayed in this same hotel every winter. They welcomed me with open arms of friendliness although I could not speak more than two words in French — *bonjour* and *merci* — hello and thank you. Maybe those are the only two words one needs to know in a foreign language to communicate sociability and approachability. Those two words and a smile were my only mode of communication. Many of the French-speaking folks could speak a little English; a couple of them could speak English rather well.

Living within fifty miles of the Canadian border for most of my life, I had long heard of how rude the people from Quebec were. This is not true per my experience. Although I do not drink wine, cannot carry a tune when singing, and cannot speak French, I was warmly invited to join them daily on the patio for music and fellowship. They invited me to dine with them at local restaurants. They invited me to the annual fiesta they held at the hotel. The street was blocked off and over a couple hundred people attended for music, dancing, wine, and food. I was invited to come back and live with them in the hotel the following year.

I was welcomed as though I was a long lost French-speaking family member.

On the day I was to leave Melaque, I learned I had been fired from my job. I was on medical leave due to back problems pending surgery. I spent the morning crying over my loss of employment at a job I thoroughly enjoyed. Then I realized, I could return to Montana in the freezing cold winter and await surgery or I could extend my stay in the warm balmy climate of southern Mexico and await surgery. I did not contemplate the decision for long. I spent the afternoon walking the streets looking for another place to rent.

A friend had given me a ride to the far end of town. I started the long walk back to my hotel. Siesta time in Mexico is not a good time to search for anything in Melaque or anywhere else in Mexico. The bungalow establishments I found open did not have any vacancies.

I entered the last hotel before the street on which the hotel was where I had stayed for the previous two weeks. This "last hotel on the block" so to speak had an open room I could afford to rent for a month. I told them I would arrive the next morning.

This new hotel had a swimming pool and beautiful garden. It was a most tranquil environment. A man from the Yukon, the region second only to British Columbia for visiting Canadians to this town (followed by residents of Quebec as third), had started a tradition of sharing the mid-day meal with the employees of the hotel. He invited me to join them. After he returned to Whitehorse, the employees and I continued to spend the two hours together every afternoon. I started to learn some Spanish during these daily two hours of fellowship and a meal.

When I returned to Montana, my mom asked me how I got along for seven weeks in a country where I did not speak the language and in an area where I knew no one. I told her it was easy to meet people. All I had to do was to greet people in friendliness and start up a conversation. She exclaimed, "Oh Honey Bee, you are more like me than I knew!"

During my years of traveling and speaking when I was in college and when I worked for the government, I had learned to meet people by simply saying hello and asking them a question about themselves. Most people like to talk about themselves. I continued the habit in Mexico on the beach or in a restaurant. Striking up a conversation in a restaurant or on the beach was not the only way I met people. There were meetings in English for the gathering of ex-drunks. A day did not go by where I did not visit with someone in English.

I was not in pain in Mexico. I had noticed on my two previous recent ventures to the country that I hurt less when I was in Mexico. I think part of the reason is the barometric pressure does not fluctuate as rapidly or as dramatically here as it does in Montana. And with the abundant sunshine, my body could absorb copious amounts of natural vitamin D. Low vitamin D levels contributes to body pain.

One of the Frenchmen at the first hotel suggested I write a book about a French-speaking tourist getting murdered in the Costa Alegre region of Mexico.

"Similar to Agatha Christie's *Ten Little Indians*?" I asked.

He nodded.

I had changed genres and had started to write thriller or murder mystery manuscripts. None of the manuscripts are finished yet. I had planned to work on these manuscripts while in Mexico.

At first I rejected his notion. But the more I thought about the man's suggestion, the more I liked the idea. I started to research what I needed to know in order to write such a book. The research went amazingly fast. Normally it takes months for me to research enough material to write a story line. I was able to start that manuscript while in Mexico that trip.

Because my name is known as a clean wholesome young adult fiction writer, when these thriller or murder mystery books are published I will use the name of my maternal grandmother, Anna Schilke, as my pen name.

I have always loved research ever since I attended college. I love learning. I read once that a scientist is forever the child asking "Why?" over and over again. Once learning the answer, they ask, "Why not?"

It is still the same for me when I research for a book.

Once when my case manager, Marna, had not heard from me for a couple of weeks, she called and asked what I had been doing.

"Researching murder," was my answer.

"WHAT!?" she exclaimed.

I explained I conducted research into the history of the Opera House in Chinook in order to write my first murder mystery short-story.

I have no desire to DO, only to learn, and to disseminate the knowledge I have acquired.

Days prior to my leaving Mexico again, I saw an ad on the website where I was a registered house-sitter, for a job in the nearby town of La Manzanilla. I had applied for every house-sitting job in Mexico that was from two weeks to two months. I had never been selected. Home owners always wanted a couple to sit for them. I am not a couple although I am as capable as a couple. This ad wanted a sitter for a year. I knew they would never choose me but I applied anyway simply because it was so near to Melaque.

The home owners changed their ad from twelve months to six months. They contacted me and told me they wanted a couple. I understood. I told them to keep me in mind anyway. They ended up hiring me. I learned later they could not get local people to work for them. They hired me because no one else applied.

After I arrived in Mexico for a six month stint, I was offered the contract to write my memoirs. I began this manuscript while house-sitting.

Since then a new chapter of my life has begun.

My Relationship with My Son's Father

When I was in my first year of college, the boys' father phoned me. The girlfriend with whom he had left Montana had cheated on him.

He said, "You never did, did you." It was not a question, rather, a statement.

No, I never cheated on him. Now that he experienced a partner cheating, he knew that I had not done so.

That conversation was the closest to an apology I ever got. It is okay. I am happy to know he knows that I never had an affair or did anything to kill our baby.

His second wife hated me. Her feelings toward me made his and my relationship with decisions that we had to make together in rearing the boys more difficult. After they divorced, I asked him why she hated me. His answer did not make sense, but, I guess it was her reasoning.

After ten years of marriage they divorced. He and I became similar to old acquaintances or comparable to distance relatives. When we saw each other maybe once or twice a year, we would ask about how so-and-so in the family was doing. We would visit like old friends.

At the end of our marriage, when we were still together, he went to a doctor who prescribed medication for his fixated thinking. When he is on his medication his thinking is somewhat normal. When he is off his medication he has obsessive thinking. When he is on his medication, his eyes are blue. When he is off of his medication, his eyes are green. His eyes were green the entire time we were married.

A person ought not hold a resentment against someone who is sick. My husband was sick when we were married and at the time of his accusations concerning our baby's death. Looking at the situation in his eyes, here was a woman he had known and had been married to for seven years, who had never smoked or drank for the entire time he knew her, suddenly smoking and drinking. And not crying over the baby's death. These things appeared to him as though I were guilty of something. Without proper medication, his mind took a twisted turn.

He went off of his medication during his second marriage and made some bad decisions. Subsequently, he lost his second marriage. At one point he made some correct choices. To deal with the ramifications of the poor choices and to heal up from the retaliation of his second divorce, he came to Montana and stayed with us for two weeks in the spring and again for two weeks in the fall.

Several months later, Matthew moved to Tennessee to live with his father for a year and a half. Toward the end of that period, Matthew returned to Montana for a friend wedding. I told him that if he ever wanted to move back to Montana I would help him do so.

Two months later, he called and asked if I would come to Tennessee and help him drive his car back to Montana.

Sure.

It did not dawn on me that my ex-husband's new girlfriend would have difficulty with the idea of me staying in their home. She and Matthew met me at the airport. She was gracious and, perhaps, a little hesitant.

A couple of days later, after Matthew and I hit the road for the long drive northwest, did he tell me how uncomfortable she was with me coming to or rather, staying in, their home. He told me how both he and his father had to convince her that it would be okay for me to stay in their home. They had to convince her that there was nothing between his father and me any longer.

I had no idea. She behaved without ire toward me.

When Andrew graduated from high school, they made the road trip to Montana for the celebration. By this time they were married.

They spent the first night in a motel in Havre.

Why did they stay in a motel, when I have enough room in the house? They were welcome in my home.

They agreed to and planned to stay one night with us.

They stayed for four days.

Andrew wanted to take his father to his grandfather's, my dad's, cabin in the Little Rocky Mountains. All four of us trooped up to the cabin for the day. At one point, the boys wanted to take their dad on a 4-wheeler trip around the mountains to show him the sights of the old abandoned gold mines and other places of interest in the area.

When they left to go on their excursion, my ex-husband's wife, and I sat around the campfire visiting. When they returned, we still sat there talking like long lost sisters.

I think this unnerved my ex-husband.

His third wife and I get along fine. I really like her. They seem to have a good marriage and to get along very well. She is southern bred and born. She is the wife he always wanted. I hope, for the sake of their marriage, he never goes off his medication again.

My Sons as Men

I cannot describe how proud I am of my sons. They have turned out to be fine upstanding young men.

Once when I congratulated myself for the way they turned out, Andrew informed me that how they are had nothing to do with how I raised them. He told me that they make their own choices.

True. However, I still think that I provided them the atmosphere in the home in which to feel confident to make their own choices. I think I gave them the foundation on which to build their own lives. Every parent should want to raise their children to be responsible in all areas of their lives, to be interdependent, to be loving toward others, and to be self-assured enough to pursue their dreams and goals.

Matthew is an Assistant Manager of a casino. He is trusted with thousands of dollars a day in maintaining the accounting books for the establishment. Often he has to help others with balancing the books when it is the responsibility of the other person to do so. Not only is he extremely competent mathematically and totally trustworthy handling large amounts of cash, he has a "people personality."

Once when I visited him at a different store, a woman walked in. His face light up and he began to talk to her as he reached for her brand of cigarettes and lottery tickets. He asked about her family and other familiar things. When she left the store with a smile on her face, I asked him who she was.

"I have no idea, Mom," was his answer

I persisted. "But you greeted her like you knew her; you asked about her children."

"Mom," he patiently explained to me, "she is a regular customer. I know what she smokes, I know what she buys. She has come in here with her children, so I know she has kids. That is all I know about her."

But … but … but … .

He continued, "Mom that is the way it is with customer service. A teller or clerk has to make every customer feel as though they are important. When a customer feels important and welcome in a store, they come back."

One of the definitions I like for the word "love" is to make the other person feel important. Matthew is savvy of this quality in human interaction. When a customer enters an establishment where Matthew works, they leave feeling as if they are important. They feel that bond of brotherly love. They feel the connection of one human being with another. They feel important. They come back.

No wonder Matthew once was given the honor of being the highest tipped Floor Walker in the chain of casinos for which he works. As a floor walker, he serves the players drinks and snacks, he sees to their needs for cash and cigarettes. He treats all people as though they matter to him, as though they are the most important person in the room. They come back.

Matthew is not materialistic. He knows that love and people are more important than things. He is generous in his expression of love toward others.

Andrew is a Computer Programmer. He works from his home three days a week and travels to the office of the international company for which he works two days a week. He has had this work schedule since his first year out of college. Like Matthew, he is totally trustworthy with his time, his talent, and his money.

Once when he came to stay with me for a week in preparation for a friend's upcoming wedding, he had to work from my office. He entered my office at 7:50 and did not leave it, not even for a bathroom break, until 4:15. When he is at work, he is at work. He does not do other things such as household chores.

Although Andrew is totally socially skilled, he is not the "people person" Matthew is. He is in the perfect career for him.

When he was in college, his advisor said to me, "You have a gifted son."

I thanked him.

He continued, "Do you know how brilliant your son is?"

No. I do not. I know Andrew is a brain; I know he is gifted with computer know-how. But, because it is not the area of my expertise, I really do not fully understand how truly intelligent is my son. I suspect he is a genius.

When Andrew was sixteen he had a teacher who suggested he do contract computer work for people. He did not think people would hire a teenager so he did not pursue a lot of contract computer work. Yet, every time he visits family, they have him do something to or on their computer. When he was in high school and his computer teacher had to be away, the school had him and another gifted computer student teach the classes. Although a paid substitute teacher was also in the classroom.

Both of my sons treat others with respect.

I think one of the reasons Kali fell in love with Andrew was that he respected her both as the beautiful woman she is and as the professional woman she is. May their love and their marriage last a life-time.

My sons have great friends. They know the importance of close cherished friendships.

Matthew became friends with a couple of older guys in Chinook. These brothers were probably ten or so years older than Matthew. He enjoyed their company so much that he had to introduce Andrew to these two guys. The two sets of brothers became fast friends. The four guys, plus a couple more people, got together every Sunday afternoon to play role playing games. This was not an excuse to drink alcohol; it was a time for laughter and friendship. It was a time to enjoy one another's company. When my sons travel to visit me, they go to Chinook to see them.

Andrew became friends with a guy nearly my age when he was in college. He introduced Matthew to the man. The three of them all live in the same town. This other guy's family invites my sons to their home for Christmas. These three men, with other male friends, get together frequently to go to the lake, to go to a movie, to go out to eat, to play paint ball wars, or to do other male bonding activities. I am grateful for this man and his friendship, and maybe his influence, in my sons' lives.

Their list of friends is as long as my list of my friends. They learned the importance of people in their lives much, much sooner or younger than I learned this life-lesson.

When I talked to Andrew about what I planned to write in this section, he said, "You know, Mom, we're not perfect."

As if I thought they were.

I know my sons are not perfect. No human is. Although they are not perfect, they are outstanding men.

It was difficult for me to learn to have adult to adult relationships with them and to quit acting the parent. They are adults. They do not need a parent (verb). I know I am important in their lives as a parent (noun).

Andrew has thanked me several times for not being a domineering, over-protective parent. He met students in college whose parents tried to dictate their children's behavior. I did not do that. I respected my sons and their decisions. I am available for consultation, but I will not, do not, tell when what to do. Bob taught me how important it was not tell others what to do; he taught me the importance of simply making a few suggestions or giving my opinion when asked.

I know also that I would not have made it through those long years of depressing debilitating illness if it were not for my sons. THEY are what I fought to live for. At first, I did not have the self-esteem to want to live for myself. My sons, at first, were the only reason I kept fighting for life. My love for them kept me alive when there seemed to be no other reason to go on living.

I once confessed to my 100% PTSD disabled buddy that I secretly looked forward to the day my sons were out of the house so I could commit suicide so great was the discouragement living my new life in physical ailment hell.

In his dry, droll manner he said, “You won’t want to do it then, either. They will still be your sons and they will still need you.” With that comment, he tossed away his cigarette and walked off.

He was right. Although I do not know if my sons need me as much as I appreciate them in my life. We need each other. We need our family even as we grow and build new families.

My sons and I do not talk all that often. Sometimes my folks will ask me what I have heard from the boys. I may not have heard anything from them for a month or so. Other times we may have just talked for hours. When they want to visit, they know I am available. When they need something, they know I will help. I am “there” for them and they are “there” for me.

Matthew and Andrew, I love you guys more than words can say.

My Assailant

I continue to see the man responsible for my PTSD when there are community or family events, such as funerals, in Malta. This is not a problem for me.

Not long ago I walked into The Stockman Bar. I glanced around mildly amazed I recognized no one in the place of business.

Then I made eye-contact with him. He stood at the bar. We nodded at each other and I looked away.

To my mild surprise, he soon stood next to me. We greeted one another and visited a few moments. He introduced me to his new wife. She and I shook hands; I said I was happy to meet her.

The classmate of mine whom I had entered the bar was ready to leave. She and I left. I had no ill feelings after having had an encounter with him.

I have no fear of him or of anyone else. I will not live as a volunteer victim after the fact. I will not wallow in martyrdom.

I am responsible for my own life and my own recovery.

I am free.

Epilogue

I now live full-time in Mexico. I have thrived here as I did when my family first moved to the ranch a half century ago.

My house in Havre is rented to a woman who needs to heal from her past. May she be able to continue her journey in inner healing in the quietness of the sanctuary I generated. May I be able to continue my journey in a like-manner.

The community I live in is south of my beloved Melaque about eight miles. Brisas de Navidad is not a town; rather it is a housing community. It is a suburb, so to speak, of El Aguacate. The church is an empty lot on which they set chairs for the service. The altar is fenced for protection from vandalism; its gates are opened when there is Mass.

I have fewer nightmares. In fact, my dreams are unlike they have ever been before. I dream of the people in my past, many of whom touched my life yet are not in this manuscript such as fellow speech and drama teammates, facebook friends, classmates, and companions in the fellowship of ex-drunks. The dreams are peaceful, loving, and kind interactions.

I live a simple life. In the beginning I thought I would have two chairs, two cups, two glasses, two of everything. I cannot live that simply. I have too many friends who stop by. I have four of almost everything necessary to welcome company.

It is impossible to fully describe the joy and happiness I feel on a daily basis. I am so grateful I never attempted to commit suicide in my depression during those many, many dark times and years and years of struggle. I made many plans of how to do so. None of the suicide plans included a gun. I like guns; guns are not dangerous, people are. Yet, I hung in there. I hung on for the ride of my life. I hung in there for my sons.

The Mexican community in which I live is a mile or so from the nearest town. There are about 200 people in Brisas, few speak English. There are three small convenience stores, a constructed but not open hospital to serve several of the surrounding towns and communities, and at least two houses where the people who live there cook for anyone who wishes to buy their meal.

There are scorpions, other deadly bugs, tarantulas, mosquitoes, and a host of different insects. It never freezes here to kill of the insects like it does in Montana. I have learned to deal with the bugs and dust. There is a lot of dust.

My condo is the last condo on the first street as the paved road gives way to a dirt trail. This trail is the short-cut to town and has heavy traffic. The traffic is cars, pick-ups, semi-trucks, and everything in between. There are bicycles, motorcycles, carts, people a foot, and horseback riders. I always stop whatever I am doing to watch the horses walk by. Some of the riders have begun to notice and greet me as I stare at their horses. Across the street is a cow pasture. The nearby ranch practices intensive grazing rotation. There are the big mean-looking-but-very-gentle Brahma cattle in the pasture for nearly a week once a month. They are corralled every night and allowed to graze during the day. I live adjacent to the community well.

The lot surrounding the well was an abandoned pile of trash. Our next-door neighbors moved here eight years ago; they said it was a mound of trash and weeds back then as well. We cleared and cleaned up the lot and turned it into a garden. I have ten banana trees, two avocado trees, two yaka trees, a pear tree, a guava tree, three papaya trees, sugar cane, non-fruiting palms, zucchini, tomatoes, jitomatoes, and plans for more plants and flowers as well as a spot delineated for grass.

My days are spent weeding and writing.

That is a joke. I wanted to write "weeding and whiting" just for fun. With the drip irrigation system installed, there is little weeding to be done. And I do not read much anymore as my instructor years ago advised caution in obtaining ideas for my writing from other authors.

Because of the voltage fluctuations when the timer starts the well to pump water for the houses three times a day, during those hours, I do not use my computer. I am forced to take a break and to do something else.

Daily I water down the dusty road to reduce the dust in our house. During the time the well is pumping, I clean house, cook, or putter in the garden. I am learning how to use the cement washboard.

Daily I walk to at least one of the stores. There is the store with the friendly, chubby owners. I call it the dirty store because … it is. They spend their time watching TV rather than cleaning their store. I buy our fresh tortillas, some fresh fruits and vegetables, and dairy products at this store. Next to it is the store run by the very soft-spoken and gentle young transvestite who changed his/her name from George to Vivianna. Vivianna's store has four computers with internet, is very clean, and is well stocked. I go there to use the internet, to buy cleaning and laundry products, cigarettes, and most other "little things" I need or want. She does not have a good selection of fresh fruits and vegetables. I have begun to visit with the owners of both of these stores. The third store is on the street in which we live; it is the biggest store. It is not well-stocked and it is clean. The woman who stands behind the till is friendly, but the older woman with glasses who is nearly always sitting outside is not. I patronize this store the least due to the unfriendliness of the woman with glasses. I buy my beans and rice here as well as a few vegetables.

Daily I thank God for my life. I thank Him for the people in my life who have given me such rich experiences in love. I thank Him for the people who taught me about love and how to love. I thank Him for guiding me throughout my life, when I allowed Him to do so. I thank Him especially for protecting me when I was on a self-destructive path.

Ever since my parents built their new home when I was thirteen, I have wanted to build my own home. Maybe someday I will. If I had my way, I would own cattle, horses, and chickens again. Maybe that will happen, I do not know and it is not important.

What is important is:

a. that I continue to trust God in every circumstance in my life; that I continue to abandon my life to His care, guidance, and protection in every instance;
b. that I continue to "suit up and show up" in the lives of others and to be available to help whenever anyone anywhere reaches out their hand for help; that I continue to communicate with those I love that I love them;
c. that I continue to hang on for the ride!

Yee Haw!

CPSIA information can be obtained at www.ICGtesting.com
Printed in the USA
267121BV00001B/4/P

9 781456 001384